BLACK LEGACY PRESS™
WWW.BLACKLEGACYPRESS.ORG

SLAVE NARRATIVES

VOLUME II
ARKANSAS NARRATIVES
PART 1

By
United States.
Work Projects Administration

Copyright © 2024 by BLACKLEGACYPRESS.ORG

All rights reserved. No part of this publication may be reproduced or transmitted in any form or by any means electronic or mechanical, including information storage and retrieval systems without permission in writing from the publisher, except for student research using the appropriate citations.

ISBN: 978-1-63652-211-1

SLAVE NARRATIVES

A Folk History of Slavery in the United States.
From Interviews with Former Slaves

**UNITED STATES.
WORK PROJECTS ADMINISTRATION**

TYPEWRITTEN RECORDS PREPARED BY
THE FEDERAL WRITERS' PROJECT
1936-1938
ASSEMBLED BY
THE LIBRARY OF CONGRESS PROJECT
WORK PROJECTS ADMINISTRATION
FOR THE DISTRICT OF COLUMBIA
SPONSORED BY THE LIBRARY OF
CONGRESS

WASHINGTON 1941

VOLUME II
ARKANSAS NARRATIVES
PART 1

Prepared by
The Federal Writers' Project of
The Works Progress Administration
For the State of Arkansas

CONTENTS

SILAS ABBOTT 1
LUCIAN ABERNATHY 3
LAURA ABROMSOM 9
AUNT ADELINE 13
ROSE ADWAY 19
LIDDIE AIKEN 23
MATTIE ALDRIDGE 27
AMSY O. ALEXANDER 29
DIANA ALEXANDER 35
FANNIE ALEXANDER 37
LUCRETIA ALEXANDER 39
ED ALLEN 49
LUCINDY ALLISON 51
JOSEPHINE AMES 55
CHARLES ANDERSON 57
NANCY ANDERSON 61
R.B. ANDERSON 65
SARAH ANDERSON 69
SELIE ANDERSON 71
W.A. ANDERSON 75
HENRY ANTHONY 77
KATIE ARBERY 79
CAMPBELL ARMSTRONG 83
CORA ARMSTRONG 91

LILLIE BACCUS	93
JOSEPH SAMUEL BADGETT	95
JEFF BAILEY	101
JAMES BAKER	107
WILLIAM BALTIMORE	113
MOSE BANKS	117
HENRY BANNER	121
JOHN W. H. BARNETT	125
JOSEPHINE ANN BARNETT	127
LIZZIE BARNETT	131
SPENCER BARNETT	135
EMMA BARR	141
ROBERT BARR	145
MATILDA BASS	149
EMMETT BEAL	151
DINA BEARD	153
ANNIE BECK	155
J.H. BECKWITH	157
ENOCH BEEL	161
SOPHIE D. BELLE	163
CYRUS BELLUS	167
BOB BENFORD	173
CARRIE BRADLEY LOGAN BENNET	177
GEORGE BENSON	183
KATO BENTON	185
JAMES BERTRAND	187
ALICE BIGGS	191

MANDY BILLINGS	193
JANE BIRCH	195
BEATRICE BLACK	197
BOSTON BLACKWELL	199
HENRY BLAKE	207
MISS ADELINE BLAKELEY	213
VERA ROY BOBO	223
LIDDIE BOECHUS	225
MAGGIE (BUNNY) BOND	227
CAROLINE BONDS	231
REV. FRANK T. BOONE	233
J.F. BOONE	243
JONAS BOONE	247
JOHN BOWDRY	249
JACK BOYD	251
MAL BOYD	255
GEORGE BRADDOX	259
GEORGE BRADDOX	263
EDWARD BRADLEY	267
RACHEL BRADLEY	273
ELIZABETH BRANNON	277
MACK BRANTLEY	281
ELLEN BRASS	287
ALICE BRATTON	291
FRANK BRILES	293
MARY ANN BROOKS	297
WATERS BROOKS	301

CASIE JONES BROWN	311
ELCIE BROWN	317
F. H. BROWN	321
GEORGE BROWN	329
J.N. BROWN	333
LEWIS BROWN	335
LEWIS BROWN	339
MAG BROWN	349
MARY BROWN	351
MATTIE BROWN	353
MOLLY BROWN	355
PETER BROWN	365
WILLIAM BROWN	371
WILLIAM BROWN	373
MAGGIE BROYLES	381
IDA BRYANT	387
BELLE BUNTIN	389
JEFF BURGESS	393
NORMAN BURKES	395
WILL BURKS, SR.	397
ADELINE BURRIS	401
JENNIE BUTLER	405
E.L. BYRD	411
EMMETT AUGASTA BYRD	413

Interviewer: Miss Irene Robertson
Person Interviewed: Silas Abbott
R.F.D.
Brinkley, Ark.
Age: 73

SILAS ABBOTT

"I was born in Chickashaw County, Mississippi. Ely Abbott and Maggie Abbott was our owners. They had three girls and two boys—Eddie and Johnny. We played together till I was grown. I loved em like if they was brothers. Papa and Mos Ely went to war together in a two-horse top buggy. They both come back when they got through.

"There was eight of us children and none was sold, none give way. My parents name Peter and Mahaley Abbott. My father never was sold but my mother was sold into this Abbott family for a house girl. She cooked and washed and ironed. No'm, she wasn't a wet nurse, but she tended to Eddie and Johnny and me all alike. She whoop them when they needed, and Miss Maggie whoop me. That the way we grow'd up. Mos Ely was 'ceptionly good I recken. No'm, I never heard of him drinkin' whiskey. They made cider and 'simmon beer every year.

"Grandpa was a soldier in the war. He fought in a battle. I don't know the battle. He wasn't hurt. He come home and told us how awful it was.

"My parents stayed on at Mos Ely's and my uncle's

family stayed on. He give my uncle a home and twenty acres of ground and my parents same mount to run a gin. I drove two mules, my brother drove two and we drove two more between us and run the gin. My auntie seen somebody go in the gin one night but didn't think bout them settin' it on fire. They had a torch, I recken, in there. All I knowed, it burned up and Mos Ely had to take our land back and sell it to pay for four or five hundred bales of cotton got burned up that time. We stayed on and sharecropped with him. We lived between Egypt and Okolona, Mississippi. Aberdeen was our tradin' point.

"I come to Arkansas railroading. I railroaded forty years. Worked on the section, then I belong to the extra gang. I help build this railroad to Memphis.

"I did own a home but I got in debt and had to sell it and let my money go.

"Times is so changed and the young folks different. They won't work only nough to get by and they want you to give em all you got. They take it if they can. Nobody got time to work. I think times is worse than they ever been, cause folks hate to work so bad. I'm talking bout hard work, field work. Jobs young folks want is scarce; jobs they could get they don't want. They want to run about and fool around an get by.

"I get $8.00 and provisions from the government."

Interviewer: Watt McKinney
Person interviewed: Lucian Abernathy, Marvell, Arkansas
Age: 85

LUCIAN ABERNATHY

"I was borned in de 'streme norf part of Mississippi nigh de Tennessee line. You mought say dat it was 'bout straddle of de state line and it wasn't no great piece from where us libed to Moscow what was de station on de ole Memfis en Charston Railroad. My white folks was de Abernathys. You neber do hear 'bout many folks wid dat name these times, leastwise not ober in dis state, but dere sure used to be heap of dem Abernathys back home where I libed and I spect dat mebbe some dere yit en cose it's bound to be some of the young uns lef' dar still, but de ole uns, Mars Luch en dem, dey is all gone.

"Mars Luch, he was my young boss. Though he name was Lucian us all called him Luch and dat was who I is named for. Ole mars, he was name Will and dat was Mars Luch's pa and my ole miss, she name Miss Cynthia and young miss, her name Miss Ellen. Ole mars an' ole miss, dey just had de two chillun, Mars Luch and Miss Ellen; dat is what libed to be grown. Mars Luch, he 'bout two year older dan me and Miss Ellen, she 'bout two year older dan Mars Luch. Miss Ellen, she married er gentman from Virginny and went dar to lib and Mars Luch, he married Miss Fannie Keith.

"Miss Fannie's folks, dey libed right nigh us on to 'j'ining place and dem was my ole man's peoples. Yas sah, boss, dat ole man you see settin' right dar now in dat chere. She was Ella Keith, dats zackly what her named when us married and she named fer Miss Fannie's ma. Dat she was. Us neber did leave our folkses eben atter de War ober and de niggers git dey freedom, yit an' still a heap of de niggers did leave dey mars' and a heap of dem didn' an' us stayed on an farmed de lan' jus' like us been doin' 'cept dey gib us a contract for part de crop an' sell us our grub 'gainst us part of de crop and take dey money outen us part of de cotton in de fall just like de bizness is done yit and I reckon dat was de startin' of de sharecrop dat is still goin' on.

"Soon atter Mars Luch good and grown an' him an' Miss Fannie done married, ole mars and ole miss, dey bofe died and Mars Luch say he gwine sell out an' lebe 'cause de lan' gittin' so poor and wore out and it takin' three an' more acres to make a bale and he tell us all dat when we wind up de crop dat fall and say, 'You boys mebbe can stay on wid whoever I sell out to er if not den you can fin' you homes wid some one close if you wants to do dat.' And den he says dat he gwine fin' him some good lan' mebbe in Arkansas down de riber from Memfis. Mighty nigh all de ole famblys lef' de place when Mars Luch sole it out.

"My pappy and my mammy, dey went to Memfis and me wid 'em. I was growed by den and was fixin' to marry Ella just es soon es I could fin' a good home. I was a country nigger en liked de farm an' en cose wasn't satisfied in town, so 'twasn't long 'fore I heered 'bout han's beein' needed down de riber in Mississippi and dats where I went en stayed for two years and boss, I sure was struck wid dat lan' what you could make a bale to a acre on an' I just knowed dat I was gwine git rich in a hurry an' so I writ er letter to Ella en her peoples tellin' dem 'bout de rich lan' and 'vising dem to come down dere where I was and I was wantin' to marry Ella den. Boss, and you know what, 'twasn't long afore I gits er letter back an' de letter says dat Ella an' her peoples is down de riber in Arkansas from Memfis at Bledsoe wid Mars Luch an' Miss Fannie where Mars Luch had done moved him an' Miss Fannie to a big plantation dey had bought down dere.

"Dat was a funny thing how dat happened an' Bledsoe, it was right 'cross de riber from where I was en had been for two years an' just soon es I git dat letter I 'range wid a nigger to take me 'cross da riber in er skift to de plantation where dey all was and 'bout fust folkses dat I see is Ella an' her peoples en lots of de famblys from de ole home place back in Tennessee an' I sure was proud to see Mars Luch en Miss Fannie. Dey had built demselves a fine house at a p'int dat was sorter like a knoll where de water don' git when de riber come out on de lan' in case of oberflow and up de rode 'bout half mile from de house, Mars Luch had de store en de gin. Dey had de boys den, dat is Mars Luch and Miss Fannie did, and de boys was named Claude an' Clarence atter Miss Fannie's two brudders.

"Dem was de finest boys dat one ever did see. At dat time Claude, he 'bout two year old and Clarence, he 'bout four er mebbe little less. Ella, she worked in da house cooking for Miss Fannie an' nussin' de chillun and she plumb crazy 'bout de chillun an' dey just as satisfied wid her as dey was wid dere mama and Ella thought more dem chillun dan she did anybody. She just crazy 'bout dem boys. Mars Luch, he gibe me job right 'way sort flunkying for him and hostling at de lot an' barn and 'twasn't long den 'fore Ella and me, us git married an' libs in a cabin dat Mars Luch had built in de back of de big house.

"Us git 'long fine for more dan a year and Mars Luch, he raise plenty cotton an' at times us ud take trip up to Memfis on de boat, on de Phil Allin what was 'bout de fineist boat on de riber in dem days and de one dat most frequent put in at us landin' wid de freight for Mars Luch and den he most ginally sont he cotton an' seed to Memfis on dis same Phil Allin.

"I jus' said, boss, dat us git 'long fine for more dan a year and us all mighty happy till Miss Fannie took sick an' died an' it mighty nigh killed Mars Luch and all of us and Mars Luch, he jus' droop for weeks till us git anxious 'bout him but atter while he git better and seam like mebbe he gwine git ober he sadness but he neber was like he used to be afore Miss Fannie died.

"Atter Miss Fannie gone, Mars Luch, he say, 'Ella, you an' Luch mus' mobe in de big house an' make you a bed in de room where de boys sleep, so's you can look atter 'em good, 'cause lots nights I gwine be out late at de gin an' store an' I knows you gwine take plumb good care of dem chillun.' An' so us fixed us bed in de big house an' de boys, dey sleeped right dar in dat room on dere bed where us could take care of 'em.

"Dat went on for 'bout two years an' den Mars Luch, he 'gun to get in bad health an' jus' wasted down like and den one night when he at de store he took down bad and dey laid him down on de bed in de back room where he would sleep on sich nights dat he didn' come home when he was so busy an' he sont a nigger on a mule for me to come up dar an' I went in he room an' Mars Luch, he say, 'Lissen, Luch, you is been a good faithful nigger an' Ella too, an' I is gonna die tonight and I wants you to send er letter to Miss Ellen in Virginny atter I is daid en tell her to come an' git de boys 'cause she is all de kin peoples dat dey habe lef' now cepn cose you an' Ella an' it mought be some time afore she gits here so you all take good en faithful care dem till she 'rives an' tell her she habe to see dat all de bizness wind up and take de boys back wid her an' keep dem till dey is growed,'

"Well, boss, us done jus' like Mars Luch tell us to do an' us sure feel sorry for dem two little boys. Dey jus' 'bout five an' seben year old den and day sure loved dere pa; day was plumb crazy 'bout Mars Luch and him 'bout dem too.

"'Bout two weeks from time dat Mars Luch daid, Miss Ellen come on de boat one night an' she stayed some days windin' up de bizness and den she lef' an' take de boys 'way wid her back to Virginny where she libed. Us sure did hate to 'part from dem chillun. Dat's been nigh on to sixty years ago but us neber forgit dem boys an' us will allus lobe dem. Dey used to sen' us presents an' sich every Christmas for seberal years and den us started movin' 'bout an' I reckon dey don' know where we's at now. I sure would like to see dem boys ag'in. I betcha I'd know dem right today. Mebbe I wouldn't, it's been so long since I seen 'em; but shucks, I know dat dey would know me."

United States. Work Projects Administration

Interviewer: Miss Irene Robertson
Person interviewed: Laura Abromsom, R.F.D., Holly Grove, Arkansas
Receives mail at Clarendon, Arkansas
Age: 74

LAURA ABROMSOM

"My mama was named Eloise Rogers. She was born in Missouri. She was sold and brought to three or four miles from Brownsville, Tennessee. Alex Rogers bought her and my papa. She had been a house girl and well cared for. She never got in contact wid her folks no more after she was sold. She was a dark woman. Papa was a ginger cake colored man. Mama talked like Alex Rogers had four or five hundred acres of land and lots of niggers to work it. She said he had a cotton factory at Brownsville.

"Mistress Barbara Ann was his wife. They had two boys and three girls. One boy George went plumb crazy and outlived 'em all. The other boy died early. Alex Rogers got my papa in Richmond, Virginia. He was took outer a gang. We had a big family. I have eight sisters and one brother.

"Pa say they strop 'em down at the carriage house and give 'em five hundred lashes. He say they have salt and black pepper mixed up in er old bucket and put it all on flesh cut up with a rag tied on a stick (mop). Alex Rogers had a nigger to put it on the place they whooped. The

Lord puts up wid such wrong doings and den he comes and rectifies it. He does that very way.

"Pa say they started to whoop him at the gin house. He was a sorter favorite. He cut up about it. That didn't make no difference 'bout it. Somehow they scared him up but he didn't git whooped thater time.

"They fed good on Alex Rogers' place. They'd buy a barrel of coffee, a barrel molasses, a barrel sugar. Some great big barrels.

"Alex Rogers wasn't a good man. He'd tell them to steal a hog and git home wid it. If they ketch you over there they'll whoop you. He'd help eat hogs they'd steal.

"One time papa was working on the roads. The neighbor man and road man was fixing up their eating. He purty nigh starved on that road work. He was hired out.

"Mama and papa spoke like they was mighty glad to get sat free. Some believed they'd git freedom and others didn't. They had places they met and prayed for freedom. They stole out in some of their houses and turned a washpot down at the door. Another white man, not Alex Rogers, tole mama and papa and a heap others out in the field working. She say they quit and had a regular bawl in the field. They cried and laughed and hollered and danced. Lot of them run offen the place soon as the man tole 'em. My folks stayed that year and another year.

"What is I been doing? Ast me is I been doing? What ain't I been doing be more like it. I raised fifteen of my own children. I got four living. I living wid one right here in dis house wid me now. I worked on the farm purty nigh all my life. I come to dis place. Wild, honey, it was! I come in 1901. Heap of changes since then.

"Present times—Not as much union 'mongst young black and white as the old black and white. They growing apart. Nobody got nothin' to give. No work. I used to could buy second-handed clothes to do my little children a year for a little or nothin'. Won't sell 'em now nor give 'em 'way neither. They don't work hard as they used to. They say they don't git nothin' outen it. They don't want to work. Times harder in winter 'cause it cold and things to eat killed out. I cans meat. We dry beef. In town this Nickellodian playing wild wid young colored folks— these Sea Bird music boxes. They play all kind things. Folks used to stay home Saturday nights. Too much running 'round, excitement, wickedness in the world now. This generation is worst one. They trying to cut the Big Apple dance when we old folks used to be down singing and praying, 'Cause dis is a wicked age times is bad and hard."

Interviewer's Comment

Mulatto, clean, intelligent.

Interviewer: Mrs. Zillah Cross Peel
Person interviewed: "Aunt Adeline" Age: 89
Home: 101 Rock Street, Fayetteville, Arkansas

AUNT ADELINE

"I was born a slave about 1848, in Hickmon County, Tennessee," said Aunt Adeline who lives as care taker in a house at 101 Rock Street, Fayetteville, Arkansas, which is owned by the Blakely-Hudgens estate.

Aunt Adeline has been a slave and a servant in five generations of the Parks family. Her mother, Liza, with a group of five Negroes, was sold into slavery to John P.A. Parks, in Tennessee, about 1840.

"When my mother's master come to Arkansas about 1849, looking for a country residence, he bought what was known as the old Kidd place on the Old Wire Road, which was one of the Stage Coach stops. I was about one year old when we came. We had a big house and many times passengers would stay several days and wait for the next stage to come by. It was then that I earned my first money. I must have been about six or seven years old. One of Mr. Parks' daughters was about one and a half years older than I was. We had a play house back of the fireplace chimney. We didn't have many toys; maybe a doll made of a corn cob, with a dress made from scraps and a head made from a roll of scraps. We were playing church. Miss Fannie was the preacher and I was the audience. We were singing "Jesus my all to Heaven is gone." When we were half way through with our song we discovered that the passengers from the stage coach had stopped to listen. We were so frightened at our audience that we both ran. But we were coaxed to come back for a dime and sing our song over. I remember that Miss Fannie used a big leaf for a book.

"I had always been told from the time I was a small child that I was a Negro of African stock. That it was no disgrace to be a Negro and had it not been for the white folks who brought us over here from Africa as slaves, we would never have been here and would have been much better off.

"We colored folks were not allowed to be taught to read or write. It was against the law. My master's folks always treated me well. I had good clothes. Sometimes I was whipped for things I should not have done just as the white children were.

"When a young girl was married her parents would always give her a slave. I was given by my master to his daughter, Miss Elizabeth, who married Mr. Blakely. I was just five years old. She moved into a new home at Fayetteville and I was taken along but she soon sent me back home to my master telling him that I was too little and not enough help to her. So I went back to the Parks home and stayed until I was over seven years old. [1]My master made a bill of sale for me to his daughter, in order to keep account of all settlements, so when he died and the estate settled each child would know how he stood.

"I was about 15 years old when the Civil War ended and was still living with Mrs. Blakely and helped care for her little children. Her daughter, Miss Lenora, later married H.M. Hudgens, and I then went to live with her and cared for her children. When her daughter Miss Helen married Professor Wiggins, I took care of her little daughter, and this made five generations that I have cared for.

"During the Civil War, Mr. Parks took all his slaves and all of his fine stock, horses and cattle and went South to Louisiana following the Southern army for protection. Many slave owners left the county taking with them their slaves and followed the army.

"When the war was over, Mr. Parks was still in the South and gave to each one of his slaves who did not want to come back to Arkansas so much money. My uncle George came back with Mr. Parks and was given a good mountain farm of forty acres, which he put in cultivation and one of my uncle's descendants still lives on the place. My mother did not return to Arkansas but went on to Joplin, Missouri, and for more than fifty years, neither one of us knew where the other one was until one day a man from Fayetteville went into a restaurant in Joplin and ordered his breakfast, and my mother who was in there heard him say he lived in Fayetteville, Arkansas. He lived just below the Hudgens home and when my mother enquired about the family he told her I was still alive and was with the family. While neither of us could read nor write we corresponded through different people. But I never saw her after I was eleven years old. Later Mr. Hudgens went to Joplin to see if she was well taken care of. She owned her own little place and when she died there was enough money for her to be buried.

"Civil War days are vivid to me. The Courthouse which was then in the middle of the Square was burned one night by a crazy Confederate soldier. The old men in the town saved him and then put him in the county jail to keep him from burning other houses. Each family was to take food to him and they furnished bedding. The morning I was to take his breakfast, he had ripped open his feather bed and crawled inside to get warm. The room was so full of feathers when I got there that his food nearly choked him. I had carried him ham, hot biscuits and a pot of coffee.

"After the War many soldiers came to my mistress, Mrs. Blakely, trying to make her free me. I told them I was free but I did not want to go anywhere, that I wanted to stay in the only home that I had ever known. In a way that placed me in a wrong attitude. I was pointed out as different. Sometimes I was threatened for not leaving but I stayed on.

"I had always been well treated by my master's folks. While we lived at the old Kidd place, there was a church a few miles from our home. My uncle George was coachman and drove my master's family in great splendor in a fine barouche to church. After the war, when he went to his own place, Mr. Parks gave him the old carriage and bought a new one for the family.

"I can remember the days of slavery as happy ones. We always had an abundance of food. Old Aunt Martha cooked and there was always plenty prepared for all the white folks as well as the colored folks. There was a long table at the end of the big kitchen for the colored folks. The vegetables were all prepared of an evening by Aunt Martha with someone to help her.

"My mother seemed to have a gift of telling fortunes. She had a brass ring about the size of a dollar with a handwoven knotted string that she used. I remember that she told many of the young people in the neighborhood many strange things. They would come to her with their premonitions.

"Yes, we were afraid of the patyroles. All colored folks were. They said that any Negroes that were caught away from their master's premises without a permit would be whipped by the patyroles. They used to sing a song:

> 'Run nigger run,
> The patyroles
> Will get you.'

"Yes'm, the War separated lots of families. Mr. Parks' son, John C. Parks, enlisted in Colonel W.H. Brooks' regiment at Fayetteville as third lieutenant. Mr. Jim Parks was killed at the Battle of Getysburg.

"I do remember it was my mistress, Mrs. Blakely, who kept the Masonic Building from being burned. The soldiers came to set it on fire. Mrs. Blakely knew that if it burned, our home would burn as it was just across the street. Mrs. Blakely had two small children who were very ill in upstairs rooms. She told the soldiers if they burned the Masonic Building that her house would burn and she would be unable to save her little children. They went away."

While Aunt Adeline is nearing ninety, she is still active, goes shopping and also tends to the many crepe myrtle bushes as well as many other flowers at the Hudgens place.

She attends to the renting of the apartment house, as caretaker, and is taken care of by members of the Blakely-Hudgens families.

Aunt Adeline talks "white folks language," as they say, and seldom associates with the colored people of the town.

[1] This statement can be verified by the will made by John P.A. Parks, and filed in Probate Court in the clerk's office in Washington County.

Interviewer: Mrs. Bernice Bowden
Person interviewed: Rose Adway
405 W. Pullen, Pine Bluff, Arkansas
Age: 76

ROSE ADWAY

"I was born three years 'fore surrender. That's what my people told me. Born in Mississippi. Let me see what county I come out of. Smith County—that's where I was bred and born.

"I know I seen the Yankees but I didn't know what they was. My mama and papa and all of 'em talked about the War.

"My papa was a water toter in durin' the War. No, he didn't serve the army—just on the farm.

"Mama was the cook for her missis in slavery times.

"I think my folks went off after freedom and then come back. That was after they had done been sot free. I can remember dat all right.

"I registered down here at the Welfare and I had to git my license from Mississippi and I didn't remember which courthouse I got my license, but I sent letters over there till I got it up. I got all my papers now, but I ain't never got no pension.

"I been through so much I can't git much in my remembrance, but I was here—that ain't no joke—I been here.

"My folks said their owners was all right. You know they was 'cause they come back. I remember dat all right.

"I been farmin' till I got disabled. After I married I went to farmin'. And I birthed fourteen head of chillun by dat one man! Fourteen head by dat one man! Stayed at home and took care of 'em till I got 'em up some size, too. All dead but five out of the fourteen head.

"My missis' name was Miss Catherine and her husband named Abe Carr.

"I went to school a little bit—mighty little. I could read but I never could write.

"And I'm about to go blind in my old age. I need help and I need it bad. Chillun ain't able to help me none 'cept give me a little bread and give me some medicine once in a while. But I'm thankful to the Lord I can get outdoors.

"I don't know what to think of this young race. That baby there knows more than I do now, nearly. Back there when I was born, I didn't know nothin'.

"I know they said it was bad luck to bring a hoe or a ax in the house on your shoulder. I heard the old folks tell dat—sure did.

"And I was told dat on old Christmas night the cows gets down on their knees and gives thanks to the Lord.

"I 'member one song:

> 'I am climbin' Jacob's ladder
> I am climbin' Jacob's ladder

I am climbin' Jacob's ladder
For the work is almost done.

'Every round goes higher and higher
Every round goes higher and higher
Every round goes higher and higher
For my work is almost done.

'Sister, now don't you get worried
Sister, now don't you get worried
Sister, now don't you get worried
For the work is almost done.'

My mother used to sing dat when she was spinnin' and cardin'. They'd spin and dye the thread with some kind of indigo. Oh, I 'member dat all right."

United States. Work Projects Administration

Interviewer: Miss Irene Robertson
Person interviewed: Liddie Aiken, Wheatley, Arkansas
Age: 62

LIDDIE AIKEN

"My mother was born in southwest Georgia close to the Alabama line. Her mother come from Virginia. She was sold with her mother and two little brothers. Her mother had been sold and come in a wagon to southwest Georgia. They was all field hands. They cleaned out new ground. They was afraid of hoop-snakes. She said they look like a hoop rolling and whatever they stuck a horn or their tail in it died. They killed trees.

"Mama said she druther plough than chop. She was a big woman and they let her plough right along by her two little brothers, Henry and Will Keller. Will et so many sweet potatoes they called him 'Tater Keller.' After he got grown we come out here. Folks called him 'Tate Keller.' Henry died. I recollect Uncle Tate.

"I was born close to Mobile, Alabama. Mama was named Sarah Keller. Grandma was called Mariah. Banks Tillman sold her the first time. Bill Keller bought them all the last time. His wife was named Ada Keller. They had a great big family but I forgot what they said about them. Mack clem up in a persimmon tree one day and the old man hollered at him, 'Get out of that tree 'fore you fall.' 'Bout then the boy turned 'loose and fell. It knocked the breath out him. It didn't kill him. Three or four of Miss Ada's children died with congestive chills. Mama said the reason they had them chills they played down at the gin pond all the time. It was shady and a pretty place and they was allowed to play in the pond. Three or four of them died nearly in a heap.

"One of the boys had a pet billy-goat. It got up on top mama's house one time. It would bleat and look down at them. They was afraid it would jump down on them if they went out. It chewed up things Aunt Beanie washed. She had them put out on bushes and might had a line too. They fattened it and killed it. Mama said Mr. Bill Keller never had nothing too good to divide with his niggers. I reckon by that they got some of the goat.

"They lived like we live now. Every family done his own cooking. I don't know how many families lived on the place.

"I know about the Yankees. They come by and every one of the men and boys went with them but Uncle Cal. He was cripple and they advised him not to start. Didn't none of the women go. Mama said she never seen but one ever come back. She thought they got killed or went on some place else.

"Mr. Keller died and Miss Ada went back to her folks. They left everything in our care that they didn't move. She took all her house things. They sold or took all their stock. They left us a few cows and pigs. I don't know how long they stayed after the old man died. His children was young; he might not been so old.

"I recollect grandma. She smoked a pipe nearly all the

time. My papa was a livery stable man. He was a fine man with stock. He was a little black man. Mama was too big. Grandma was taller but she was slick black. He lived at Mobile, Alabama. I was the onliest child mama had. Uncle 'Tate Keller' took grandma and mama to Mobile. He never went to the War. He was a good carpenter and he worked out when he didn't have a lot to do in the field. He was off at work when all the black men and boys left Mr. Bill. He never went back after they left till freedom.

"They didn't know when freedom took place. They was all scattering for two years about to get work and something to eat. Tate come and got them. They went off in a wagon that Tate made for his master, Bill Keller. We come to Tupelo, Mississippi from Mobile when I was a little bit of a girl. Then we made one crop and come to Helena. Uncle Tate died there and mama died at Crocketts Bluff. My papa died back in Mobile, Alabama. He was breaking a young horse and got throwed up side a tree. He didn't live long then.

"I got three boys now and I had seben—all boys. They farms and do public work. Tom is in Memphis. Pete is in Helena and I live wid Macon between here (Wheatley) and Cotton Plant. We farm. I done everything could be thought of on a farm. I ploughed some less than five year ago. I liked to plough. My boy ploughs all he can now and we do the chopping. We all pick cotton and get in the corn. We work day laborers now.

"If I was young the times wouldn't stand in my way. I could make it. I don't know what is the trouble lessen some wants too much. They can't get it. We has a living and thankful for it. I never 'plied for no help yet.

"I still knits my winter stockings. I got knitting needles and cards my own mother had and used. I got use for them. I wears clothes on my body in cold weather. One reason you young folks ain't no 'count you don't wear enough clothes when it is cold. I wear flannel clothes if I can get holt of them.

"Education done ruint the world. I learnt to read a little. I never went to school. I learnt to work. I learnt my boys to go with me to the field and not to be ashamed to sweat. It's healthy. They all works."

Interviewer: Miss Irene Robertson
Person Interviewed: Mattie Aldridge
Hazen, Arkansas
Age: 60?

MATTIE ALDRIDGE

"My mother's old owner named Master Sanders. She born somewhere in Tennessee. I heard her say she lived in Mississippi. I was born in Tennessee. My pa was born in Mississippi. I know he belong to the Duncans. His name George Washington Duncan. There ain't nary drap white blood in none us. I got four brothers. I do remembers grandma. She set and tell us tales bout old times like you want to know. Been so long I forgotten. Ma was a house girl and pa a field hand. Way grandma talked it must of been hard to find out what white folks wanted em to do, cause she couldn't tell what you say some times. She never did talk plain.

"They was glad when freedom declared. They said they was hard on em. Whoop em. Pa was killed in Crittenden County in Arkansas. He was clearin' new ground. A storm come up and a limb hit him. It killed him. Grandma and ma allus say like if you build a house you want to put all the winders in you ever goin' to want. It bad luck to cut in and put in nother one. Sign of a death. I ain't got no business tellin' you bout that. White folks don't believe in signs.

"I been raisin' up childern—'dopted childern, washin', ironin', scourin', hoein', gatherin' corn, pickin' cotton, patchin', cookin'. They ain't nothin' what I ain't done.

"No'm, I sure ain't voted. I don't believe in women votin'. They don't know who to vote for. The men don't know neither. If folks visited they would care more bout the other an wouldn't be so much devilment goin' on."

Interviewer: Samuel S. Taylor.
Person Interviewed: Amsy O. Alexander
2422 Center Street, Little Rock, Arkansas
Age: 74

AMSY O. ALEXANDER

[HW: Helps Build Railroad]

"I was born in the country several miles from Charlotte in Macklenberg, County, North Carolina in 1864.

"My father's name was John Alexander and my mother was Esther McColley. That was her maiden name of course.

"My father's master was named Silas Alexander and my mother belonged to Hugh Reed. I don't know just how she and my father happened to meet. These two slaveholders were adjoining neighbors, you might say.

"My father and my mother married during the war. I was the first child. I had three half brothers and three half sisters from the father's side. I didn't have no whole brothers and sisters. I am the only one on my mother's side. My father was not in the war.

"I don't know that the pateroles bothered him very much. My father and mother were well treated by our master and then both she and my father were quiet and their masters were good to them naturally.

"During slavery times, my father was a farmer. My mother farmed too. She was a hand in the field. They lived in a little log cabin, one room. They had a bed in there, a few chairs and a homemade table. They had a plank floor. I only know what I heard my people speak of. I don't know what was what for myself because I was too young.

"From what I can understand they had a big room at the house and the slaves came there and ate there. They had a colored woman who prepared their meals. The children mostly were raised on pot liquor. While the old folk were working the larger young uns mongst the children would take care of the little ones.

"Their masters never forced any breeding. I have heard of that happening in other places but I never heard them speak of it in connection with our master.

"When the master came back from the war, they told the slaves they were free. After slavery my people stayed on and worked on the old plantation. They didn't get much. Something like fifty cents a day and one meal. My folks didn't work on shares.

"Back there in North Carolina times got tight and it seemed that there wasn't much doing. Agents came from Arkansas trying to get laborers. So about seven or eight families of us emigrated from North Carolina. That is how my folks got here.

"The Ku Klux were bad in North Carolina too. My people didn't have any trouble with them in Arkansas, though. They weren't bothered so much in North Carolina because of their owners. But they would come around and see them. They came at night. We came to Arkansas in the winter of 1897.

"I went to public school after the war, in North Carolina. I didn't get any further than the eighth grade. My father and mother didn't get any schooling till after the war. They could read a little but they picked it up themselves during slavery. I suppose their Master's children learned it to them.

"My father never did see any army service. I have heard him speak of seeing soldiers come through though. They looted the place and took everything they wanted and could carry.

"When I first come to this state, I settled in Drew County and farmed. I farmed for three years. During the time I was there, I got down sick with slow fever. When I got over that I decided that I would move to higher ground. There was a man down there who recommended Little Rock and so I moved here. I have been here forty-nine years. That is quite a few days.

"I belong to the Presbyterian Church and have been a member of that church for fifty-five years. I have never gotten out publicly, but I even do my little preaching round in the house here.

"When I came to Little Rock, I came in a very dull season. There wasn't even a house to be rented. It was in the winter. I had to rent a room at "Jones" hall on Ninth and Gaines streets and paid one dollar a day for it. I stayed there about a month. Finally there was a vacant house over on Nineteenth street and Common and I moved there. Then I commenced to look for work and I walked the town over daily. No results whatever. Finally I struck a little job with the contractor here digging ditches, grubbing stumps, grading streets and so forth. I worked with him for three years and finally I got a job with the street car company, as laborer in the Parks. I worked at that job two years. Finally I got a job as track laborer. I worked there a year. Then I was promoted to track foreman. I held that seven years.

"I quit that then and went to the railroads. I helped to build the Choctaw Oklahoma and Gulf Railway. When the road was completed, I made the first trip over it as Porter. I remained there till August 9, 1928. During that time I was operated on for prostatitis and doctors rendered me unfit for work, totally disabled; so that is my condition today.

"I think the future looks bright. I think conditions will get better. I believe that all that is necessary for betterment is cooperation.

"I believe the younger generation—the way it looks—is pretty bad. I think we haven't done anything like as much as we could do in teaching the youngsters. We need to give them an idea of things. They don't know. Our future depends on our children If their minds aren't trained, the future will not be bright. Our leaders should lecture to these young people and teach them. We have young people who dodge voting because of the poll tax. That is not the right attitude. I don't know what will become of us if our children are not better instructed. The white people are doing more of this than we are.

"There was a time when children didn't know but what the foot was all there was of a chicken. The foot was all they had ever seen. But young folks nowaday should be taught everything."

United States. Work Projects Administration

Interviewer: Miss Irene Robertson
Person interviewed: Diana Alexander, Brinkley, Arkansas
Age: 74

DIANA ALEXANDER

"I was born in Mississippi close to Bihalia. Our owner was Myers(?) Bogan. He had a wife and children. Mama was a field woman. Her name was Sarah Bogan and papa's name was Hubberd Bogan.

"I heard them talk about setting the pot at the doors and having singing and prayer services. They all sung and prayed around the room. I forgot all the things they talked about. My parents lived on the same place after freedom a long time. They said he was good to them.

"Dr. Bogan in Forrest City, Arkansas always said I was his brother's child. He was dead years ago, so I didn't have no other way of knowing.

"The only thing I can recollect about the War was once my mistress took me and her own little girl upstairs in a kind of ceiling room (attic). They had their ham meat and jewelry locked up in there and other fine stuff. She told us to sit down and not move, not even grunt. Me and Fannie had to be locked up so long. It was dark. We both went to sleep but we was afraid to stir. The Yankees come then but I didn't get to see them. I didn't want to be took away by 'em. I was big enough to know that. I heard 'em say we was near 'bout eat out at the closing of the War. I thought it muster been the Yankees from what they was talking about, eating us out.

"I been washing and ironing and still doing it. All my life I been doing that 'ceptin' when I worked in the field.

"Me and my daughter is paying on this house (a good house). I been making my own living—hard or easy. I don't get no relief aid. Never have. I 'plied for the old people's pension. Don't get it."

Interviewer's Comment

This must be Myers Bogan, yet she told me Bogan Myers. Later she said Dr. Bogan of Forrest City was thus and so.

Interviewer: Miss Irene Robertson
Person interviewed: Fannie Alexander, Helena, Arkansas
Age: 62

FANNIE ALEXANDER

"I was an orphant child. My mother-in-law told me during slavery she was a field hand. One day the overseer was going to whoop one of the women 'bout sompin or other and all the women started with the hoes to him and run him clear out of the field. They would killed him if he hadn't got out of the way. She said the master hadn't put a overseer over them for a long time. Some of 'em wouldn't do their part and he put one of the men on the place over the women. He was a colored foreman. The women worked together and the men worked together in different fields. My mother-in-law was named Alice Drummond. She said they would cut the hoecakes in half and put that in your pan, then pour the beef stew on top. She said on Christmas day they had hot biscuits. They give them flour and things to make biscuit at home on Sundays. When they got through eating they take their plate and say, 'Thank God for what I received.' She said they had plenty milk. The churns was up high—five gallon churns. Some churns was cedar wood. The children would churn standing on a little stool. It would take two to churn. They would change about and one brushed away the flies. She lived close to Meridian and Canton.

"My mother talked the bright side to her children.

She was born in Tennessee. She had two older sisters sold from her. She never seen them no more. They was took to Missouri. Mother was never sold. She was real bright color. She died when I was real little. From what I know I think my parents was industrious. Papa was a shoemaker. He worked on Sunday to make extra money to buy things outside of what his master give them for his family. Now I can remember that much. My papa was a bright color like I am but not near as light as mama. He had a shop when I was little but he wasn't 'lowed to keep it open on Sunday. I heard him tell about working on Sundays during slavery and how much he made sometimes. He tanned his own leather.

"I went to Mississippi and married. Folks got grown earlier than they do now and I married when I was a young girl 'bout seventeen. We come to Arkansas. I sewed for white and colored. I cooked some. I taught school in the public schools. I taught opportunity school two years. I had a class at the church in day and at the schoolhouse at night. I had two classes.

"John Hays was mama's owner in Tennessee."

Interviewer: Samuel S. Taylor
Person interviewed: Lucretia Alexander
1708 High Street. Little Rock, Arkansas
Age: 89

LUCRETIA ALEXANDER

"I been married three times and my last name was Lucretia Alexander. I was twelve years old when the War began. My mother died at seventy-three or seventy-five. That was in August 1865—August the ninth. She was buried August twelfth. The reason they kept her was they had refugeed her children off to different places to keep them from the Yankees. They couldn't get them back. My mother and her children were heir property. Her first master was Toliver. My mother was named Agnes Toliver. She had a boy and a girl both older than I were. My brother come home in '65. I never got to see my sister till 1869.

"My father died in 1881 and some say he was one hundred twelve and some say one hundred six. His name was Beasley, John Beasley, and he went by John Beasley till he died.

"My mother died and left four living children. I was the youngest.

"I got religion in 1865. I was baptized seventy-three years ago this August.

"I ain't got nary living child. My oldest child would

have been sixty-four if he were living. They claim my baby boy is living, but I don't know. I have four children.

"The first overseer I remember was named Kurt Johnson. The next was named Mack McKenzie. The next one was named Pink Womack. And the next was named Tom Phipps. Mean! Liked meanness! Mean a man as he could be. I've seen him take them down and whip them till the blood run out of them.

"I got ten head of grandchildren. And I been grandmother to eleven head. I been great-grandmother to twelve head of great-grandchildren. I got one twenty-three and another nineteen or twenty. Her father's father was in the army. She is the oldest. Lotas Robinson, my granddaughter, has four children that are my great-grandchildren. Gayden Jenkins, my grandson, has two girls. I got a grandson named Dan Jenkins. He is the father of three boys. He lives in Cleveland. He got a grandson named Mark Jenkins in Memphis who has one boy. The youngest granddaughter—I don't remember her husband's name—has one boy. There are four generations of us.

"I been here. You see I took care of myself when I was young and tried to do right. The Lord has helped me too. Yes, I am going on now. I been here a long time but I try to take care of myself. I was out visiting the sick last time you come here. That's the reason I missed you. I tries to do the best I can.

"I am stricken now with the rheumatism on one side. This hip.

"My mother was treated well in slavery times. My father was sold five times. Wouldn't take nothin'. So they sold him. They beat him and knocked him about. They put him on the block and they sold him 'bout beatin' up his master. He was a native of Virginia. The last time they sold him they sold him down in Claiborne County, Mississippi. Just below where I was born at. I was born in Copiah County near Hazlehurst, about fifteen miles from Hazlehurst. My mother was born in Washington County. Virginia. Her first master was Qualls Tolliver. Qualls moved to Mississippi and married a woman down there and he had one son, Peachy Toliver. After he died, he willed her to Peachy. Then Peachy went to the Rebel army and got killed.

"My mother's father was a free Indian named Washington. Her mother was a slave. I don't know my father's father. He moved about so much and was sold so many times he never did tell me his father. He got his name from the white folks. When you're a slave you have to go by your owner's name.

"My master's mother took me to the house after my mother died. And the first thing I remember doing was cleaning up. Bringing water, putting up mosquito-bars, cooking. My master's mother was Susan Reed. I have done everything but saw. I never sawed in my life. The hardest work I did was after slavery. I never did no hard work during slavery. I used to pack water for the plow hands and all such as that. But when my mother died, my mistress took me to the house.

"But Lawd! I've seen such brutish doin's—runnin' niggers with hounds and whippin' them till they was bloody. They used to put 'em in stocks. When they didn't put 'em in stocks, used to be two people would whip 'em—the overseer and the driver. The overseer would be a man named Elijah at our house. He was just a poor white man. He had a whip they called the BLACK SNAKE.

"I remember one time they caught a man named George Tinsley. They put the dogs on him and they bit 'im and tore all his clothes off of 'im. Then they put 'im in the stocks. The stocks was a big piece of timber with hinges in it. It had a hole in it for your head. They would lift it up and put your head in it. There was holes for your head, hands and feet in it. Then they would shut it up and they would lay that whip on you and you couldn't do nothin' but wiggle and holler, 'Pray, master, pray!' But when they'd let that man out, he'd run away again.

"They would make the slaves work till twelve o'clock on Sunday, and then they would let them go to church. The first time I was sprinkled, a white preacher did it; I think his name was Williams.

"The preacher would preach to the white folks in the forenoon and to the colored folks in the evening. The white folks had them hired. One of them preachers was named Hackett; another, Williams; and another, Gowan. There was five of them but I just remember them three. One man used to hold the slaves so late that they had to go to the church dirty from their work. They would be sweaty and smelly. So the preacher 'buked him 'bout it. That was old man Bill Rose.

"The niggers didn't go to the church building; the preacher came and preached to them in their quarters. He'd just say, 'Serve your masters. Don't steal your master's turkey. Don't steal your master's chickens. Don't steal your master's hawgs. Don't steal your master's meat. Do whatsomeever your master tells you to do.' Same old thing all the time.

"My father would have church in dwelling houses and they had to whisper. My mother was dead and I would go with him. Sometimes they would have church at his house. That would be when they would want a real meetin' with some real preachin'. It would have to be durin' the week nights. You couldn't tell the difference between Baptists and Methodists then. They was all Christians. I never saw them turn nobody down at the communion, but I have heard of it. I never saw them turn no pots down neither; but I have heard of that. They used to sing their songs in a whisper and pray in a whisper. That was a prayer-meeting from house to house once or twice— once or twice a week.

"Old Phipps whipped me once. He aimed to kill me but I got loose. He whipped me about a colored girl of his'n that he had by a colored woman. Phipps went with a colored woman before he married his wife. He had a girl named Martha Ann Phipps. I beat Martha 'bout a pair of stockings. My mistress bought me a nice pair of stockings from the store. You see, they used to knit the stockings. I wore the stockings once; then I washed them and put them on the fence to dry. Martha stole them and put them on. I beat her and took them off of her. She ran and told her father and he ran me home. He couldn't catch me, and he told me he'd get me. I didn't run to my father. I run to my mistress, and he knew he'd better not do nothin' then. He said, 'I'll get you, you little old black some thin'.' Only he didn't say 'somethin'.' He didn't get me then.

"But one day he caught me out by his house. I had

gone over that way on an errand I needn't have done. He had two girls hold me. They was Angeline and Nancy. They didn't much want to hold me anyhow. Some niggers would catch you and kill you for the white folks and then there was some that wouldn't. I got loose from them. He tried to hold me hisself but he couldn't. I got away and went back to my old mistress and she wrote him a note never to lay his dirty hands on me again. A little later her brother, Johnson Chatman, came there and ran him off the place. My old mistress' name was Susan Chatman before she married. Then she married Toliver. Then she married Reed. She married Reed last—after Toliver died.

"One old lady named Emily Moorehead runned in and held my mother once for Phipps to whip her. And my mother was down with consumption too. I aimed to git old Phipps for that. But then I got religion and I couldn't do it. Religion makes you forgit a heap of things.

"Susan Reed, my old mistress, bought my father and paid fifteen hundred dollars for him and she hadn't never seen 'im. Advertising. He had run away so much that they had to advertise and sell 'im. He never would run away from Miss Susan. She was good to him till she got that old nigger beater Phipps. Her husband, Reed, was called a nigger spoiler. My father was an old man when Phipps was on overseer and wasn't able to fight much then.

"Phipps sure was a bad man. He wasn't so bad neither; but the niggers was scared of him. You know in slave times, sometimes when a master would git too bad, the niggers would kill him—tote him off out in the woods somewheres and git rid of him. Two or three of them would git together and scheme it out, and then two or three of them would git him way out and kill 'im. But they didn't nobody ever pull nothin' like that on Phipps. They was scared of him.

"One time I saw the Yankees a long way off. They had on blue uniforms and was on coal black horses. I hollered out, 'Oh, I see somethin'.' My mistress said, 'What?' I told her, and she said, 'Them's the Yankees.' She went on in the house and I went with her. She sacked up all the valuables in the house. She said, 'Here,' and she threw a sack of silver on me that was so heavy that I went right on down to the ground. Then she took hold of it and holp me up and holp me carry it out. I carried it out and hid it. She had three buckskin sacks—all full of silver. That wasn't now; that was in slavery times. During the War, Jeff Davis gave out Confederate money. It died out on the folks' hands. About twelve hundred dollars of it died out on my father's hands. But there wasn't nothin' but gold and silver in them sacks.

"I heard them tell the slaves they were free. A man named Captain Barkus who had his arm off at the elbow called for the three near-by plantations to meet at our place. Then he got up on a platform with another man beside him and declared peace and freedom. He p'inted to a colored man and yelled, 'You're free as I am.' Old colored folks, old as I am now, that was on sticks, throwed them sticks away and shouted.

"Right after freedom I stayed with that white woman I told you about. I was with her about four years. I worked for twelve dollars a month and my food and clothes. Then I figured that twelve dollars wasn't enough and I went to work in the field. It was a mighty nice woman. Never hit me in her life. I never have been whipped by a white woman. She was good to me till she died. She died after I had my second child—a girl child.

"I have been living in this city fifteen years. I come from Chicot County when I come here. We come to Arkansas in slavery times. They brought me from Copiah County when I was six or eight years old. When Mrs. Toliver married she came up here and brought my mother. My mother belonged to her son and she said, 'Agnes (that was my mother's name), will you follow me if I buy your husband?' Her husband's name was John Beasley. She said, 'Yes.' Then her old mistress bought Beasley and paid fifteen hundred dollars to get my mother to come with her. Then Peachy went to war and was shot because he come home of a furlough and stayed too long. So when he went back they killed him. My mother nursed him when he was a baby. Old man Toliver said he didn't want none of us to be sold; so they wasn't none of us sold. Maybe there would have been if slavery had lasted longer; but there wasn't.

"Mother really belonged to Peachy, but when Peachy died, then she fell to her mistress.

"I have been a widow now for thirty years. I washed and ironed and plowed and hoed—everything. Now I am gittin' so I ain't able to do nothin' and the Relief keeps me alive. I worked and took care of myself and my last husband and he died, and I ain't married since. I used to take a little boy and make ten bales of cotton. I can't do it now. I used to be a woman in my day. I am my mother's seventh child.

"I don't buy no hoodoo and I don't believe in none, but a seventh child can more or less tell you things that are a long way off. If you want to beat the devil you got to do right. God's got to be in the plan. I tries to do right. I am not perfect but I do the best I can. I ain't got no bottom teeth, but my top ones are good. I have a few bottom ones. The Lawd's keepin' me here for somepin. I been with 'im now seventy-three years."

Interviewer's Comment

I'll bet the grandest moment in the life of Sister Alexander's mother was when her mistress said, "Agnes, will you follow me if I buy your husband?" Fifteen hundred dollars to buy a rebellious slave in order to unite a slave couple. It's epic.

United States. Work Projects Administration

Interviewer: Miss Irene Robertson
Person interviewed: Ed Allen, Des Arc, Ark.
Age: ?

ED ALLEN

"I know that after freedom they took care of my pa and ma and give em a home long as they lived. Ma died wid young mistress here in Des Arc.

"The present generation is going to the bad. Have dealings wid em, not good to you. Young folks ain't nice to you like they used to be.

"White boys and colored boys, whole crowd of us used to go in the river down here all together, one got in danger help him out. They don't do it no more. We used to play base ball together. All had a good time. We never had to buy a ball or a bat. Always had em. The white boys bought them. I don't know as who to blame but young folk changed."

United States. Work Projects Administration

Interviewer: Miss Irene Robertson
Person interviewed: Lucindy Allison, Marked Tree, Arkansas
With children at Biscoe, Arkansas
Age: 61

LUCINDY ALLISON

"Ma was a slave in Arkansas. She said she helped grade a hill and help pile up a road between Wicksburg and Wynne. They couldn't put the road over the hill, so they put all the slaves about to grade it down. They don't use the road but it's still there to show for itself.

"She was a tall rawbony woman. Ma was a Hillis and pa's name was Adam Hillis. He learned to trap in slavery and after freedom he followed that for a living. Ma was a sure 'nough field hand. Mama had three sets of children. I don't know how many she did have in all. I had eleven my own self. Grandma was named Tempy and I heard them tell about when she was sold. She and mama went together. They used to whoop the slaves when they didn't work up peart.

"When the 'Old War' come on and the Yankees come they took everything and the black men folks too. They come by right often. They would drive up at mealtime and come in and rake up every blessed thing was cooked. Have to go work scrape about and find something else to eat. What they keer 'bout you being white or black? Thing they was after was filling theirselves up. They done white folks worse than that. They burned their cribs and fences up and their houses too about if they got mad. Things didn't suit them. If they wanted a colored man to go in camp with them and he didn't go, they would shoot you down like a dog. Ma told about some folks she knowd got shot in the yard of his own quarters.

"Us black folks don't want war. They are not war kind of folks. Slavery wasn't right and that 'Old War' wasn't right neither.

"When my children was all little I kept Aunt Mandy Buford till she died. She was a old slave woman. Me and my husband and the biggest children worked in the field. She would sit about and smoke. My boys made cob pipes and cut cane j'ints for 'er to draw through. Red cob pipes was the prettiest. Aunt Mandy said her master would be telling them what to do in the field and he say to her, 'I talking to you too.' She worked right among the men at the same kind of work. She was tall but not large. She carried children on her right hip when she was so young she dragged that foot when she walked. The reason she had to go with the men to the field like she did was 'cause she wasn't no multiplying woman. She never had a chile in all her lifetime. She said her mother nearly got in bad one time when her sister was carrying a baby. She didn't keep up. Said the riding boss got down, dug a hole with the hoe to lay her in it 'cause she was so big in front. Her mother told him if he put her daughter there in that hole she'd cop him up in pieces wid her hoe. He found he had two to conquer and he let her be. But he had to leave 'cause he couldn't whoop the niggers.

"If I could think of all she tole I'd soon have enough to fill up that book you're getting up. I can't recollect who she belong to, and her old talk comes back to me now and then. She talked so much we'd get up and go on off to keep from hearing her tell things over so many times.

"Folks like me what got children think the way they do is all right. I don't like some of my children's ways but none of us perfect. I tells 'em right far as I knows. Times what makes folks no 'count. Times gets stiff around Biscoe. Heap of folks has plenty. Some don't have much—not enough. Some don't have nothing.

"I don't believe in women voting. That ruined the country. We got along very well till they got to tinkering with the government."

United States. Work Projects Administration

Interviewer: Pernella Anderson
Person interviewed: Josephine Ames. Fordville, Arkansas
Age: not given.

JOSEPHINE AMES

Ah wuz bo'n de first year niggers wuz free. Wuz born in Caledonia at de Primm place. Mah ma belonged tuh George Thompson. After mah ma died ah stayed wid de Wommacks, a while. Aftuh dat mah pa taken me home. Pa's name wuz Jesse Flueur. Ah worked lak er slave. Ah cut wood, sawed logs, picked 400 pounds uv cotton evah day. Ah speck ah married de first time ah wuz about fo'teen years ole. Ah been mahrid three times. All mah husband's is daid. Ole man England and ole man Cullens run business places and ole man Wooley. His name wuz reason Wooley. De Woolies got cemetery uv dey own right dar near de Cobb place. No body is buried in dar but de fambly uv Wooleys. Ole man Allen Hale, he run er store dar too. He is yet livin right dar. He is real ole. De ole Warren Mitchell place whar ah use tuh live is Guvment land. Warren Mitchell, he homesteaded the place. We lived dar and made good crops. De purtiest dar wuz eround, but not hit's growed up. Don lived dar and made good crops. De purtiest dar wuz eround. Dar is whah all mah chillun wuz bo'n. Ah use tuh take mah baby an walk tuh El Dorado to sevice. Ah use tuh come tuh El Dorado wid a oman by de name of Sue Foster. Nothin but woods when dey laid de railroad heah. Dey built dem widh horses and axes. Ah saw em when dey whoop de hosses and oxen till dey fall out working dem when dey laid dat steel. Ah wuz at de first buryin uv de fust pussen buried in Caledonia graveyard. Huh name wuz Joe Ann Polk. We set up wid huh all night and sing and pray. An when we got nearly tuh de church de bells started tolling and de folks started tuh singin. When evah any body died dey ring bells tuh let yo know some body wuz daid. A wuz born on Christmas day, an ah had two chilluns born on Christmas Day. Dey wuz twins and one uv em had two teeth and his hair hung down on her shoulders when hit wuz born but hit did not live but er wek.

Interviewer: Miss Irene Robertson
Person interviewed: Charles Anderson. Helena, Arkansas
Age: 77 or 78, not sure

CHARLES ANDERSON

"I was born in Bloomfield, Kentucky. My parents had the same owners. Mary and Elgin Anderson was their names. They was owned by Isaac Stone. Davis Stone was their son. They belong to the Stones as far back as they could remember. Mama was darker than I am. My father was brighter than I am. He likely had a white father. I never inquired. Mama had colored parents. Master Stone walked with a big crooked stick. He nor his son never went to war. Masters in that country never went. Two soldiers were drafted off our place. I saw the soldiers, plenty of them and plenty times. There never was no serious happenings.

"The Federal soldiers would come by, sleep in the yard, take our best horses and leave the broken down ones. Very little money was handled. I never seen much. Master Stone would give us money like he give money to Davis. They prized fine stock mostly. They needed money at wheat harvest time only. When a celebration or circus come through he give us all twenty-five or thirty cents and told us to go. There wasn't many slaves up there like down in this country. The owners from all I've heard was crueler and sold them off oftener here.

"Weaving was a thing the women prided in doing—

being a fast weaver or a fine hand at weaving. They wove pretty coverlets for the beds. I see colored spreads now makes me think about my baby days in Kentucky.

"Freedom was something mysterious. Colored folks didn't talk it. White folks didn't talk it. The first I realized something different, Master Stone was going to whip a older brother. He told mama something I was too small to know. She said, 'Don't leave this year, son. I'm going to leave.' Master didn't whip him.

"Master Stone's cousin kept house for him. I remember her well. They were all very nice to us always. He had a large farm. He had twenty servants in his yard. We all lived there close together. My sister and mama cooked. We had plenty to eat. We had beef in spring and summer. Mutton and kid on special occasions. We had hog in the fall and winter. We had geese, ducks, and chickens. We had them when we needed them. We had a field garden. He raised corn, wheat, oats, rye, and tobacco.

"Once a year we got dressed up. We got shirts, a suit, pants and shoes, and what else we needed to wear. Then he told them to take care of their clothes. They got plenty to do a year. We didn't have fine clothes no time. We didn't eat ham and chicken. I never seen biscuit—only sometimes.

"I seen a woman sold. They had on her a short dress, no sleeves, so they could see her muscles, I reckon. They would buy them and put them with good healthy men to raise young slaves. I heard that. I was very small when I seen that young woman sold and years later I heard that was what was done.

"I don't know when freedom came on. I never did know. We was five or six years breaking up. Master Stone never forced any of us to leave. He give some of them a horse when they left. I cried a year to go back. It was a dear place to me and the memories linger with me every day.

"There was no secret society or order of Ku Klux in reach of us as I ever heard.

"I voted Republican ticket. We would go to Jackson to vote. There would be a crowd. The last I voted was for Theodore Roosevelt. I voted here in Helena for years. I was on the petit jury for several years here in Helena.

"I farmed in your state some (Arkansas). I farmed all my young life. I been in Arkansas sixty years. I come here February 1879 with distant relatives. They come south. When I come to Helena there was but one set of mechanics. I started to work. I learned to paint and hang wall paper. I've worked in nearly every house in Helena.

"The present times are gloomy. I tried to prepare for old age. I had a apartment house and lost it. I owned a home and lost it. They foreclosed me out.

"The present generation is not doing as well as I have.

"My health knocked me out. My limbs swell, they are stiff. I have a bad bladder trouble.

"I asked for help but never have got none. If I could got a little relief I never would lost my house. They work my wife to death keeping us from starving. She sewed till they cut off all but white ladies. When she got sixty-five they let her go and she got a little job cooking. They never give us no relief."

Interviewer: Miss Irene Robertson
Person interviewed: Nancy Anderson
Street H, West Memphis, Arkansas
Age: 66

NANCY ANDERSON

"I was born at Sanitobia, Mississippi. Mother died when I was a child. I was three months old, they said, when I lost her. Father lived to be very old. My mother was Ella Geeter and my stepmother was Lucy Evans. My father's name was Si Hubbard. My parents married after the War. I remembers Grandma Harriett Hubbard. She said she was sold. She was a cook and she raised my papa up with white folks. Her children was sold with her. Papa was sold too at the same time. Papa fired a steam gin. They ground corn and ginned cotton.

"I stayed with Sam Hall's family. She was good to me. I had a small bed by the fireplace. She kept me with two of her own children. Some of the girls and boys I was raised up with live at Sanitobia now and have fine homes. When we would be playing they would take all the toys from me. Miss Fannie would say, 'Poor Nancy ain't got no toys.' Then they would put them on the floor and we would all play. They had a little table. We all eat at it. We had our own plates. We all eat out of tin plates and had tin cups.

"They couldn't keep me at home when papa married. I slipped off across the pasture. There was cows and hogs in there all the time. I wasn't afraid of them. I would get behind Miss Fannie and hide in her dress tail when they come after me. They let me stay most of the time for about five years. Sam Hall was good to my father and Miss Fannie about raised me after my mother died. She made me mind but she was good to me.

"Grandma lived with papa. She was part Indian. As long as papa lived he share cropped and ginned. He worked as long as he was able to hit a lick. He died four miles east out from Sanitobia on Mr. Hayshaws place. What I told you is what I know. He said he was sold that one time. Hubbards had plenty to eat and wear. He was a boy and they didn't want to stunt the children. Papa was a water boy and filed the hoes for the chopping hands. He carried a file along with them hoeing and would sharpen their hoes and fetch 'em water in their jugs. Aunt Sallie, his sister, took keer of the children.

"Papa went to the War. He could blow his bugle and give all the war signals. He got the military training. Him and his friend Charlie Grim used to step around and show us how they had to march to orders. His bugle had four joints. I don't know what went with it. From what they said they didn't like the War and was so glad to get home.

"Between the big farms they had worm fences (rail fences) and gates. You had to get a pass from your master to go visiting. The gates had big chains and locks on them. Some places was tollgates where they traveled over some man's land to town. On them roads the man owned the place charged. He kept some boy to open and shut the gate. They said the gates was tall.

"Some of the slaves that had hard masters run off and stay in the woods. They had nigger dogs and would run them—catch 'em. He said one man (Negro) was hollowing down back of the worm fence close to where they was working. They all run to him. A great long coachwhip snake was wrapped 'round him, his arms and all, and whooping him with its tail. It cut gashes like a knife and the blood poured. The overseer cut the snake's head off with his big knife and they carried him home bleeding. His master didn't whoop him, said he had no business off in the woods. He had run off. His master rubbed salt in the gashes. It nearly killed him. It burnt him so bad. That stopped the blood. They said sut (soot) would stopped the blood but it would left black mark. The salt left white marks on him. The salt helped kill the pison (poison). Some masters and overseers was cruel. When they was so bad marked they didn't bring a good price. They thought they was hard to handle.

"Aunt Jane Peterson, old friend of mine, come to visit me nearly every year after she got so old. She told me things took place in slavery times. She was in Virginia till after freedom. She had two girls and a boy with a white daddy. She told me all about how that come. She said no chance to run off or ever get off, you had to stay and take what come. She never got to marry till after freedom. Then she had three more black children by her husband. She said she was the cook. Old master say, 'Jane, go to the lot and get the eggs.' She was scared to go and scared not to go. He'd beat her out there, put her head between the slip gap where they let the hogs into the pasture from the lot down back of the barn. She say, 'Old missis whip me. This ain't right.' He'd laugh. Said she bore three of his children in a room in the same house his family lived in. She lived in the same house. She had a room so as she could build fires and cook breakfast by four o'clock sometimes, she said. She was so glad freedom come on and soon as she heard it she took her children and was gone, she said. She had no use for him. She was scared to death of him. She learned to pray and prayed for freedom. She died in Cold Water, Mississippi. She was so glad freedom come on before her children come on old enough to sell. Part white children sold for more than black children. They used them for house girls.

"I don't know Ku Klux stories enough to tell one. These old tales leave my mind. I'm 66 and all that was before my time.

"Times is strange—hard, too. But the way I have heard they had to work and do and go I hardly ever do grumble. I've heard so much. I got children and I do the best I can by them. That is all I can do or say."

Interviewer: Samuel S. Taylor
Person interviewed: R.B. Anderson
Route 4, Box 68 (near Granite)
Little Rock, Arkansas
Age: 75

R.B. ANDERSON

[HW: The Brooks-Baxter War]

"I was born in Little Rock along about Seventeenth and Arch Streets. There was a big plantation there then. Dr. Wright owned the plantation. He owned my mother and father. My father and mother told me that I was born in 1862. They didn't know the date exactly, so I put it the last day in the year and call it December 30, 1862.

"My father's name was William Anderson. He didn't go to the War because he was blind. He was ignorant too. He was colored. He was a pretty good old man when he died.

"My mother's name was Minerva Anderson. She was three-fourths Indian, hair way down to her waist. I was in Hot Springs blacking boots when my mother died. I was only about eight or ten years old then. I always regretted I wasn't able to do anything for my mother before she died. I don't know to what tribe her people belonged.

"Dr. Wright was awful good to his slaves.

"I don't know just how freedom came to my folks. I

never heard my father say. They were set free, I know. They were set free when the War ended. They never bought their freedom.

"We lived on Tenth and near to Center in a one-room log house. That is the earliest thing I remember. When they moved from there, my father had accumulated enough to buy a home. He bought it at Seventh and Broadway. He paid cash for it—five hundred and fifty dollars. That is where we all lived until it was sold. I couldn't name the date of the sale but it was sold for good money—about three thousand eight hundred dollars, or maybe around four thousand. I was a young man then.

"I remember the Brooks-Baxter War.

"I remember the King White fooled a lot of niggers and armed them and brought them up here. The niggers and Republicans here fought them and run them back where they come from.

"I know Hot Springs when the main street was a creek. I can't remember when I first went there. The government bath-house was called 'Ral Hole', because it was mostly people with bad diseases that went there.

"After the War, my father worked for a rich man named Hunter. He was yardman and took care of the horse. My mother was living then.

"Scipio Jones and I were boys together. We slept on pool tables many a time when we didn't have no other place to sleep. He was poor when he was a boy and glad to get hold of a dime, or a nickel. He and I don't speak today because he robbed me. I had a third interest in my place. I gave him money to buy my place in for me. It was up for sale and I wanted to get possession. He gave me some papers to sign and when I found out what was happening, he had all my property. My wife kept me from killing him."

Interviewer's Comment

Occupation: Grocer, bartender, porter, general work

United States. Work Projects Administration

Interviewer: Mrs. Bernice Bowden
Person interviewed: Sarah Anderson
3815 W. Second Avenue, Pine Bluff, Arkansas
Age: 78?

SARAH ANDERSON

"I don't know when I was born. When the Civil War ended, I was bout four or five years old.

"I jes' remember when the people come back—the soldiers—when the War ended. We chillun run under the house. That was the Yankees.

"I was born in Bibb County, Georgia. That's where I was bred and born.

"I been in Arkansas ever since I was fourteen. That was shortly after the Civil War, I reckon. We come here when they was emigratin' to Arkansas. I'm tellin' you the truth, I been here a long time.

"I member when the soldiers went by and we chillun run under the house. It was the Yankee cavalry, and they made so much noise. Dat's what the old folks told us. I member dat we run under the house and called our self hidin'.

"My master was Madison Newsome and my missis was Sarah Newsome. Named after her? Must a done it. Ma and her chillun was out wallowin' in the dirt when the Yankees come by. Sometimes I stayed in the house with my white folks all night.

"My mother and father say they was well treated. That's what they say.

"Old folks didn't low us chillun round when they was talkin' bout their business, no ma'am.

"We stayed with old master a good while after freedom—till they commenced emigratin' from Georgia to Arkansas. Yes ma'am!

"I'm the mother of fourteen chillun—two pairs of twins. I married young—bout fifteen or sixteen, I reckon. I married a young fellow. I say we was just chaps. After he died, I married a old settled man and now he's dead.

"I been livin' a pretty good life. Seems like the white folks just didn't want me to get away from their chillun.

"All my chillun dead cept one son. He was a twin."

Interviewer: Miss Irene Robertson
Person interviewed: Selie Anderson, Holly Grove, Arkansas
Age: 78

SELIE ANDERSON

"I was born near Decatur, Alabama and lived there till I was fifteen years old. Course I members hearin' em talk bout Mars Newt. I named fur my ma's old mistress—Miss Selie Thompson and Mars Newt Thompson. Pa died when I was three years old. He was a soldier. Ma had seven children. They have bigger families then than they have now. Ma name Emmaline Thompson. Pa name Sam Adair. I can't tell you about him. I heard em say his pa was a white man. He was light skinned. Old folks didn't talk much foe children so I don't know well nough to tell you bout him. Ma was a cook and a licensed midwife in Alabama. She waited on both black and white. Ma never staid at home much. She worked out. I come to Mississippi after I married and had one child. Ma and all come. Ma went to Tom McGehee's to cook after freedom. She married old man named Lewis Chase and they worked on where he had been raised. His name was Lewis Sprangle. He looked after the stock and drove the carriage. Daniel Sprangle had a store and a big farm. He had three girls and three boys, I was their house girl. Mama lived on the place and give me to em cause they could do better part by me than she could. I was six years old when she give me to em. They lernt me to sweep, knit, crochet, piece quilts. She lernt her children thater way sometimes. Miss Nancy Sprangle didn't treat me no different from her own girls. Miss Dora married Mr. Pitt Loney and I was dressed up and held up her train (long dress and veil). I stayed with Miss Dora after she married. One of the girls married Mr. John Galbreth. I married and went home then come to Mississippi. Mrs. Gables, Mr. Gables was old people but they had two adopted boys. I took them boys to the field to work wid my children. She sewed for me and my children. Her girls cooked all we et in busy times. They done work at the house but they didn't work in the field.

"I been married five times. Every time I married I married at home. Mighty little marryin' goin' on now—mighty little. Mama stayed wid Mr. Sprangle till we all got grown. Miss Nancy's girls married so that all the way I knowd how to do. I had a good time. I danced every chance I got. I been well blessed all my life till I'm gettin' feeble now.

"Papa run the gin on Mr. Sprangle's place, then he went to war, come back foe he died. I recken he come home sick cause he died pretty soon.

"I jess can member this Ku Klux broke down our door wid hatchets. It scared us all to death. They didn't do nuthin' to us. They was huntin' Uncle Jeff. He wasn't bout our house. He was ox driver fer Mr. Sprangle. Him and a family of pore white folks got to fussin' bout a bridle. Some of em was dressed up when they come to our house ma said. After that Mr. Kirby killed him close to his home startin' out one mornin' to work. His name was Uncle Jeff Saxon. Ma knowd it was some of the men right on Mr. Sprangle's place whut come to our house.

"I live wid my daughter. I get $8 from the Welfare.

"If they vote for better it be all right. I never seen no poles. I don't know how they vote. I'm too old to start up votin'.

"Lawd you got me now. The times changed and got so fast. It all beyond me. I jes' listens. I don't know whut goner happen to this young generation."

United States. Work Projects Administration

Interviewer: Samuel S. Taylor
Person interviewed: W.A. Anderson (dark brown)
3200 W. 18th Street, Little Rock, Arkansas
Age: 78
Occupation: House and yard man

W.A. ANDERSON

[HW: Serves the "Lawd"]

"I don't know nothin' about slavery. You know I wouldn't know nothin' bout it cause I was only four years old when the war ended. All I know is I was born in slavery; but I don't know nothin' bout it.

"I don't remember nothin' of my parents. Times was all confused and old folks didn't talk before chilun. They didn't have time. Besides, my mother and father were separated.

"I was born in Arkansas and have lived here all my life. But I don't gossip and entertain. I just moved in this house last week. Took a wheelbarrow and brought all these things here myself.

"Those boys out there jus' threw a stone against the house. I thought the house was falling. I work all day and when night comes, I'm tired.

"I don't have no wife, no children, nothin'; nobody to help me out. I don't ask the neighbors nothin' cept to clear out this junk they left here.

"I ain't goin' to talk about the Ku Klux. I got other things to think about. It takes all my time and strength to do my work and live a Christian. Folks got so nowadays they don't care bout nothin'. I just live here and serve the Lawd."

Interviewer's Comments

Anderson is separated from his wife who left him. He lost his home a short time ago. A few months ago, he was so sick he was expected to die. He supports himself through the friendliness of a few white people who give him odds and ends of work to do.

I made three calls on him, helped him set up his stoves and his beds and clear up his house a little bit since he had just moved into it and had a good deal of work to do. His misfortunes have made him unwilling to talk just now, but he will give a good interview later I am certain.

Interviewer: Miss Irene Robertson
Person interviewed: Henry Anthony; R.F.D. #1 Biscoe, Arkansas
Age: 84

HENRY ANTHONY

"I was born at Jackson, North Carolina. My master and mistress named Betsy and Jason Williams but my pa's name was Anthony. My young master was a orderly seargent. He took me wid him to return some mules and wagons. He showed me what he want done an I followed him round wid wagons. The wagons hauled ammunition and provisions. Pa worked for the master and ma cooked. They got sold to Lausen Capert. When freedom come they went back and stayed a month or two at Williams then we all went back to John Odom. We stayed round close and farmed and worked till they died. I married and when I had four or five children I heard ob dis country. I come on immigration ticket to Mr. Aydelott here at Biscoe. Train full of us got together and come. One white man got us all up and brought us here to Biscoe. I farmed for Mr. Aydelott four or five years, then for Mr. Bland, Mr. Scroggin.

"I never went to school a day in my life. I used to vote here in Biseoe right smart. I let the young folks do my votin. They can tell more about it. I sho do not think it is the woman's place to vote an hold all the jobs from the men. Iffen you don't in the Primary cause you don't know nuf to pick out a man, you sho don't know nuthin er tall bout votin in the General lection. In fact it ain't no good to our race nohow.

"The whole world gone past my judgment long ago. I jess sets round to see what they say an do next. It is bad when you caint get work you able to do on that's hard on the old folks. I could saved. I did save right smart. Sickness come on. Sometimes you have a bad crop year, make nuthin, but you have to live on. Young folks don't see no hard times if they keep well an able to work.

"I get commodities and $6 a month. I do a little if I can.

"One time my son bought a place fo me and him. He paid all cept $70. I don't know whut it cost now. It was 47 acres. I worked on it three years. He sold it and went to the sawmill. He say he come out square on it. I didn't wanter sell it but he did."

Interviewer: Mrs. Bernice Bowden
Person interviewed: Katie Arbery
815 W. Thirteenth, Pine Bluff, Arkansas
Age: 80

KATIE ARBERY

"I am eighty years old. My name 'fore I was a Arbery was Baxter. My mother was a Baxter. Born in Union County.

"My mother's first people was Baxter and my grandmother was a Baxter and they just went by that name; she never did change her name.

"The boss man—that was what they called our master—his name was Paul McCall. He was married twice. His oldest son was Jim McCall. He was in the War. Yes ma'am, the Civil War.

"Paul McCall raised me up with his chillun and I never did call him master, just called him pappy, and Jim McCall, I called him brother Jim. Just raised us all up there in the yard. My grandmother was the cook.

"There wasn't no fightin' in Union County but I 'member when the Yankees was goin' through and singin'

> 'The Union forever, hurrah, boys, hurrah
> We'll rally 'round the flag, boys,
> Shouting the battle cry of freedom.'

(She sang this—ed.)

And I 'member this one good:

> 'Old buckwheat cakes and good strong butter
> To make your lips go flip, flip, flutter.
> Look away, look away, look away, Dixie land.'

"Pappy used to play that on his fiddle and have us chillun tryin' to dance. Used to call us chillun and say, 'You little devils, come up here and dance' and have us marchin'.

"My cousin used to be a quill blower. Brother Jim would cut fishin' canes and plat 'em together—they called 'em a pack—five in a row, just like my fingers. Anybody that knowed how could sure make music on 'em. Tom Rollins, that was my baby uncle, he was a banjo picker.

"I can remember a heap a things that happened, but 'bout slavery, I didn't know one day from another. They treated us so nice that when they said freedom come, I thought I was always free.

"I heered my grandmother talk about sellin' 'em, but I was just a little kid and I didn't know what they was talkin' about. I heered 'em say, 'Did you know they sold Aunt Sally away from her baby?' I heered 'em talkin', I know that much.

"After freedom, our folks stayed right on Paul McCall's place. My grandmother cooked for the McCalls till I was eight or nine years old, then she cooked for the McCrays—they was all relatives—till I was twenty-one. Then I married.

"Paul McCall first married in the Baxter family and then he married into the McCray family. I lived on the McCall place till I was grown. They all come from Alabama. Yes'm, they come befo' the war was.

"Chillun in dem days paid attention. People raised chillun in dem days. Folks just feeds 'em now and lets 'em grow up.

"I looks at the young race now and they is as wise as rabbits.

"I never went to school but three months, but I never will forget that old blue back McGuffey's. Sam Porter was our teacher and I was scared of him. I was so scared I couldn't learn nothin'.

"As far as I can remember I have been treated nice everywhere I been. Ain't none of the white folks ever mistreated me.

"Lord, we had plenty to eat in slavery days—and freedom days too.

"One time when my mother was cookin' for Colonel Morgan and my oldest brother was workin' some land, my mother always sent me over with a bucket of milk for him. So one day she say. 'Snooky, come carry your brother's milk and hurry so he can have it for dinner.' I was goin' across a field; that was a awful deer country. I had on a red dress and was goin' on with my milk when I saw a old buck lookin' at me. All at once he went 'whu-u-u', and then the whole drove come up. There was mosely trees (I think she must have meant mimosa—ed.) in the field and I run and climbed up in one of 'em. A mosely tree grows crooked; I don't care how straight you put it in the ground, it's goin' to grow crooked. So I climb up in the mosely tree and begin to yell. My brother heard me and come 'cause he knowed what was up. He used to say, 'Now, Snipe, when you come 'cross that mosely field, don't you wear that old red dress 'cause they'll get you down and tear that dress off you.' I liked the dress 'cause he had give it to me. I had set the milk down at the foot of the tree and it's a wonder they didn't knock it over, but when my brother heard me yell he come a runnin', with a gun and shot one of the deer. I got some of the venison and he give some to Colonel Morgan, his boss man. Colonel Morgan had fought in the war.

"The reason I can't tell you no more is, since I got old my mind goes this and that a way.

"But I can tell you all the doctors that doctored on me. They give me up to die once. I had the chills from the first of one January to the next We had Dr. Chester and Dr. McCray and Dr. Lewis—his name was Perry—and Dr. Green and Dr. Smead. Took quinine till I couldn't hear, and finally Dr. Green said, 'We'll just quit givin' her medicine, looks like she's goin' to die anyway.' And then Dr. Lewis fed me for three weeks steady on okra soup cooked with chicken. Just give me the broth. Then I commenced gettin' better and here I am.

"But I can't work like I used to. When I was young I could work right along with the men but I can't do it now. I wish I could 'cause they's a heap a things I'd like that my chillun and grandchillun can't get for me.

"Well, good-bye, come back again sometime."

Interviewer: Samuel S. Taylor
Person interviewed: Campbell Armstrong
802 Schiller Street, Little Rock, Arkansas
Age: 86

CAMPBELL ARMSTRONG

[HW: Boys liked corn shuckings]

"I couldn't tell you when I was born. I was born a good while before freedom. I was a boy about ten years old in the time of the Civil War. That would make me about eighty-five or six years old.

"My father's name was Cy Armstrong. My mother's name was Gracie Armstrong. I don't know the names of my grandparents. They was gone when I got here. My sister died right there in the corner of the next room.

House and Furniture

"I used to live in an old log house. Take dirt and dob the cracks. The floors were these here planks. We had two windows and one door. That was in Georgia, in Houston County, on old Dempsey Brown's place. I know him—know who dug his grave.

"They had beds nailed up to the side of the house. People had a terrible time you know. White folks had it all. When I come along they had it and they had it ever since I been here. You didn't have no chance like folks have nowadays. Just made benches and stools to sit on.

Made tables out of planks. I never saw any cupboards and things like that. Them things wasn't thought about then. The house was like a stable then. But them log houses was better than these 'cause the wind couldn't get through them.

Work as a Boy

"I wasn't doin' nothin' but totin' water. I toted water for a whole year when I was a boy about eight years old. I was the water boy for the field hands. Later I worked out in the fields myself. They would make me sit on my mammy's row to help keep her up.

Free Negroes

"You better not say you were free them days. If you did, they'd tell you to get out of there. You better not stop on this side of the Mason Dixie Line either. You better stop on the other side. Whenever a nigger got so he couldn't mind, they'd take him down and whip him. They'd whip the free niggers just the same as they did the slaves.

Marriage

"You see that broom there? They just lay that broom down and step over it. That was all the marriage they knowed about.

Corn Shuckings

"The boys used to just get down and raise a holler and shuck that corn. Man, they had fun! They sure liked to go to those corn shuckings. They danced and went on. They'd give 'em whiskey too. That's all I know about it.

Rations

"They'd weigh the stuff out and give it to you and you better not go back. They'd give you three pounds of meat and a quart of meal and molasses when they'd make it. Sometimes they would take a notion to give you something like flour. But you had to take what they give you. They give out the rations every Saturday. That was to last you a week.

Patrollers

"I was at a ball one night. They had fence rails in the fire. Patroller knocked at the door, stepped in and closed it behind him. Nigger pulled a rail out of the fire and stuck it 'gainst the patroller and that patroller stepped aside and let that nigger get by. Niggers used to tie ropes across the road so that the patrollers' horses would trip up.

Mulattoes

"I never seed any mulattoes then. That thing is something that just come up. Old Dempsey Brown, if he seed a white man goin' 'round with the nigger women on his place, he run him away from there. But that's gwine on in the full now.

"That ought not to be. If God had wanted them people to mix, he'd have mixed 'em. God made 'em red and white and black. And I'm goin' to stay black. I ain't climbed the fence yet and I won't climb it now. I don't know. I don't believe in that. If you are white be white, and if you are black be black. Children need to go out and play but these boys ought not to be 'lowed to run after these girls.

Whippings

"Your overseer carried their straps with them. They had 'em with 'em all the time. Just like them white folks do down to the County Farm. Used to use a man just like he was a beast. They'd make him lay down on the ground and whip him. They'd had to shoot me down. That is the reason I tend to my business. If he wouldn't lay down they'd call for help and strap him down and stretch him out. Put one man on one arm and another on the other. They'd pull his clothes down and whip the blood out of him. Them people didn't care what they done since they didn't do right.

Freedom

"When I first heard them talking about freedom, I didn't know what freedom was. I was there standin' right up and looking at 'em when they told us we was free. And master said, 'You all free now. You can go where you want to.'

"They never give you a thing when they freed you. They give you some work to do. They never looked for nothin' only to go to work. The white folks always had the best of it.

"When Abe Lincoln first freed 'em, they all stood together. If this one was ill the others went over and sit up with him. If he needed something they'd carry it to him. They don't do that now. They done well then. As soon as they quit standing together then they had trouble.

Wages Then

"Fellow said to me, 'Campbell, I want you to split up them blocks and pile 'em up for me.' I said, 'What you goin' to pay me?' He said, 'I'll pay you what is right.' I said, 'That won't do; you have to tell me what you goin' to give me before I start to work.' And he said to me, 'You can git to hell out of here.'

Selling and Buying Slaves

"They'd put you up on the block and sell you. That is just what they'd do—sell you. These white folks will do anything,—anything they want to do. They'd take your clothes off just like you was some kind of a beast.

"You used to be worth a thousand dollars then, but you're not worth two bits now. You ain't worth nothin' when you're free.

Refugees—Jeff Davis

"They used to come to my place in droves. Wagons would start coming in in the morning and they wouldn't stop coming in till two or three in the evening. They'd just be travelin' to keep out the way of the Yankees. They caught old Jeff Davis over in Twiggs County. That's in Georgia. Caught him in Buzzard's Roost. That was only about four or five miles from where I was. I was right down yonder in Houston County. Twigg County and Houston County is adjoinin'. I never saw any of the soldiers but they was following them though.

Voters

"I have seen plenty of niggers voting. I wasn't old enough to vote in Georgia. I come in Arkansas and I found out how the folks used themselves and I come out that business. They was selling themselves just like cattle and I wouldn't have nothing to do with that.

"I knew Jerry Lawson, who was Justice of Peace. He was a nigger, a low-down devil. Man, them niggers done more dirt in this city. The Republicans had this city and state. I went to the polls and there was very few white folks there. I knew several of them niggers—Mack Armstrong, he was Justice of Peace. I can't call the rest of them. Nothing but old thieves. If they had been people, they'd been honest. Wouldn't sell their brother. It is bad yet. They still stealin' yet.

Ku Klux

"That's another devil. Man, I'll tell you we seen terrible times. I don't know nothing much about 'em myself. I know one thing. Abe Lincoln said, 'Kill him wherever you see him.'

Self-Support and Support of Aged Slaves in Slave Times

"A white man asked me how much they givin' me. I said, 'Eight dollars.' He said, 'You ought to be gittin' twenty-five.' I said, 'Maybe I ought to be but I ain't.'

"I ain't able to do no work now. I ain't able to tote that wood hardly. I don't git as much consideration as they give the slaves back yonder. They didn't make the old people in slavery work when they was my age. My daddy when he was my age, they turned him out. They give him a rice patch where he could make his rice. When he died, he had a whole lot of rice. They stopped putting all the slaves out at hard labor when they got old. That's one thing. White folks will take care of their old ones. Our folks won't do it. They'll take a stick and kill you. They don't recognize you're human. Their parents don't teach them. Folks done quit teaching their children. They don't teach them the right thing no more. If they don't do, then they ought to make them do.

Little Rock

"I been here about twenty years in Little Rock. I went and bought this place and paid for it. Somebody stole seventy-five dollars from me right here in this house.

And that got me down. I ain't never been able to git up since.

"I paid a man for what he did for me. He said, 'Well, you owe me fifteen cents.' When he got done he said, 'You owe me fifty cents.' You can't trust a man in the city.

"I was living down in England. That's a little old country town. I come here to Little Rock where I could be in a city. I done well. I bought this place.

"I reckon I lived in Arkansas about thirty years before I left and come here to Little Rock. When I left Georgia, I come to Arkansas and settled down in Lonoke County, made crops there. I couldn't tell you how long I stayed there. I didn't keep no record of it at all. I come out of Lonoke County and went into Jefferson.

"Man, I was never in such shape as I am in now. That devilish stock law killed me. It killed all the people. Nobody ain't been able to do nothin' since they passed the stock law. I had seventy-five hogs and twenty cows. They made a law you had to keep them chickens up, keep them hogs up, keep them cows up. They shoots at every right thing, and the wrong things they don't shoot at. God don't uphold no man to set you up in the jail when you ain't done nothin'. You didn't have no privilege then (slave time), and you ain't got none now."

Interviewer: Pernella Anderson, colored.
Person interviewed: Cora Armstrong, colored., Arkansas

CORA ARMSTRONG

"I was born in the Junction city community and belonged to the Cooks. I was ten years old at surrender. Mother and father had 12 children and we lived in a one room log cabin and cooked on a fireplace and oven. Mos and Miss Cook did not allow ma and pa to whip me. When ever I do something and I knew I was going to get a whipping I would make it to old Miss. She would keep me from getting that whipping. I was a devilish boy. I would do everything in the world I could think of just for devilment. Old mos was sure good to his slaves. I never went to school a day in my life. Old Miss would carry me to church sometimes when it was hot so we could fan for her. We used palmeter fan leaves for fans. We ate pretty good in slavery time, but we did not have all of this late stuff. Some of our dishes was possum stew, vegetables, persimmon pie and tato bread. Ma did not allow us to sit around grown folks. When they were talking she always made us get under the bed. Our bed was made from pine poles. We children slept on pallets on the floor. The way slaves married in slavery time they jumped over the broom and when they separated they jumped backward over the broom. Times were better in slavery time to my notion than they are now because they did not go hungry, neither necked. They ate common and wore one kind of clothes."

A duck, a bullfrog and a skunk went to a circus, the duck and the bullfrog got in, why didn't the skunk get in?

(Answer). The duck had a bill, the bullfrog had a greenback but the skunk had nothing but a scent.

If your father's sister is not your aunt what kin is she to you? (your mother).

What is the difference between a four quart measure and a side saddle? (Answer). They both hold a gallon. (a gal on)

Interviewer: Miss Irene Robertson
Person interviewed: Lillie Baccus, Madison, Arkansas
Age: 73

LILLIE BACCUS

"I'll tell you what I heard. I was too little to remember the Civil War. Mama's owner was ---- Dillard. She called him 'Master' Dillard. Papa's owner was ---- Smith. He called him 'Master' Smith. Mama was named Ann and papa Arthur Smith. I was born at West Point, Mississippi. I heard ma say she was sold. She said Pattick sold her. She had to leave her two children Cherry and Ann. Mama was a field hand. So was grandma yet she worked in the house some she said. After freedom Cherry and Ann come to mama. She was going to be sold agin but was freed before sold.

"Mama didn't live only till I was about three years old, so I don't know enough to tell you about her. Grandma raised us. She was sold twice. She said she run out of the house to pick up a star when the stars fell. They showered down and disappeared.

"The Yankees camped close to where they lived, close to West Point, Mississippi, but in the country close to an artesian well. The well was on their place. The Yankees stole grandma and kept her at their tent. They meant to take her on to wait on them and use but when they started to move old master spicioned they had her hid down there. He watched out and seen her when they was going to load her up. He went and got the head man to make them give her up. She was so glad to come home. Glad to see him cause she wanted to see him. They watched her so close she was afraid they would shoot her leaving. She lived to be 101 years old. She raised me. She used to tell how the overseer would whip her in the field. They wasn't good to her in that way.

"I have three living children and eleven dead. I married twice. My first husband is living. My second husband is dead. I married in day time in the church the last time. All else ever took place in my life was hard work. I worked in the field till I was too old to hit a tap. I live wid my children. I get $8 and commodities.

"I come to Arkansas because they said money was easy to get—growed on bushes. I had four little children to make a living for and they said it was easier.

"I think people is better than they was long time ago. Times is harder. People have to buy everything they have as high as they is, makes money scarce nearly bout a place as hen's teeth. Hens ain't got no teeth. We don't have much money I tell you. The Welfare gives me $8."

Interviewer: Samuel S. Taylor
Person interviewed: Joseph Samuel Badgett
1221 Wright Avenue, Little Rock, Arkansas
Age: 72

JOSEPH SAMUEL BADGETT

[HW: Mother was a Fighter]

"My mother had Indian in her. She would fight. She was the pet of the people. When she was out, the pateroles would whip her because she didn't have a pass. She has showed me scars that were on her even till the day that she died. She was whipped because she was out without a pass. She could have had a pass any time for the asking, but she was too proud to ask. She never wanted to do things by permission.

Birth

"I was born in 1864. I was born right here in Dallas County. Some of the most prominent people in this state came from there. I was born on Thursday, in the morning at three o'clock, May the twelfth. My mother has told me that so often, I have it memorized.

Persistence of Slave Customs

"While I was a slave and was born close to the end of the Civil War, I remember seeing many of the soldiers down here. I remember much of the treatment given to the slaves. I used to say 'master' myself in my day. We had to do that till after '69 or '70. I remember the time when I couldn't go nowhere without asking the 'white folks.' I wasn't a slave then but I couldn't go off without asking the white people. I didn't know no better.

"I have known the time in the southern part of this state when if you wanted to give an entertainment you would have to ask the white folks. Didn't know no better. For years and years, most of the niggers just stayed with the white folks. Didn't want to leave them. Just took what they give 'em and didn't ask for nothing different.

"If I had known forty years ago what I know now!

First Negro Doctor in Tulip, Arkansas

"The first Negro doctor we ever seen come from Little Rock down to Tulip, Arkansas. We were all excited. There were plenty of people who didn't have a doctor living with twenty miles of them. When I was fourteen years old, I was secretary of a conference.

Schooling

"What little I know, an old white woman taught me. I started to school under this old woman because there weren't any colored teachers. There wasn't any school at Tulip where I lived. This old lady just wanted to help. I went to her about seven years. She taught us a little every year—'specially in the summer time. She was high class—a high class Christian woman—belonged to the Presbyterian church. Her name was Mrs. Gentry Wiley.

"I went to school to Scipio Jones once. Then they opened a public school at Tulip and J.C. Smith taught there two years in the summer time. Then Lula Baily taught there one year. She didn't know no more than I did. Then Scipio came. He was there for a while. I don't remember just how long.

"After that I went to Pine Bluff. The County Judge at that time had the right to name a student from each district. I was appointed and went up there in '82 and '83 from my district. It took about eight years to finish Branch Normal at that time. I stayed there two years. I roomed with old man John Young.

"You couldn't go to school without paying unless you were sent by the Board. We lived in the country and I would go home in the winter and study in the summer. Professor J.C. Corbin was principal of the Pine Bluff Branch Normal at that time. Dr. A.H. Hill, Professor Booker, and quite a number of the people we consider distinguished were in school then. They finished, but I didn't. I had to go to my mother because she was ill. I don't claim to have no schooling at all.

"Forty Acres and a Mule"

"My mother received forty acres of land when freedom came. Her master gave it to her. She was given forty acres of land and a colt. There is no more to tell about that. It was just that way—a gift of forty acres of land and a colt from her former master.

"My mother died. There is a woman living now that lost it (the home). Mother let Malinda live on it. Mother lived with the white folks meanwhile. She didn't need the property for herself. She kept it for us. She built a nice log house on it. Fifteen acres of it was under cultivation when it was given to her. My sister lived on it for a long time. She mortgaged it in some way I don't know how. I remember when the white people ran me down there some years back to get me to sign a title to it. I didn't have to sign the paper because the property had been deeded to Susan Badgett and HEIRS; lawyers advised me not to sign it. But I signed it for the sake of my sister.

Father and Master

"My mother's master was named Badgett—Captain John Badgett. He was a Methodist preacher. Some of the Badgetts still own property on Main Street. My mother's master's father was my daddy.

Marriage

"I was married July 12, 1889. Next year I will have been married fifty years. My wife's name was Elizabeth Owens. She was born in Batesville, Mississippi. I met her at Brinkley when she was visiting her aunt. We married in Brinkley. Very few people in this city have lived together longer than we have. July 12, 1938, will make forty-nine years. By July 1939, we will have reached our fiftieth anniversary.

Patrollers, Jayhawkers, Ku Klux, and Ku Klux Klan

"Pateroles, Jayhawkers, and the Ku Klux came before the war. The Ku Klux in slavery times were men who would catch Negroes out and keep them if they did not collect from their masters. The Pateroles would catch Negroes out and return them if they did not have a pass. They whipped them sometimes if they did not have a pass. The Jayhawkers were highway men or robbers who stole slaves among other things. At least, that is the way the people regarded them. The Jayhawkers stole and pillaged, while the Ku Klux stole those Negroes they caught out. The word 'Klan' was never included in their name.

"The Ku Klux Klan was an organization which arose after the Civil War. It was composed of men who believed in white supremacy and who regulated the morals of the neighborhood. They were not only after Jews and Negroes, but they were sworn to protect the better class of people. They took the law in their own hands.

Slave Work

"I'm not so certain about the amount of work required of slaves. My mother says she picked four hundred pounds of cotton many a day. The slaves were tasked and given certain amounts to accomplish. I don't know the exact amount nor just how it was determined.

Opinions

"It is too bad that the young Negroes don't know what the old Negroes think and what they have done. The young folks could be helped if they would take advice."

Interviewer's Comment

Badgett's distinctions between jayhawkers, Ku Klux, patrollers, and Ku Klux Klan are most interesting.

I have been slow to catch it. All my life, I have heard persons with ex-slave background refer to the activities of the Ku Klux among slaves prior to 1865. I always thought that they had the Klux Klan and the patrollers confused.

Badgett's definite and clear-cut memories, however, lead me to believe that many of the Negroes who were slaves used the word Ku Klux to denote a type of persons who stole slaves. It was evidently in use before it was applied to the Ku Klux Klan.

The words "Ku Klux" and "Ku Klux Klan" are used indiscriminately in current conversation and literature. It is also true that many persons in the present do, and in the past did, refer to the Ku Klux Klan simply as "Ku Klux."

It is a matter of record that the organization did not at first bear the name "Ku Klux Klan" throughout the South. The name "Ku Klux" seems to have grown in application as the organization changed from a moral association of the best citizens of the South and gradually came under the control of lawless persons with lawless methods—whipping and murdering. It is antecedently reasonable that the change in names accompanying a change in policy would be due to a fitness in the prior use of the name.

The recent use of the name seems mostly imitation and propaganda.

Histories, encyclopedias, and dictionaries, in general, do not record a meaning of the term Ku Klux as prior to the Reconstruction period.

Slave Narratives

STATE—Arkansas
NAME OF WORKER—Samuel S. Taylor
ADDRESS—Little Rock, Arkansas
DATE—December, 1938
SUBJECT—Ex-slave

JEFF BAILEY

[TR: Repetitive information deleted from subsequent pages.]

Circumstances of Interview

1. Name and address of informant—Jeff Bailey, 713 W. Ninth Street, Little Rock.

2. Date and time of interview--

3. Place of interview—713 W. Ninth Street, Little Rock.

4. Name and address of person, if any, who put you in touch with informant--

5. Name and address of person, if any, accompanying you--

6. Description of room, house, surroundings, etc.

Personal History of Informant

1. Ancestry—father, Jeff Wells; mother, Tilda Bailey.

2. Place and date of birth—born in 1861 in Monticello, Arkansas.

3. Family--

4. Places lived in, with dates—reared in Monticello. Lived in Pine Bluff thirty-two years, then moved to Little Rock and has lived here thirty-two years.

5. Education, with dates--

6. Occupations and accomplishments, with dates—Hostler

7. Special skills and interests--

8. Community and religious activities--

9. Description of informant--

10. Other points gained in interview--

Text of Interview (Unedited)

[HW: A Hostler's Story]

"I was born in Monticello. I was raised there. Then I came up to Pine Bluff and stayed there thirty-two years. Then I came up here and been here thirty-two years. That is the reason the white folks so good to me now. I been here so long, I been a hostler all my life. I am the best hostler in this State. I go down to the post office they give me money. These white folks here is good to me.

"What you writing down? Yes, that's what I said. These white folks like me and they good to me. They give me anything I want. You want a drink? That's the best bonded whiskey money can buy. They gives it to me. Well, if you don't want it now, come in when you do.

"I lost my wife right there in that corner. I was married just once. Lived with her forty-three years. She died here five months ago. Josie Bailey! The white folks thought the world and all of her. That is another reason they give me so much. She was one of the best women I ever seen.

"I gits ten dollars a month. The check comes right up to the house. I used to work with all them money men. Used to handle all them horses at the post office. They ought to give me sixty-five dollars but they don't. But I gits along. God is likely to lemme live ten years longer. I worked at the post office twenty-two years and don't git but ten dollars a month. They ought to gimme more.

"My father's name was Jeff Wells. My mother's name was Tilda Bailey. She was married twice. I took her master's name. Jeff Wells was my father's name. Governor Bailey ought to give me somethin'. I got the same name he has. I know him.

"My father's master was Stanley—Jeff Stanley. That was in slavery time. That was my slave time people. I was just a little bit of a boy. I am glad you are gittin' that to help the colored people out. Are they goin' to give the old slaves a pension? What they want to ask all these questions for then? Well, I guess there's somethin' else besides money that's worth while.

"My father's master was a good man. He was good to him. Yes Baby! Jeff Wells, that my father's name. I was a little baby settin' in the basket 'round in the yard and they would put the cotton all 'round me. They carried me out where they worked and put me in the basket. I couldn't pick no cotton because I was too young. When they got through they would put me in that big old wagon and carry me home. There wasn't no trucks then. Jeff Wells (that was my father), when they got through pickin' the cotton, he would say, 'Put them children in the wagon; pick 'em up and put 'em in the wagon.' I was a little bitty old boy. I couldn't pick no cotton then. But I used to pick it after the surrender.

"I remember what they said when they freed my father. They said, 'You're free. You children are free. Go on back there and work and let your children work. Don't work them children too long. You'll git pay for your work.' That was in the Monticello courthouse yard. They said, 'You're free! Free!'

"My mistress said to me when I got back home, 'You're free. Go on out in the orchard and git yoself some peaches.' They had a yard full of peaches. Baby did I git me some peaches. I pulled a bushel of 'em.

Ku Klux Klan

"The Ku Klux run my father out of the fields once. And the white people went and got them 'bout it. They said, 'Times is hard, and we can't have these people losin' time out of the fields. You let these people work.' A week after that, they didn't do no mo. The Ku Klux didn't. Somebody laid them out. I used to go out to the fields and they would ask me, 'Jeff Bailey, what you do in' out here?' I was a little boy and you jus' ought to seen me gittin' 'way frum there. Whooo-eeee!

"I used to pick cotton back yonder in Monticello. I can't pick no cotton now. Naw Lawd! I'm too old. I can't do that kind of work now. I need help. Carl Bailey knows me. He'll help me. I'm a hostler. I handle horses. I used to pick cotton forty years ago. My mother washed clothes right after the War to git us children some thin' to eat. Sometimes somebody would give us somethin' to help us out.

"Tilda Bailey, that was my mother. She and my father belonged to different masters. Bailey was her master's name. She always called herself Bailey and I call myself Bailey. If I die, I'll be Bailey. My insurance is in the name of Bailey. My father and mother had about eight children. They raised all their children in Monticello. You ever been to Monticello? I had a good time in Monticello. I was a baby when peace was declared. Just toddling 'round.

"My father drank too much. I used to tell him about it. I used to say to him, 'I wouldn't drink so much whiskey.' But he drank it right on. He drank hisself to death.

"I believe Roosevelt's goin' to be President again. I believe he's goin' to run for a third term. He's goin' to be dictator. He's goin' to be king. He's goin' to be a good dictator. We don't want no more Republic. The people are too hard on the poor people. President Roosevelt lets everybody git somethin'. I hope he'll git it. I hope he'll be dictator. I hope he'll be king. Yuh git hold uh some money with him.

"You couldn't ever have a chance if Cook got to be governor. I believe Carl Bailey's goin' to be a good governor. I believe he'll do better. They put Miz Carraway back; I believe she'll do good too."

Extra Comment

Jeff Bailey talked like a man of ninety instead of a man of seventy-six or seven. It was hard to get him to stick to any kind of a story. He had two or three things on his mind and he repeated those things over and over again—Governor Bailey, Hostler, Post Office. He had to be pried loose from them. And he always returned the next sentence.

Interviewer: Mary D. Hudgins.
Person Interviewed: James Baker Aged: 81
Home: With daughter who owns home at 941 Wade St.

JAMES BAKER

The outskirts of eastern Hot Springs resemble a vast checkerboard—patterned in Black and White. Within two blocks of a house made of log-faced siding—painted a spotless white and provided with blue shutters will be a shack which appears to have been made from the discard of a dozen generations of houses.

Some of the yards are thick with rusting cans, old tires and miscelaneous rubbish. Some of them are so gutted by gully wash that any attempt at beautification would be worse than useless. Some are swept—farm fashion—free from surface dust and twigs. Some attempt—others achieve grass and flowers. Vegetable gardens are far less frequent then they should be, considering space left bare.

The interviewer frankly lost her way several times. One improper direction took her fully half a mile beyond her destination. From a hilltop she could look down on less elevated hills and into narrow valleys. The impression was that of a cheaply painted back-drop designed for a "stock" presentation of "Mrs. Wiggs of the Cabbage Patch."

Moving along streets, alleys and paths backward "toward town" the interviewer reached another hill. Almost a quarter of a mile away she spied an old colored man sunning himself on the front porch of a well kept cottage. Somthing about his white hair and erectly-slumped bearing screamed "Ex-slave" even at that distance. A negro youth was passing.

"I beg your pardon, can you tell me where to find Wade Street and James Baker?" "Ya—ya—ya—s ma'am. Dat—dat—dat's de house over da—da—da—da—r. He—he—he lives at his daughter's" "Could that be he on the porch?" "Ya—ya—yas ma'am. Dat—dat—dat's right."

"Yes, ma'am I'm James Baker. Yes ma'am I remembers about the war. You want to talk to me about it. Let me get you a chair. You'd rather sit right there on the step? All right ma'am.

I was born in Hot Spring county, below Melvern it was. I was borned on the farm of a man named Hammonds. But I was pretty little when he sold me to some folks named Fenton. Wasn't with them so very long. You know how it goes—back in them days. When a girl or a boy would marry, why they'd givem them as many black folks as they could spare. I was give to one of the daughters when she married. She was Mrs. Samuel Gentry.

I wasn't so very big before the war. So I didn't have to work in the fields. Just sort of played around. Can't remember very much about what happened then. We never did see no fighting about. They was men what passed through. They was soldiers. They come backwards and forewards. I was about as big as that boy you see there"—pointing to a lad about 8 years old—"some of them they was dressed in blue—sort of blue. We was told that they was Federals. Then some of them was in grey—them was the Southerners.

No, we wasn't scared of them—either of them. They didn't never bother none of us. Didn't have anything to be scared of not at all. It wasn't really Malvern we was at—that was sort of before Malvern come to be. Malvern didn't grow up until after the railroad come through. The town was across the river, sort of this side. It was called Rockport. Ma'am—you know about Rockport"—a delighted chuckle. "Yes, ma'am, don't many folks now-a-days know about Rockport. Yes ma'am the river is pretty shoaly right there. Pretty shoaly. Yes ma'am there was lots of doings around Rockport. Yes ma'am. Dat's right. Before Garland county was made, Rockport was the capitol O—I mean de county seat of Hot Spring County. Hot Springs was in that county at that time. There was big doings in town when they held court. Real big doings.

No, ma'am I didn't do nothing much when the war was over. No, I didn't go to be with my daddy. I moved over to live with a man I called Uncle Billy—Uncle Billy Bryant he was. He had all his family with him. I stayed with him and did what he told me to—'til I grew up. He was always good to me—treated me like his own children.

Uncle Billy lived at Rockport. I liked living with him. I remember the court house burned down—or blowed down—seems like to me it burned down. Uncle Billy got the job of cleaning bricks. I helped him. That was when they moved over to Malvern—the court house I mean. No—no they didn't. Not then, that was later—they didn't build the railroad until later. They built it back—sort of simple like—built it down by Judge Kieth's.

No ma'am. I don't remember nothing about when they built the railroad. You see we lived across the river—and I guess—well I just didn't know nothing about it. But Rockport wasn't no good after the railroad come in. They moved the court house and most of the folks moved away. There wasn't nothing much left.

I started farming around there some. I moved about quite a bit. I lived down sort of by Benton too for quite a spell. I worked around at most any kind of farming.

'Course most of the time we was working at cotton and corn. I's spent most of my life farming. I like it. Moved around pretty considerable. Sometimes I hired out—sometimes I share cropped—sometimes I worked thirds and fourths. What does I mean by hired out—I means worked for wages. Which way did I like best—I'll take share-cropping. I sort of like share-cropping.

I been in Hot Springs for 7 years. Come to be with my daughter." (An interruption by a small negro girl—neatly dressed and bright-eyed. Not content with watching from the sidelines she had edged closer and squatted comfortably within a couple of feet of the interviewer. A wide, pearly grin, a wee pointing forefinger and, "Granddaddy, that lady's got a tablet just like Aunt Ellen. See, Granddaddy.") "You mustm't bother the lady. Didn't your mother tell you not to stop folks when they is talking."—the voice was kindly and there was paternal pride in it. A nickle—tendered the youngster by the interviewer—and guaranteed to produce a similar tablet won a smile and childish silence.

"Yes, ma'am, I lives with my daughter—her name is Lulu Mitchell. She owns her house—yes ma'am it helps.

But it's sure hard to get along. Seems like it's lots harder now than it used to be when I was gitting started. Lulu works—she irons. Another daughter lives right over there. Her name's Ellen. She works too—at what she can get to do. She owns her house too.

Three of my daughters is living. Been married twice—I has. Didn't stay with the last one long. Yes ma'am I been coming backwards and forewards to Hot Springs all my life—you might say. 'Twasn't far over and I kept a'coming back. Been living all around here. It's pretty nice being with my daughter. She's good to me. I loves my granddaughter. We has a pretty hard time—Harder dan what I had when I was young—but then it do seem like it's harder to earn money dan what it was when I was young."

Interviewer: R.S. Taylor
Person Interviewed: Uncle William Baltimore
Resident: Route #1, Pine Bluff, Arkansas, Jefferson County. Age: 103.

WILLIAM BALTIMORE

"You wants to know how old I is? I'se lived a long time. I'se goin' on 104. My gran'mammy was over 100 years. My mamma was 100. My pappy was 96. They was twelve chilluns. I don't know if any of my sisters or brothers is livin'. Don't know if one of my friends back in my boy days is livin'. I'se like a poor old leaf left hangin' to a tree.

"Yes—I sho do member back befo' the war. I was borned on the Dr. Waters place about twelve miles out of Pine Bluff on the east side of Noble Lake. My gran'mammy and gran'pappy and my mamma and my pappy were slaves on de Walker plantation. I was not bought or sold—just lived on de old plantation. I wasn't whipped neither but once I mighty near got a beatin'. Want to hear about it? I likes to tell.

"Dr. Waters had a good heart. He didn't call us 'slaves'. He call us 'servants'. He didn't want none of his niggers whipped 'ceptin when there wasn't no other way. I was grown up pretty good size. Dr. Waters liked me cause I could make wagons and show mules. Once when he was going away to be gone all day, he tole me what to do while he was gone. The overseer wasn't no such good man as old master. He wanted to be boss and told me what to do. I tole him de big boss had tole me what to do and I was goin' to do it. He got mad and said if I didn't do what he said I'd take a beating. I was a big nigger and powerful stout. I tole the overseer fore he whipped me he's show himself a better man than I was. When he found he was to have a fight he didn't say no more about the whipping.

"I worked on de plantation till de war broke. Then I went into the army with them what called themselves secesh's. I didn't fight none, never give me a gun nor sword. I was a servant. I cooked and toted things. In 1863 I was captured by the Yankees and marched to Little Rock and sworn in as a Union Soldier. I was sure enough soldier now. I never did any fighting but I marched with the soldiers and worked for them whatever they said.

"We marched from Pine Bluff on through Ft. Smith and the Indian Territory of Oklahoma. Then we went to Leavenworth Kansas and back to Jefferson County, Arkansas. And all that walking I did on these same foots you see right here now.

"On this long march we camped thirty miles from Ft. Smith. We had gone without food three days and was powerful hongry. I started out to get something to eat. I found a sheep, I was tickled. I laughed. I could turn the taste of that sheep meat under my tongue. When I got to camp with the sheep I had to leave for picket duty. Hungrier than ever, I thought of that sheep all the time. When I got back I wanted my chunk of meat. It had been killed, cooked, eat up. Never got a grease spot on my finger from my sheep.

"When time come for breaking up the army I went

back to Jefferson county and set to farmin'. I was free now. I didn't do so well on the land as I didn't have mules and money to live on. I went to Dersa County and opened up a blacksmith shop. I learned how to do this work when I was with Dr. Waters. He had me taught by a skilled man. I learned to build wagons too.

"I made my own tools. Who showed me how? Nobody. When I needed a hack saw I made it out of a file—that was all I had to make it of. I had to have it. Once I made a cotton scraper out of a piece of hardwood. I put a steel edge on it. O yes I made everything. Can I build a wagon—make all the parts? Every thing but the hubs for the wheels.

"You say I don't seem to see very well. Ha-ha! I don't see nuthin' at all. I'se been plum blind for 23 years. I can't see nothin'. But I patches my own clothes. You don't know how I can thread the needle? Look here." I asked him to let me see his needle threader. He felt around in a drawer and pulled out a tiny little half arrow which he had made of a bit of tin with a pair of scissors and fine file. He pushed this through the eye of the needle, then hooked the thread on it and pulled it back again threading his needle as fast as if he had good eyesight. "This is a needle threader. I made it myself. Watch me thread a needle. Can't I do it as fast as if I had a head full of keen eyes? My wife been gone twenty years. She went blind too. I had to do something. My patches may not look so pretty but they sure holt (hold).

"You wants to know what I think of the way young folks is doing these days? They'se goin' to fast. So is their papas and mammas. Dey done forgot dey's a God and a day of settlin'. Den what dances pays de fiddler. I got religion long time ago—jined de Baptist church in 1870 and haven't never got away from it. I'se tried to tote fair with God and he's done fair by me.

"Does I get a pension? I shure do. It was a lucky day when de Yankees got me. Ef they hadn't I don't know what'd become of me. After I went blind I had hard times. Folks, white folks and all, brought me food. But that wasn't any good way to get along. Sometimes I ate, sometimes I didn't. So some of my white, friends dug up my record with the Yankees and got me a pension. Now I'm setting pretty for de rest of my life. Yes—O yes I'se older dan most folks get. Still I may be still takin' my grub here when some of these young whiskey drinkin razzin' around young chaps is under the dirt. It pays to I don know of any bad spots in me yet. It pays to live honest, work hard, stay sober. God only knows what some of these lazy, triflin' drinkin' young folks is comin' to."

Interviewer: Pernella M. Anderson
Person interviewed: Mose Banks
Douglas Addition, El Dorado, Arkansas
Age: 69

MOSE BANKS

"My name is Mose Banks and I am sixty-nine years old. I was born in 1869. I was born four years after freedom but still I was a slave in a way. My papa stayed with his old miss and master after freedom until he died and he just died in 1918, so we all stayed with him too. I had one of the best easiest times in my life. My master was name Bob Stevenson and he was a jewel. Never meaned us, never dogged, never hit one of us in his life. He bought us just like he bought my papa. He never made any of the girls work in the field. He said the work was too hard. He always said splitting rails, bushing, plowing and work like that was for men. That work makes no count women.

"The girls swept yards, cleaned the house, nursed, and washed and ironed, combed old miss' and the children's hair and cut their finger and toe nails and mended the clothes. The womens' job was to cook, attend to the cows, knit all the socks for the men and boys, spin thread, card bats, weave cloth, quilt, sew, scrub and things like that.

"The little boys drove up the cows, slopped the hogs, got wood and pine for light, go to the spring and get water. After a boy was twelve then he let him work in the fields. My main job was hitching the horse to the buggy for old Miss Stevenson, and put the saddle on old master's saddle horse.

"I was very small but when the first railroad come through old master took us to see the train. I guess it was about forty or fifty miles because it took us around four days to make the round trip. The trains were not like they are now. The engine was smaller and they burned wood and they had what they called a drum head and they didn't run very fast, and could not carry many cars. It was a narrow gauge road and the rails were small and the road was dirt. It was not gravel and rocks like it is now. It was a great show to me and we all had something to talk about for a long time. People all around went to see it and we camped out one night going and coming and camped one night at the railroad so we could see the train the next day. A man kept putting wood in the furnace in order to keep a fire. Smoke come out of the drum head. The drum head was something like a big washpot or a big old hogshead barrel. An ox team was used for most all traveling. You did not see very many horses or mules.

"The white children taught us how to read and I went to school too.

"I went to church too. We did not have a church house; we used a brush arbor for service for a long time. In the winter we built a big fire in the middle and we sat all around the fire on small pine logs. Later they built a log church, so we had service in there for years.

"We did not live near a school, so old mistress and the children taught us how to read and write and count. I never went to school in my life and I bet you, can't none of these children that rub their heads on college walls beat me reading and counting. You call one and ask them to divide ninety-nine cows and one bob-tailed bull by two, and they can't answer it to save their lives without a pencil and paper and two hours' figuring when it's nothing to say but fifty.

"Wasn't no cook stoves and heaters until about 1890 or 1900. If there was I did not know about them. They cooked on fireplace and fire out in the yard on what they called oven and we had plenty of plain grub. We stole eggs from the big house because we never got any eggs.

"The custom of marrying was just pack up and go on and live with who you wanted to; that is the Negroes did—I don't know how the white people married. This lawful marrying came from the law since man made law.

"When anybody died everybody stopped working and moaned and prayed until after the burying.

"I can say there is as much difference between now and sixty years ago as it is in day and night."

United States. Work Projects Administration

Interviewer: S. S. Taylor
Person interviewed: Henry Banner
County Hospital
Little Rock, Ark.
Age: ?

HENRY BANNER

[HW: Forty Acres and a Mule]

"I was sold the third year of the war for fifteen years old. That would be in 1864. That would make my birthday come in 1849. I must have been 12 year old when the war started and sixteen when Lee surrendered. I was born and raised in Russell County, Ol' Virginny. I was sold out of Russell County during the war. Ol' Man Menefee refugeed me into Tennessee near Knoxville. They sold me down there to a man named Jim Maddison. He carried me down in Virginny near Lynchburg and sold me to Jim Alec Wright. He was the man I was with in the time of the surrender. Then I was in a town called Liberty. The last time I was sold, I sold for $2,300,—more than I'm worth now.

"Police were for white folks. Patteroles were for niggers. If they caught niggers out without a pass they would whip them. The patteroles were for darkies, police for other people.

"They run me once, and I ran home. I had a dog at home, and there wasn't no chance them gettin' by that dog. They caught me once in Liberty, and Mrs. Charlie

Crenchaw, Ol' John Crenchaw's daughter, came out and made them turn me loose. She said, 'They are our darkies; turn them loose.'

"One of them got after me one night. I ran through a gate and he couldn't get through. Every time I looked around, I would see through the trees some bush or other and think it was him gaining on me. God knows! I ran myself to death and got home and fell down on the floor.

"The slaves weren't expecting nothing. It got out somehow that they were going to give us forty acres and a mule. We all went up in town. They asked me who I belonged to and I told them my master was named Banner. One man said, 'Young man, I would go by my mama's name if I were you.' I told him my mother's name was Banner too. Then he opened a book and told me all the laws. He told me never to go by any name except Banner. That was all the mule they ever give me.

"I started home a year after I got free and made a crop. I had my gear what I had saved on the plantation and went to town to get my mule but there wasn't any mule.

"Before the war you belonged to somebody. After the war you weren't nothin' but a nigger. The laws of the country were made for the white man. The laws of the North were made for man.

"Freedom is better than slavery though. I done seed both sides. I seen darkies chained. If a good nigger killed a white overseer, they wouldn't do nothin' to him. If he was a bad nigger, they'd sell him. They raised niggers to sell; they didn't want to lose them. It was just like a mule killing a man.

"Yellow niggers didn't sell so well. There weren't so many of them as there are now. Black niggers stood the climate better. At least, everybody thought so.

"If a woman didn't breed well, she was put in a gang and sold. They married just like they do now but they didn't have no license. Some people say that they done this and that thing but it's no such a thing. They married just like they do now, only they didn't have no license.

"Ol' man came out on April 9, 1865. and said, 'General Lee's whipped now and dam badly whipped. The war is over. The Yankees done got the country. It is all over. Just go home and hide everything you got. General Lee's army is coming this way and stealing everything they can get their hands on.' But General Lee's army went the other way.

"I saw a sack of money setting near the store. I looked around and I didn't see nobody. So I took it and carried it home. Then I hid it. I heard in town that Jeff Davis was dead and his money was no good. I took out some of the money and went to the grocery and bought some bread and handed her five dollar bill. She said, 'My goodness, Henry, that money is no good; the Yankees have killed it.' And I had done gone all over the woods and hid that money out. There wasn't no money. Nobody had anything. I worked for two bits a day. All our money was dead.

"The Yankees fed the white people with hard tacks (at Liberty, Virginia). All around the country, them that didn't have nothin' had to go to the commissary and get hard tacks.

"I started home. I went to town and rambled all around but there wasn't nothin' for me.

"I was set free in April. About nine o'clock in the morning when we went to see what work we would do, ol' man Wright called us all up and told us to come together. Then he told us we were free. I couldn't get nothing to do; so I jus' stayed on and made a crop."

Interviewer: Miss Irene Robertson
Person interviewed: John W. H. Barnett, Marianna, Arkansas
Age: 81

JOHN W. H. BARNETT

"I was born at Clinton Parish, Louisiana. I'm eighty-one years old. My parents and four children was sold and left six children behind. They kept the oldest children. In that way I was sold but never alone. Our family was divided and that brought grief to my parents. We was sold on a block at New Orleans. J.J. Gambol (Gamble?) in north Louisiana bought us. After freedom I seen all but one of our family. I don't recollect why that was.

"For three weeks steady after the surrender people was passing from the War and for two years off and on somebody come along going home. Some rode and some had a cane or stick walking. Mother was cooking a pot of shoulder meat. Them blue soldiers come by and et it up. I didn't get any I know that. They cleaned us out. Father was born at Eastern Shore, Maryland. He was about half Indian. Mother's mother was a squaw. I'm more Indian than Negro. Father said it was a white man's war. He didn't go to war. Mother was very dark. He spoke a broken tongue.

"We worked on after freedom for the man we was owned by. We worked crops and patches. I didn't see much difference then. I see a big change come out of it.

We had to work. The work didn't slacken a bit. I never owned land but my father owned eighty acres in Drew County. I don't know what become of it. I worked on the railroad section, laid crossties, worked in stave mills. I farmed a whole lot all along. I hauled and cut wood.

"I get ten dollars and I sells sassafras and little things along to help out. My wife died. My two sons left just before the World War. I never hear from them. I married since then.

"Present times—I can't figure it out. Seems like a stampede. Not much work to do. If I was young I reckon I could find something to do.

"Present generation—Seem like they are more united. The old ones have to teach the young ones what to do. They don't listen all the time. The times is strange. People's children don't do them much good now seems like. They waste most all they make some way. They don't make it regular like we did farming. The work wasn't regular farming but Saturday was ration day and we got that."

Interviewer: Miss Irene Robertson
Person interviewed: Josephine Ann Barnett,
R.F.D., De Valls Bluff, Arkansas
Age: 75 or 80

JOSEPHINE ANN BARNETT

"I do not knows my exact age. I judge I somewhere between 75 and 80 years old. I was born close to Germantown, Tennessee. We belong, that is my mother, to Phillip McNeill and Sally McNeill. My mother was a milker. He had a whole heap of hogs, cattle and stock. That not all my mother done. She plowed. Children done the churnin'.

"The way it all come bout I was the onliest chile my mother had. Him and Miss Sallie left her to help gather the crop and they brought me in the buggy wid them. I set on a little box in the foot of the buggy. It had a white umbrella stretched over it. Great big umbrella run in between them. It was fastened to the buggy seat. When we got to Memphis they loaded the buggy on the ship. I had a fine time coming. When we got to Bucks Landing we rode to his place in the buggy. It is 13 miles from here (De Valls Bluff). In the fall nearly all his slaves come out here. Then when my mother come on. I never seen my papa after I left back home [TR: Crossed out: (near Germantown)]. My father belong to Boston Hack. He wouldn't sell and Mr. McNeill wouldn't sell and that how it come.

"I muster been five or six years old when I come out

here to Arkansas. My grandma was a midwife. She was already out here. She had to come with the first crowd cause some women was expecting. I tell you it sho was squally times. This country was wild. It was different from Tennessee or close to Germantown where we come from. None of the slaves liked it but they was brought.

"The war come on direckly after we got here. Several families had the slaves drove off to Texas to save them. Keep em from following the Yankee soldiers right here at the Bluff off. I remember seein' them come up to the gate. My mother and two aunts went. His son and some more men drove em. After freedom them what left childern come back. I stayed with my grandma while they gone. I fed the chickens, shelled corn, churned, swept. I done any little turns they sent me to do.

"One thing I remember happened when they had scrimmage close—it mighter been the one on Long Prairie—they brought a young boy shot through his lung to Mr. Phillip McNeill's house. He was a stranger. He died. I felt so sorry for him. He was right young. He belong to the Southern army. The Southern army nearly made his place their headquarters.

"Another thing I remember was a agent was going through the country settin' fire to all the cotton. Mr. McNeill had his cotton—all our crop we made. That man set it afire. It burned more than a week big. He burned some left at the gin not Mr. McNeill's. It was fun to us children but I know my grandma cried and all the balance of the slaves. Cause they got some Christmas money and clothes too when the cotton was sold.

"The slaves hated the Yankees. They treated them

mean. They was having a big time. They didn't like the slaves. They steal from the slaves too. Some poor folks didn't have slaves.

"After freedom my mother come back after me and we come here to De Valls Bluff and I been here ever since. The Yankee soldiers had built shacks and they left them. They would do. Some was one room, log, boxed and all sorts. They give us a little to eat to keep us from starvin'. It sho was a little bit too. My mother got work about.

"The first schoolhouse was a colored school. We had two rooms and two teachers sent down from the North to teach us. If they had a white school I didn't know it. They had one later on. I was bout grown. Mr. Proctor and Miss Rice was the first teachers. We laughed bout em. They was rough looking, didn't look like white folks down here we'd been used to. They thought they sho was smart. Another teacher come down here was Mr. Abner. White folks wouldn't have nothin' to do with em. We learned. They learned us the ABC's and to write. I can read. I learned a heap of it since I got grown just trying. They gimme a start.

"Times is hard in a way. Prices so high. I never had a hard time in my life. I get $40 a month. It is cause my husband was a soldier here at De Valls Bluff.

"I do not vote. I ain't goiner vote.

"I don't know what to think of the young generation. They are on the road to ruin seems like. I speakln' of the real young folks. They do like they see the white girls and boys doin'. I don't know what to become of em. The women outer stay at home and let the men take care of em. The women seems like taking all the jobs. The colored folks cookin' and making the living for their men folks. It ain't right—to me. But I don't care how they do. Things ain't got fixed since that last war." (World War).

Interviewer: Mrs. Rosa B. Ingram
Person interviewed: Lizzie Barnett; Conway, Arkansas
Age: 100?

LIZZIE BARNETT

"Yes; I was born a slave. My old mammy was a slave before me. She was owned by my old Miss, Fanny Pennington, of Nashville, Tennessee. I was born on a plantation near there. She is dead now. I shore did love Miss Fanny.

"Did you have any brothers and sisters, Aunt Liz.?"

"Why, law yes, honey, my mammy and Miss Fanny raised dey chillun together. Three each, and we was jes' like brothers and sisters, all played in de same yard. No, we did not eat together. Dey sot us niggers out in de yard to eat, but many a night I'se slept with Miss Fanny.

"Mr. Pennington up and took de old-time consumption. Dey calls it T.B. now. My mammy nursed him and took it from him and died before Mr. Abe Lincoln ever sot her free.

"I have seen hard times, Miss, I shore have.

"In dem days when a man owned a plantation and had children and they liked any of the little slave niggers, they were issued out to 'em just like a horse or cow.

"'Member, honey, when de old-time war happened between the North and South, The Slavery War. It was so long ago I just can 'member it. Dey had us niggers scared to death of the Bluejackets. One day a man come to Miss Fanny's house and took a liking to me. He put me up on a block an' he say, 'How old is dis nigger?' An' she say 'five' when she know well an' good I was ten. No, he didn't get me. But I thought my time had come.

"Yes, siree, I was Miss Fanny's child. Why wouldn't I love her when I sucked titty from her breast when my mammy was working in the field? I shore did love Miss Fanny.

"When de nigger war was over and dey didn't fit (fight) any longer, Abe Lincoln sot all de niggers free and den got 'sassinated fer doin it.

"Miss, you don't know what a hard life we slaves had, cause you ain't old enough to 'member it. Many a time I've heard the bull whips a-flying, and heard the awful cries of the slaves. The flesh would be cut in great gaps and the maggits (maggots) would get in them and they would squirm in misery.

"I want you to know I am not on Arkansas born nigger. I come from Tennessee. Be sure to put that down. I moved to Memphis after Miss Fanny died.

"While I lived in Memphis, de Yellow Fever broke out. You have never seed the like. Everything was under quarantine. The folks died in piles and de coffins was piled as high as a house. They buried them in trenches, and later they dug graves and buried them. When they got to looking into the coffins, they discovered some had turned over in dey coffins and some had clawed dey eyes out and some had gnawed holes in dey hands. Dey was buried alive!

"Miss, do you believe in ha'nts? Well, if you had been in Memphis den you would. Dey was jes' paradin' de streets at nite and you'd meet dem comin at you round de dark corners and all de houses everywhere was ha'nted. I've seed plenty of 'em wid my own eyes, yes, siree.

"Yes, the times were awful in Memphis endurin the plague. Women dead lying around and babies sucking their breasts. As soon as the frost came and the quarantine was lifted, I came to Conway, 1867. But I am a Tennessee nigger.

"When I cams to Conway there were few houses to live in. No depot. I bought this piece of land to build my shanty from Mr. Jim Harkrider for $25.00. I worked hard for white folks and saved my money and had this little two-room house built (mud chimney, and small porch and one small window). It is about to fall down on me, but it will last as long as I live. At first, I lived and cooked under a bush (brush) arbor. Cooked on the coals in an iron skillet. Here it it, Miss.

"Part ob de time after de nigger war (Civil) I lived in Hot Springs. President 'Kinley had a big reservation over there and a big hospital for the sick and wounded soldiers. Den de war broke out in Cuba and dere was a spatch (dispatch) board what de news come over dat de war was on. Den when dat war was over and 'Kinley was tryin to get us niggers a slave pension dey up and 'sassinated him.

"After Mr. Lincoln sot de slaves free, dey had Northern teachers down South and they were called spies and all left the country.

"I don't know 'sactly how old I am. Dey say I am 100. If Miss Fanny was livin' she could settle it. But I have had a hard life. Yes mam. Here I is living in my shanty, 'pendin' on my good white neighbors to feed me and no income 'cept my Old Age Pension. Thank God for Mr. Roosevelt. I love my Southern white friends. I am glad the North and South done shook hands and made friends. All I has to do now is sit and look forward to de day when I can meet my old mammy and Miss Fanny in the Glory Land. Thank God."

Interviewer: Miss Irene Robertson
Person interviewed: Spencer Barnett (blind), Holly Grove, Ark.
Age: 81

SPENCER BARNETT

"I was born April 30, 1856. It was wrote in a old Bible. I am 81 years old. I was born 3 miles from Florence, Alabama. The folks owned us was Nancy and Mars Tom Williams. To my recollection they had John, William, and Tom, boys; Jane, Ann, Lucy, and Emma, girls. In my family there was 13 children. My parents name Harry and Harriett Barnett.

"Mars Tom Williams had a tanning yard. He bought hides this way: When a fellow bring hides he would tan em then give him back half what he brought. Then he work up the rest in shoes, harness, whoops, saddles and sell them. The man all worked wid him and he had a farm. He raised corn, cotton, wheat, and oats.

"That slavery was bad. Mars Tom Williams wasn't cruel. He never broke the skin. When the horn blowed they better be in place. They used a twisted cowhide whoop. It was wet and tied, then it mortally would hurt. One thing you had to be in your place day and night. It was confinin'.

"Sunday was visiting day.

"One man come to dinner, he hit a horse wid a rock and run way. He missed his dinner. He come back fo dark and went tole Mars Tom. He didn't whoop him. I was mighty little when that took place.

"They worked on Saturday like any other day. One man fixed out the rations. It didn't take long fer to go git em.

"The women plowed like men in plow time. Some women made rails. When it was cold and raining they spun and wove in the house. The men cut wood under a shed or side the barn so it knock off the wind. Mars Tom Williams had 12 grown men and women. I was too little to count but I heard my folks call am over by name and number more times en I got fingers and toes. He would hire em out to work some.

"When freedom come on I was on Hawkin Lankford Simpson place. It was 3 or 5 miles from town. They had a big dinner-picnic close by. It was 4 or 5 day of August. A lot of soldiers come by there and said, 'You niggers air free.' It bout broke up the picnic. The white folks broke off home. Them wanted to go back went, them didn't struck off gone wild. Miss Lucy and Mr. Bob Barnett give all of em stayed some corn and a little money. Then he paid off at the end of the year. Then young master went and rented at Dilly Hunt place. We stayed wid him 3 or 4 years then we went to a place he bought. Tom Barnett come to close to Little Rock. Mars William started and died on the way in Memphis. We come on wid the family. Guess they are all dead now. Wisht I know or could find em. Tom never married. He was a soldier. One of the boys died fo the war started.

"My brother Joe married Luvenia Omsted and Lewis Omsted married my sister Betsy and Mars Tom Williams swapped the women. My ma was a cook for the white folks how I come to know so much bout it all. Boys wore loose shirts till they was nine or ten years old. The shirt come to the calf of the leg. No belt.

"We had plenty common eating. They had a big garden and plenty milk. They cooked wid the eggs mostly. They would kill a beef and have a week of hog killing. They would kill the beef the hardest weather that come. The families cooked at night and on Sunday at the log cabins. They cook at night for all next day. The old men hauled wood.

"When I was a little boy I could hear men runnin' the slaves wid hounds in the mountains. The landmen paid paddyrollers to keep track of slaves. Keep em home day and night.

"We took turns bout going to white church. We go in washin' at the creek and put on clean clothes. She learned me a prayer. Old mistress learned me to say it nights I slept up at the house. I still can say it:

> 'Now I lay me down to sleep
> I pray the Lord my soul to keep
> If I should die fo I wake
> I pray the Lord my soul to take.'

"The slaves at our places had wheat straw beds. The white folks had fine goose feather beds. We had no idle days. Had a long time at dinner to rest and rest and water the teams. Sometimes we fed them. Old mistress had two peafowls roosted in the Colonial poplar trees. She had a pigeon house and a turkey house. I recken chicken and goose house, too. When company come you take em to see the farm, the garden, the new leather things jes' made and to see the little ducks, calves, and colts. Folks don't care bout seeing that now.

"The girls went to Florence to school. All I can recollect is them going off to school and I knowed it was Florence.

"The Yankees burned the big house. It was a fine house. Old mistress moved in the overseer's house. He was a white man. He moved somewhere else. The Yankees made raids and took 15 or 20 calves from her at one time. They set the tater house afire. They took the corn. Old mistress cried more on one time. The Yankees starved out more black faces than white at their stealing. After that war it was hard for the slaves to have a shelter and enough eatin' that winter. They died in piles bout after that August I tole you bout. Joe Innes was our overseer when the house burned.

"The Ku Klux come to my house twice. They couldn't get filled up wid water. They scared us to death. I heard a lot of things they done.

"I don't vote. I voted once in all my life fo some county officers.

"I been in Arkansas since February 5, 1880. I come to Little Cypress. I worked for Mr. Clark by the month, J.W. Crocton's place, Mr. Kitchen's place. I was brakeman on freight train awhile. I worked on the section. I farmed and worked in the timber. I don't have no children; I never been married. I wanted to work by the month all my life. I sells mats (shuck mats) $1.00 and I bottom chairs 50¢. The Social Welfare gives me $10.00. That is 10¢ a meal.

That woman next door boards me—table board—for 50¢ a day. I make all I can outer fust one thing and another." (He is blind—cataracts.)

United States. Work Projects Administration

Interviewer: Miss Irene Robertson
Person interviewed: Emma Barr, Madison, Arkansas
Age: 65

EMMA BARR

"My parents belong to two people. Mama was born in Mississippi I think and papa come from North Carolina. Papa's master was Lark Hickerson. Mama was sold from Dr. Ware to Dr. Pope. She was grown when she was sold. She was the mother of twenty-seven children. She had twins three times.

"During the Civil War she was run from the Yankees and had twins on the road. They died or was born dead and she nearly died. They was buried between twin trees close to Hernando, Mississippi. Her last owner was Dr. Pope, ten miles south of Augusta, Arkansas. I was born there and raised up three miles south of Augusta, Arkansas.

"When mama was sold she left her people in Mississippi but after freedom her sisters, Aunt Mariah and Aunt Mary, come here to mama. Aunt Mariah had no children. Aunt Mary had four boys, two girls. She brought her children. Mama said her husband when Dr. Ware owned her was Maxwell but she married my papa after Dr. Pope bought her.

"Dr. Ware had a fine man he bred his colored house women to. They didn't plough and do heavy work. He was hostler, looked after the stock and got in wood. The women hated him, and the men on the place done as well. They hated him too. My papa was a Hickerson. He was a shoemaker and waited on Dr. Pope. Dr. Pope and Miss Marie was good to my parents and to my auntees when they come out here.

"I am the onliest one of mama's children living. Mama was sold on the block and cried off I heard them say when they lived at Wares in Mississippi. Mama was a house girl, Aunt Mary cooked and my oldest sister put fire on the skillet and oven lids. That was her job.

"Mama was lighter than I am. She had Indian blood in her. One auntee was half white. She was lighter than I am, had straight hair; the other auntee was real dark. She spun and wove and knit socks. Mama said they had plenty to eat at both homes. Dr. Pope was good to her. Mama went to the white folks church to look after the babies. They took the babies and all the little children to church in them days.

"Mama said the preachers told the slaves to be good and bedient. The colored folks would meet up wid one another at preaching same as the white folks. I heard my auntees say when the Yankees come to the house the mistress would run give the house women their money and jewelry and soon as the Yankees leave they would come get it. That was at Wares in Mississippi.

"I heard them talk about slipping off and going to some house on the place and other places too and pray for freedom during the War. They turned an iron pot upside down in the room. When some mens' slaves was caught on another man's place he was allowed to whoop them and send them home and they would git another whooping. Some men wouldn't allow that; they said they would tend to their own slaves. So many men had to leave home to go to war times got slack.

"It was Judge Martin that owned my papa before he was freed. He lived close to Augusta, Arkansas. When he was freed he lived at Dr. Pope's. He was sold in North Carolina. Dr. Pope and Judge Martin told them they was free. Mama stayed on with Dr. Pope and he paid her. He never did whoop her. Mama told me all this. She died a few years ago. She was old. I never heard much about the Ku Klux. Mama was a good speller. I was a good speller at school and she learned with us. I spelled in Webster's Blue Back Speller.

"We children stayed around home till we married off. I nursed nearly all my life. Me and my husband farmed ten years. He died. I don't have a child. I wish I did have a girl. My cousin married us in the church. His name was Andrew Baccus.

"After my husband died I went to Coffeeville, Kansas and nursed an old invalid white woman three years, till she died. I come back here where I was knowed. I'm keeping this house for some people gone off. Part of the house is rented out and I get $8 and commodities. I been sick with the chills."

Interviewer: S.S. Taylor
Person interviewed: Robert Barr
3108 West 18th St.
Little Rock, Ark.
Age: 73
Occupation: Preaching

ROBERT BARR

[HW: A Preacher Tells His Story]

"I am a minister of the Gospel. I have been preaching for the last thirty years. I am batching here. A man does better to live by himself. Young people got the devil in them now a days. Your own children don't want you around.

"I got one grand-daughter that ain't never stood on the floor. Her husband kicked her and hit her and she ain't never been able to stand up since. I got another daughter that ain't thinking about marrying. She just goes from one man to the other.

"The government gives me a pension. The white folks help me all along. Before I preached, I fiddled, danced, shot craps, did anything.

"My mother was born in Chickasaw, Mississippi. She was born a slave. Old man Barr was her master. She was a Lucy Appelin and she married a Barr. I don't know whether she stood on the floor and married them as they do now or not. They tell me that they just gave them to them in those days. My mother said that they didn't know anything about marriage then. They had some sort of a way of doing. Ol' Massa would call them up and say, 'You take that man, and go ahead. You are man and wife.' I don't care whether you liked it or didn't. You had to go ahead. I heard em say: 'Nigger ain't no more'n a horse or cow,' But they got out from under that now. The world is growing more and more civilized. But when a nigger thinks he is something, he ain't nothin'. White folks got all the laws and regulations in their hands and they can do as they please. You surrender under em and go along and you are all right. If they told a woman to go to a man and she didn't, they would whip her. You didn't have your own way. They would make you do what they wanted. They'd give you a good beating too.

"My father was born in Mississippi. His name was Simon Barr. My mother and father both lived on the same plantation. In all groups of people they went by their master's name. Before she married, my mother's master and mistress were Appelins. When she got married—got ready to marry—the white folks agreed to let them go together. Old Man Barr must have paid something for her. According to my mother and father, that's the way it was. She had to leave her master and go with her husband's master.

"According to my old father and mother, the Patteroles went and got the niggers when they did something wrong. They lived during slave time. They had a rule and government over the colored and there you are. When they caught niggers out, they would beat them. If you'd run away, they'd go and get you and beat you and put you back. When they'd get on a nigger and beat him, the colored folks would holler, 'I pray, Massa.' They had to have a great war over it, before they freed the nigger. The Bible says there is a time for all things.

"My mother and father said they got a certain amount when they was freed. I don't know how much it was. It was only a small amount. After a short time it broke up and they didn't get any more. I get ten dollars pension now and that is more than they got then.

"I heard Old Brother Page in Mississippi say that the slaves had heard em say they were going to be free. His young mistress heard em say he was going to be free and she walked up and hocked and spit in his face. When freedom came, old Massa came out and told them.

"I have heard folks talk of buried treasure. I'll bet there's more money under the ground than there is on it. They didn't have banks then, and they put their money under the ground. For hundreds of years, there has been money put under the ground.

"I heard my mother talk about their dances and frolics then. I never heard her speak of anything else. They didn't have much freedom. They couldn't go and come as they pleased. You had to have a script to go and come. Niggers ain't free now. You can't do anything; you got nothin'. This whole town belongs to white folks, and you can't do nothin'. If nigger get to have anything, white folks will take it.

"We raised our own food. We made our own flour. We wove our own cloth. We made our clothes. We made our meal. We made our sorghum cane molasses. Some of them made their shoes, made their own medicine, and went around and doctored on one another. They were more healthy then than they are now. This generation don't live hardly to get forty years old. They don't live long now.

"I came to Arkansas about thirty-five years ago. I got right into ditches. The first thing I did was farm. I farmed about ten years. I made about ten crops. Mississippi gave you more for your crops than Arkansas."

Interviewer: Mrs. Bernice Bowden
Person interviewed: Matilda Bass
1100 Palm Street, Pine Bluff, Arkansas
Age: 80

MATILDA BASS

"Yes ma'am, I was eight years old when the Old War ceasted.

"Honey, I've lived here twenty years and I don't know what this street is.

"I was born in Greenville, Mississippi. They took my parents and carried 'em to Texas to keep 'em from the Yankees. I think they stayed three years 'cause I didn't know 'em when they come back.

"I 'member the Yankees come and took us chillun and the old folks to Vicksburg. I 'member the old man that seed after the chillun while their parents was gone, he said I was eight when freedom come. We didn't know nothin' 'bout our ages—didn't have 'nough sense.

"My parents come back after surrender and stayed on my owner's place—John Scott's place. We had three masters—three brothers.

"I been in Arkansas twenty years—right here. I bought this home.

"I married my husband in Mississippi. We farmed.

"The Lord uses me as a prophet and after my husband died, the Lord sent me to Arkansas to tell the people. He called me out of the church. I been out of the church now thirty-three years. Seems like all they think about in the churches now is money, so the Lord called me out."

Interviewer: Miss Irene Robertson
Person interviewed: Emmett Beal, Biscoe, Arkansas
Age: 78

EMMETT BEAL

"I was born in Holloman County, Bolivar, Tennessee. Master Dr. Jim May owned my set er folks. He had two girls and two boys. I reckon he had a wife but I don't recollect seeing her. Ma suckled me; William May with me. Ely and Seley and Susie was his children.

"I churned for mama in slavery. She tied a cloth around the top so no flies get in. I better hadn't let no fly get in the churn. She take me out to a peach tree and learn me how to keep the flies outen the churn next time.

"Mama was Dr. May's cook. We et out the dishes but I don't know how all of 'em done their eating. They eat at their houses. Dr. May had a good size bunch of hands, not a big crowd. We had straw beds. Made new ones every summer. In that country they didn't 'low you to beat yo' hands up. I heard my folks say that more'n one time.

"Dr. May come tole 'em it was freedom. They could get land and stay—all 'at wanted to. All his old ones kept on wid him. They sharecropped and some of them got a third. I recollect him and worked for him.

"The Ku Klux didn't bother none of us. Dr. May wouldn't 'low them on his place.

"Mama come out here in 1880. I figured there better land out here and I followed her in 1881. We paid our own ways. Seem like the owners ought to give the slaves something but seem like they was mad 'cause they set us free. Ma was named Viney May and pa, Nick May.

"Pa and four or five brothers was sold in Memphis. He never seen his brothers no more. They come to Arkansas.

"Pa and Dr. May went to war. The Yankees drafted pa and he come back to Dr. May after he fit. He got his lip split open in the War. Dr. May come home and worked his slaves. He didn't stay long in war.

"I reckon they had plenty to eat at home. They didn't run to the stores every day 'bout starved to death like I has to do now. Ma said they didn't 'low the overseers to whoop too much er Dr. May would turn them off.

"Er horse stomped on my foot eight years ago. I didn't pay it much 'tention. It didn't hurt. Blood-p'ison come in it and they took me to the horsepital and my leg had to come off, (at the knee).

"We have to go back to Africa to vote all the 'lections. Voting brings up more hard feelings."

Interviewer: Pernella Anderson, colored.
Person interviewed: Dina Beard, Douglas Addition, Arkansas

DINA BEARD

Yes I was born in slavery time. I was born September 2, 1862 in the field under a tree. I don't know nothing about slavery. I was too young to remember anything about slavery. But I tell you this much, times ain't like they used to be. There was easy living back in the 18 hundred years. People wore homemade clothes, what I mean homespun and lowell clothes. My ma spun and weaved all of her cloth. We wore our dresses down to our ankles in length and my dresses was called mother hubbards. The skirts had about three yards circumference and we wore plenty of clothes under our dress. We did not go necked like these folks do now. Folk did not know how we was made. We did not show our shape, we did not disgrace ourself back in 1800. We wore our hair wrapped and head rags tied on our head. I went barefooted until I was a young missie then I wore shoes in the winter but I still went barefooted in the summer. My papa was a shoemaker so he made our shoes. We raised everything that we ate when I was a chap. We ate a plenty. We raised plenty of whippowell peas. That was the only kind of peas there was then. We raised plenty Moodie sweet potatoes they call them nigger chokers now. We had cows so we had plenty of milk and butter. We cooked on the fireplace. The first stove I cooked on was a white woman's stove, that was 1890.

I never chanced to go to school because where we lived there wasn't no school. I worked all of the time. In fact that was all we knew. White people did not see where negroes needed any learning so we had to work. We lived on a place with some white people by the name of Dunn. They were good people but they taken all that was made because we did not know. I ain't never been sick in my life and I have never had a doctor in my life. I am in good health now.

We traveled horseback in the years of 1800. We did not ride straddle the horse's back we rode sideways. The old folks wore their dreses dragging the ground. We chaps called everybody old that married. We respected them because they was considered as being old. Time has made a change.

Interviewer: Miss Irene Robertson
Person interviewed: Annie Beck, West Memphis, Arkansas
Age: 50

ANNIE BECK

"I was born in Mississippi. Mama was born in Alabama and sold to Holcomb, Mississippi. Her owner was Master Beard. She was a field woman. They took her in a stage-coach. Their owner wanted to keep it a secret about freedom. But he had a brother that fussed with him all the time and he told the slaves they was all free. Mama said they was pretty good always to her for it to be slavery, but papa said his owners wasn't so good to him. He was sold in Richmond, Virginia to Master Thomas at Grenada, Mississippi. He was a plain farming man."

United States. Work Projects Administration

Interviewer: Bernice Bowden
Person interviewed: J.H. Beckwith
619 North Spruce Street, Pine Bluff, Arkansas
Age: 68

J.H. BECKWITH

"No ma'm I was not born in the time of slavery. I was sixty-eight last Friday. I was born November 18, 1870 in Johnson County, North Carolina.

"My mother was born in Georgia and her name was Gracie Barum. Father was born in North Carolina. His name was Rufus Beckwith. He belonged to Doctor Beckwith and mother, I think, belonged to Tom Barum. Barum was just an ordinary farmer. He was just a second or third class farmer—just poor white folks. I think my mother was the only slave he owned.

"My father had to walk seven miles every Saturday night to see my mother, and be back before sunrise Monday.

"My parents had at least three or four children born in slavery. I know my father said he worked at night and made shoes for his family.

"My father was a mulatto. He had a negro mother and a white father. He had a mechanical talent. He seemed to be somewhat of a genius. He had a productive mind. He could do blacksmithing, carpenter work, brick work and shoe work.

"Father was married twice. He raised ten children by each wife. I think my mother had fifteen children and I was the the thirteenth child. I am the only boy among the first set, called to the ministry. And there was one in the second set. Father learned to read and write after freedom.

"After freedom he sent my oldest brother and sister to Hampton, Virginia and they were graduated from Hampton Institute and later taught school. They were graduated from the same school Booker T. Washington was. He got his idea of vocational education there.

"I haven't had much education. I went as far as the eighth grade. The biggest education I have had was in the Conference.

"I joined the Little Rock General Conference at Texarkana in 1914. This was the Methodist Episcopal, North, and I was ordained as a deacon and later an elder by white bishops. Then in 1930 I joined the African Methodist.

"By trade I am a carpenter and bricklayer. I served an apprentice under my father and under a German contractor.

"I used to be called the best negro journeyman carpenter between Monroe, Louisiana and Little Rock, Arkansas.

"I made quite a success in my trade. I have a couple of United States Patent Rights. One is a brick mold holding ten bricks and used to make bricks of concrete. The other is a sliding door. (See attached drawings) [TR: Drawings missing.]

"I was in the mercantile business two and one-half years in Sevier County. I sold that because it was too confining and returned to the carpenter's trade. I still practice my trade some now.

"I have not had to ask help from anyone. I have helped others. I own my home and I sent my daughter to Fisk University where she was graduated. While there she met a young man and they were later married and now live in Chicago. They own their home and are doing well.

"In my work in the ministry I am trying to teach my people to have higher ideals. We have to bring our race to that high ideal of race integrity. I am trying to keep the negro from thinking he is hated by the upper class of white people. What the negro needs is self-consciousness to the extent that he aspires to the higher principles in order to stand on an equal plane in attainment but not in a social way.

"At present, the negro's ideals are too low for him to visualize the evils involved in race mixture. He needs to be lifted in his own estimation and learn that a race cannot be estimated by other races—by anything else but their own ideals.

"The younger generation is off on a tangent. They'll have to hit something before they stop.

"The salvation of our people—of all people—white and colored, is leadership. We've got to have vision and try to give the people vision. Not to live for ourselves but for all. The present generation is selfish. The life should flow out and as it flows out it makes room for more life. If it does not flow out, it congeals and ferments. Selfishness is just like damming a stream.

"I think Woodrow Wilson won the World War with his fourteen points of democracy. If the people of foreign countries had not that old imperialism sentiment, the Jew would not be where he is today."

Interviewer's Comment

This man is the best informed and most sensible negro I have interviewed. In the room where I interviewed him, were a piano, a radio, many ferns, a wool rug, chairs, divan, and a table on which were books including a set of the Standard History of the World. I asked if he had read the history and he replied, "Not all of it but I have read the volumes pertaining to the neolithic age."

On the walls were several pictures and two tapestries.

The house was a good frame one and electric current was used.

Interviewer: Miss Irene Robertson
Person interviewed: Enoch Beel; Green Grove, Hazen, Arkansas
Age: 79

ENOCH BEEL

"Yes maam I was born a slave, born in slavery times. I wer born in Hardman County, Tennessee. My own daddy was a Union soldier and my mama was a cook fer the mistress. We belonged to Miss Viney and Dr. Jim Mass. My daddy drawed a pension fer bein a soldier till he die. He went off to wait on some men he know. Then he met some men wanted him to join the army. They said then he get paid and get a bounty. No maam he never got a red cent. He come back broke as he went off. He say he turned loose soon as he could and mustered out and lef them right now. He had no time to ax em no questions. That what he said! We stayed on that place till I was big nuf to do a days work. We had no other place to go. There was plenty land and no stock. Houses to stay in got scarce. If a family had a place to stay at when that war ended he counted hisself lucky I tell you. Heap of black an white jes ramlin round through the woods an over the roads huntin a little to eat or a little sumpin to do. If you stay in the field workin about puttin back the fences an round yo own house you wouldn't be hurt.

"The Ku Kluxes war not huntin work theirselves. They was keepin order at the gatherins and down the public roads. Folks had came toted off all the folks made in the crops till they don't call nuthin stealin'. They whooped em and made em ride on rails. I don't know all the carrings on did take place. I sho would been scared if I seed em comin to me. We left Dr. Mass and went to Grain, Tennessee. I had three sisters and half-brothers. I don't remember how many, some dead. I farmed all my life. Everybody said the land was so much better and newer out in Arkansas. When I married I come to Tomberlin and worked fer Sam Dardnne bout twelve years. Then I rented from Jim Hicks at England. I rented from one of the Carlley boys and Jim Neelam. When I very fust come here I worked at Helena on a farm one year. When I got my leg taken off it cost bout all I ever had cumlated. I lives on my sister's place. Henry Bratcher's wife out at Green Grove. The Wellfare give me $8 cause I caint get bout.

"I don't know bout the times. It is so unsettled. Folks want work caint get it and some won't work that could. You caint get help so you can make a crop of your own no more, fer sometimes is close."

Interviewer: Miss Irene Robertson
Person interviewed: Sophie D. Belle, Forrest City, Arkansas
Age: 77

SOPHIE D. BELLE

"I was born near Knoxville, Georgia. My mother was a professional pastry cook. She was a house woman during slavery. She was owned by Lewis Hicks and Ann Hicks. They had Saluda, Mary, Lewis, and Oscar.

"Mother was never sold. Mr. Hicks reared her. She was three-fourths Indian. Her father was George Hicks. Gordon carried him to Texas. Mr. Bob Gordon was mean. He asked Mr. Hicks to keep mother and auntie while he went to Texas, Mr. Gordon was so mean. My mother had two little girls but my sister died while small.

"I never saw any one sold. I never saw a soldier. But I noticed the grown people whispering many times. Mother explained it to me, they had some news from the War. Aunt Jane said she saw them pass in gangs. I heard her say, 'Did you see the soldiers pass early this morning?' I was asleep. Sometimes I was out at play when they passed.

"Master Hicks called us all up at dinner one day to the big house. He told us, 'You are free as I am.' I never had worked any then. No, they cried and went on to their homes. Aunt Jane was bad to speak out, she was so much Indian. She had three children. She went to another place to live. She was in search of her husband and thought he might be there at Ft. Valley.

"Mother stayed on another year. Mr. Hicks was good to us. None of the children ever worked till they was ten or twelve years old. He had a lot of slaves and about twenty-five children on the place growing. He had just a big plantation. He had a special cook, Aunt Mariah, to cook for the field hands. They eat like he did. Master Hicks would examine their buckets and a great big split basket. If they didn't have enough to eat he would have her cook more and send to them. They had nice victuals to eat. He had a bell to ring for all the children to be put to bed at sundown and they slept late. He said, 'Let them grow.' Their diet was milk and bread and eggs. We had duck eggs, guinea eggs, goose eggs, and turkey eggs.

"I don't know what all the slaves had but mother had feather beds. They saved all kind of feathers to make pillows and bed and chair cushions. We always had a pet pig about our place. Master Hicks kept a drove of pea-fowls. He had cows, goats, sheep. We children loved the lambs. Elvira attended to the milk. She had some of the girls and boys to milk. Uncle Dick, mother's brother, was Mr. Hicks' coachman. He was raised on the place too.

"I think Master Hicks and his family was French, but, though they were light-skin people. They had light hair too, I think.

"One day a Frenchman (white) that was a doctor come to call. My Aunt Jane said to me, 'He is your papa. That is your papa.' I saw him many times after that. I am considered eight-ninth white race. One little girl up at the courthouse asked me a question and I told her she was too young to know about such sin. (This girl was twenty-four years old and the case worker's stenographer.)

"Master Hicks had Uncle Patrick bury his silver and gold in the woods. It was in a trunk. The hair and hide was still on the trunk when the War ceased. He used his money to pay the slaves that worked on his place after freedom.

"I went to school to a white man from January till May and mother paid him one dollar a month tuition. After I married I went to school three terms. I married quite young. Everyone did that far back.

"I married at Aunt Jane's home. We got married and had dinner at one or two o'clock. Very quiet. Only a few friends and my relatives. I wore a green wool traveling dress. It was trimmed in black velvet and black beads. I married in a hat. At about seven o'clock we went to ny husband's home at Perry, Georgia. He owned a new buggy. We rode thirty miles. We had a colored minister to marry us. He was a painter and a fine provider. He died. I had no children.

"I came to Forrest City 1874. There was three dry-goods and grocery stores and two saloons here—five stores in all. I come alone. Aunt Jane and Uncle Sol had migrated here. My mother come with me. There was one railroad through here. I belong to the Baptist church.

"I married the second time at Muskogee, Oklahoma. My husband lived out there. He was Indian-African. He was a Baptist minister. We never had any children. I never had a child. They tell me now if I had married dark men

I would maybe had children. I married very light men both times.

"I washed and ironed, cooked and kept house. I sewed for the public, black and white. I washed and ironed for Mrs. Grahan at Crockettsville twenty-three years and three months. I inherited a home here. Owned a home here in Forrest City once. I live with my cousin here. He uses that house for his study. He is a Baptist minister. (The church is in front of their home—a very nice new brick church—ed.) I'm blind now or I could still sew, wash and iron some maybe.

"I get eight dollars from the Social Welfare. I do my own cooking in the kitchen. I am seventy-seven years old. I try to live as good as my age. Every year I try to live a little better, 'A little sweeter as the years go by.'"

Interviewer: Samuel S. Taylor
Person interviewed: Cyrus Bellus
1320 Pulaski Street, Little Rock, Arkansas
Age: 73

CYRUS BELLUS

[HW: Made Own Cloth]

"I was born in Mississippi in 1865 in Jefferson County. It was on the tenth of March. My father's name was Cyrus Bellus, the same as mine. My mother's name was Matilda Bellus.

"My father's master was David Hunt. My father and mother both belonged to him. They had the same master. I don't know the names of my grandfather and mother. I think they were Jordons. No, I know my grandmother's name was Annie Hall, and my grandfather's name was Stephen Hall. Those were my mother's grandparents. My father's father was named John Major and his mother was named Dinah Major. They belonged to the Hunts. I don't know why the names was different. I guess he wasn't their first master.

Slave Sales, Whippings, Work

"I have heard my folks talk about how they were traded off and how they used to have to work. Their master wouldn't allow them to whip his hands. No, it was the mistress that wouldn't allow them to be whipped. They had hot words about that sometimes.

"The slaves had to weave cotton and knit sox. Sometimes they would work all night, weaving cloth, and spinning thread. The spinning would be done first. They would make cloth for all the hands on the place.

"They used to have tanning vats to make shoes with too. Old master didn't know what it was to buy shoes. Had a man there to make them.

"My father and mother were both field hands. They didn't weave or spin. My grandmother on my mother's side did that. They were supposed to pick—the man, four hundred pounds of cotton, and the woman three hundred. And that was gittin' some cotton. If they didn't come up to the task, they was took out and give a whipping. The overseer would do the thrashing. The old mistress and master wouldn't agree on that whipping.

Fun

"The slaves were allowed to get out and have their fun and play and 'musement for so many hours. Outside of those hours, they had to be found in their house. They had to use fiddles. They had dancing just like the boys do now. They had knockin' and rasslin' and all such like now.

Church

"So for as serving God was concerned, they had to take a kettle and turn it down bottom upward and then old master couldn't hear the singing and prayin'. I don't know just how they turned the kettle to keep the noise from goin' out. But I heard my father and mother say they did it. The kettle would be on the inside of the cabin, not on the outside.

House, Furniture, Food

"The slaves lived in log houses instead of ones like now with weather-boarding. The two ends duffed in. They always had them so they would hold a nice family. Never had any partitions to make rooms. It was just a straight long house with one window and one door.

"Provisions were weighed out to them. They were allowed four pounds of meat and a peck of meal for each working person. They only provided for the working folks. If I had eight in a family, I would just get the same amount. There was no provisions for children.

"But all the children on the place were given something from the big house. The working folks ate their breakfast before daylight in the log cabin where they lived. They ate their supper at home too. They was allowed to get back home by seven or eight o'clock. The slaves on my place never ate together. I don't know anything about that kind of feeding.

"They had nurses, old folks that weren't able to work any longer. All the children would go to the same place to be cared for and the old people would look after them. They wasn't able to work, you know. They fed the children during the day.

How Freedom Came

"My father and mother and grandmother said the overseer told them that they were free. I guess that was in 1865, the same year I was born. The overseer told them that they didn't have any owner now. They was free folks. The boss man told them too—had them to come up to the big house and told them they had to look out for themselves now because they were free as he was.

Right After the War

"Right after emancipation, my folks were freed. The boss man told them they could work by the day or sharecrop or they could work by groups. A group of folks could go together and work and the boss man would pay them so much a day. I believe they worked for him a good while—about seven or eight years at least. They was in one of the groups.

Earliest Recollections

"My own earliest recollections was of picking cotton in one of those squads—the groups I was telling you about. After that, the people got to renting land and renting stock for themselves. They sharecropped then. It seems to me that everybody was satisfied. I don't remember any one saying that he was cheated or beat out of anything.

Schooling

"We had a public school to open in Jefferson County, Mississippi. We called it Dobbins Bridge. There was a bridge about a mile long built across the creek. We had two colored women for teachers. Their names was Mary Howard and Hester Harris. They only used two teachers in that school. I attended there three years to those same two women.

"We had a large family and I quit to help take care of it.

Ku Klux

"I don't think there was much disturbance from the Ku Klux on that plantation. The colored folks didn't take much part in politics.

Later Life

"I stopped school and went to work for good at about fifteen years. I worked at the field on that same plantation I told you about. I worked there for just about ten years. Then I farmed at the same place on shares. I stayed there till I was 'bout twenty-six years old. Then I moved to Wilderness Place in the Cotton Belt in Mississippi. I farmed there for two years.

"I farmed around Greenville, Mississippi for a while. Then I left Greenville and came to Arkansas. I come straight to Little Rock. The first thing I did I went into the lumber grading. I wasn't trained to it, but I went into it at the request of the men who employed me. I stayed in that eight years. I learned the lumber grading and checking. Checking is seeing the size and width and length and kind of lumber and seeing how much of it there is in a car without taking it out, you know.

"I married about 1932. My wife is dead. We never had any children.

"I haven't worked any now in five years. I have been to the hospital in the east end. I get old age assistance—eight dollars and commodities."

Interviewer: Mrs. Bernice Bowden
Person interviewed: Bob Benford
209 N. Maple Street, Pine Bluff, Arkansas
Age: 79

BOB BENFORD

"Slavery-time folks? Here's one of em. Near as I can get at it, I'se seventy-nine. I was born in Alabama. My white folks said I come from Perry County, Alabama, but I come here to this Arkansas country when I was small.

"My old master was Jim Ad Benford. He was good to us. I'm goin' to tell you we was better off then than now. Yes ma'am, they treated us right. We didn't have to worry bout payin' the doctor and had plenty to eat.

"I recollect the shoemaker come and measured my feet and directly he'd bring me old red russet shoes. I thought they was the prettiest things I ever saw in my life.

"Old mistress would say, 'Come on here, you little niggers' and she'd sprinkle sugar on the meat block and we'd just lick sugar.

"I remember the soldiers good, had on blue suits with brass buttons.

"I'se big enough to ride old master's hoss to water. He'd say, 'Now, Bob, don't you run that hoss' but when I got out of sight, I was bound to run that hoss a little.

"I didn't have to work, just stayed in the house with my mammy. She was a seamstress. I'm tellin' you the truth now. I can tell it at night as well as daytime.

"We lived in Union County. Old master had a lot of hands. Old mistress' name was Miss Sallie Benford. She just as good as she could be. She'd come out to the quarters to see how we was gettin' along. I'd be so glad when Christmas come. We'd have hog killin' and I'd get the bladders and blow em up to make noise—you know. Yes, lady, we'd have a time.

"I recollect when Marse Jim broke up and went to Texas. Stayed there bout a year and come back. [HW: migration?]

"When the war was over I recollect they said we was free but I didn't know what that meant. I was always free.

"After freedom mammy stayed there on the place and worked on the shares. I don't know nothin' bout my father. They said he was a white man.

"I remember I was out in the field with mammy and had a old mule. I punched him with a stick and he come back with them hoofs and kicked me right in the jaw—knocked me dead. Lord, lady, I had to eat mush till I don't like mush today. That was old Mose—he was a saddle mule.

"Me? I ain't been to school a day in my life. If I had a chance to go I didn't know it. I had to help mammy work. I recollect one time when she was sick I got into a fight and she cried and said, 'That's the way you does my child' and I know she died next week.

"After that I worked here and there. I remember the first run I worked for was Kinch McKinney of El Dorado.

"I remember when I was just learnin' to plow, old mule knew five hundred times more than I did. He was graduated and he learnt me.

"I made fifty-seven crops in my lifetime. Me and Hance Chapman—he was my witness when I married—we made four bales that year. That was in 1879. His father got two bales and Hance and me got two. I made money every year. Yes ma'am, I have made some money in my day. When I moved from Louisiana to Arkansas I sold one hundred eighty acres of land and three hundred head of hogs. I come up here cause my chillun was here and my wife wanted to come here. You know how people will stroll when they get grown. Lost everything I had. Bought a little farm here and they wouldn't let me raise but two acres of cotton the last year I farmed and I couldn't make my payments with that. Made me plow up some of the prettiest cotton I ever saw and I never got a cent for it.

"Lady, nobody don't know how old people is treated nowdays. But I'm livin' and I thank the Lord. I'm so glad the Lord sent you here, lady. I been once a man and twice a child. You know when you're tellin' the truth, you can tell it all the time.

"Klu Klux? The Lord have mercy! In '74 and '75 saw em but never was bothered by a white man in my life. Never been arrested and never had a lawsuit in my life. I can go down here and talk to these officers any time.

"Yes ma'am, I used to vote. Never had no trouble. I don't know what ticket I voted. We just voted for the man we wanted. Used to have colored men on the grand jury—half and half—and then got down to one and then knocked em all out.

"I never done no public work in my life but when you said farmin' you hit me then.

"Nother thing I never done. I bought two counterpins once in my life on the stallments and ain't never bought nothin' since that way. Yes ma'am, I got a bait of that stallment buying. That's been forty years ago.

"I know one time when I was livin' in Louisiana, we had a teacher named Arvin Nichols. He taught there seventeen years and one time he passed some white ladies and tipped his hat and went on and fore sundown they had him arrested. Some of the white men who knew him went to court and said what had he done, and they cleared him right away. That was in the '80's in Marion, Louisiana, in Union Parish."

Interviewer: Miss Irene Robertson
Person interviewed: Carrie Bradley Logan Bennet, Helena, Arkansas
Age: 79 plus

CARRIE BRADLEY LOGAN BENNET

"I was born not a great piece from Mobile but it was in Mississippi in the country. My mother b'long to Massa Tom Logan. He was a horse trader. He got drowned in 1863—durin' of the War, the old war. His wife was Miss Liza Jane. They had several children and some gone from home I jus' seed when they be on visits home. The ones at home I can recollect was Tiney, John, Bill, and Alex. I played wid Tiney and nursed Bill and Alex was a baby when Massa Tom got drowned.

"We never knowed how Massa Tom got drowned. They brought him home and buried him. His horse come home. He had been in the water, water was froze on the saddle. They said it was water soaked. They thought he swum the branch. Massa Tom drunk some. We never did know what did happen. I didn't know much 'bout 'em.

"He had two or three families of slaves. Ma cooked, washed and ironed for all on the place. She went to the field in busy times. Three of the men drove horses, tended to 'em. They fed 'em and curried and sheared 'em. Ma said Massa Tom sure thought a heap of his niggers and fine stock. They'd bring in three or four droves of horses and mules, care fer 'em, take 'em out sell 'em. They go out and get droves, feed 'em up till they looked like different from what you see come there. He'd sell 'em in the early part of the year. He did make money. I know he muster. My pa was the head blacksmith on Masaa Tom's place, them other men helped him along.

"I heard ma say no better hearted man ever live than Massa Tom if you ketch him sober. He give his men a drink whiskey 'round every once in awhile. I don't know what Miss Liza Jane could do 'bout it. She never done nothin' as ever I knowed. They sent apples off to the press and all of us drunk much cider when it come home as we could hold and had some long as it lasts. It turn to vinegar. I heard my pa laughing 'bout the time Massa Tom had the Blue Devils. He was p'isoned well as I understood it. It muster been on whiskey and something else. I never knowed it. His men had to take keer of 'em. He acted so much like he be crazy they laughed 'bout things he do. He got over it.

"Old mistress—we all called her Miss Liza Jane—whooped us when she wanted to. She brush us all out wid the broom, tell us go build a play house. Children made the prettiest kinds of play houses them days. We mede the walls outer bark sometimes. We jus' marked it off on the ground out back of the smokehouse. We'd ride and bring up the cows. We'd take the meal to a mill. It was the best hoecake bread can be made. It was water ground meal.

"We had a plenty to eat, jus' common eatin'. We had good cane molasses all the tine. The clothes was thin 'bout all time 'ceptin' when they be new and stubby. We got new clothes in the fall of the year. They last till next year.

"I never seed Massa Tom whoop nobody. I seen Miss Liza Jane turn up the little children's dresses and whoop 'em with a little switch, and straws, and her hand. She 'most blister you wid her bare hand. Plenty things we done to get whoopin's. We leave the gates open; we'd run the calves and try to ride 'em; we'd chunk at the geese. One thing that make her so mad was for us to climb up in her fruit trees and break off a limb. She wouldn't let us be eating the green fruit mostly 'cause it would make us sick. They had plenty trees. We had plenty fruit to eat when it was ripe. Massa Tom's little colored boys have big ears. He'd pull 'em every time he pass one of 'em. He didn't hurt 'em but it might have made their ears stick out. They all had big ears. He never slapped nobody as ever I heard 'bout.

"I don't know how my parents was sold. I'm sure they was sold. Pa's name ivas Jim Bradley (Bradly). He come from one of the Carolinas. Ma was brought to Mississippi from Georgia. All the name I heard fer her was Ella Logan. When freedom cone on, I heard pa say he thought he stand a chance to find his folks and them to find him if he be called Bradley. He did find some of his brothers, and ma had some of her folks out in Mississippi. They come out here hunting places to do better. They wasn't no Bradleys. I was little and I don't recollect their names. Seem lack one family we called Aunt Mandy Thornton. One was Aunt Tillie and Uncle Mack. They wasn't Thorntons. I knows that.

"My folks was black, black as I is. Pa was stocky, guinea man. Ma was heap the biggest. She was rawbony and tall. I love to see her wash. She could bend 'round the easier ever I seed anybody. She could beat the clothes in a hurry. She put out big washings, on the bushes and a cord they wove and on the fences. They had paling fence 'round the garden.

"Massa Tom didn't have a big farm. He had a lot of mules and horses at times. They raised some cotton but mostly corn and oats. Miss Liza Jane left b'fore us. We all cried when she left. She shut up the house and give the women folks all the keys. We lived on what she left there and went on raising more hogs and tending to the cows. We left everything. We come to Hernando, Mississippi. Pa farmed up there and run his blacksmith shop on the side. My parents died close to Horn Lake. Mama was the mother of ten and I am the mother of eight. I got two living, one here and one in Memphis. I lives wid 'em and one niece in Natches I live with some.

"I was scared to death of the Ku Klux Klan. They come to our house one night and I took my little brother and we crawled under the house and got up in the fireplace. It was big 'nough fer us to sit. We went to sleep. We crawled out next day. We seen 'em coming, run behind the house and crawled under there. They knocked about there a pretty good while. We told the folks about it. I don't know where they could er been. I forgot it been so long. I was 'fraider of the Ku Klux Klan den I ever been 'bout snakes. No snakes 'bout our house. Too many of us.

"I tried to get some aid when it first come 'bout but I quit. My children and my niece take keer or me. I ain't wantin' fer nothin' but good health. I never do feel good. I done wore out. I worked in the field all my life.

"A heap of dis young generation is triflin' as they can be. They don't half work. Some do work hard and no 'pendence to be put in some 'em. 'Course they steal 'fo' dey work. I say some of 'em work. Times done got so fer 'head of me I never 'speck to ketch-up. I never was scared of horses. I sure is dese automobiles. I ain't plannin' no rides on them airplanes. Sure you born I ain't. Folks ain't acting lack they used to. They say so I got all I can get you can do dout. It didn't used to be no sich way. Times is heap better but heap of folks is worse 'an ever folks been before."

United States. Work Projects Administration

Interviewer: Mrs. Bernice Bowden
Person interviewed: George Benson,
Ezell Quarters, Pine Bluff, Arkansas
Age: 80
Occupation: Cotton Farmer

GEORGE BENSON

"I was here in slavery days—yes ma'm, I was here. When I come here, colored people didn't have their ages. The boss man had it. After surrender, boss man told me I ought to keep up with my age, it'd be a use to me some day, but I didn't do it.

"I member the soldiers would play with me when they wasn't on duty. That was the Yankees.

"I was born down here on Dr. Waters' place. Born right here in Arkansas and ain't been outa Arkansas since I was born. So far as I know, Dr. Waters was good to us. I don't know how old I was. I know I used to go to the house with my mother and piddle around.

"My father jined the Yankees and he died in the army. I heered the old people talkin', sayin' we was goin' to be free. You know I didn't have much sense cause I was down on the river bank and the Yankees was shootin' across the river and I said, 'John, you quit that shootin'!' So you know I didn't have much sense.

"I can remember old man Curtaindall had these nigger dogs. Had to go up a tree to keep em from bitin' you. Dr. Waters would have us take the cotton and hide it in the swamp to keep the Yankees from burnin' it but they'd find it some way.

"Never went to school over two months in all my goin's. We always lived in a place kinda unhandy to go to school. First teacher I had was named Mr. Bell. I think he was a northern man.

"All my life I been farmin'—still do. Been many a day since I sold a bale a cotton myself. White man does the ginnin' and packin'. All I do is raise it. I'm farmin' on the shares and I think if I raise four bales I ought to have two bales to sell and boss man two bales, but it ain't that way.

"I voted ever since I got to be a man grown. That is—as long as I could vote. You know—got so now they won't let you vote. I don't think a person is free unless he can vote, do you? The way this thing is goin', I don't think the white man wants the colored man to have as much as the white man.

"When I could vote, I jus' voted what they told me to vote. Oh Lord, yes, I voted for Garfield. I'se quainted with him—I knowed his name. Let's see—Powell Clayton—was he one of the presidents? I voted for him. And I voted for McKinley. I think he was the last one I voted for.

"I been farmin' all my life and what have I got? Nothin'. Old age pension? I may be in glory time I get it and then what would become of my wife?"

Interviewer: Mrs. Bernice Bowden
Person interviewed: Kato Benton
Creed Taylor Place, Tamo Pike
Pine Bluff, Arkansas
Age: 78

KATO BENTON

"I was born in South Carolina before the War. I ain't no baby. I wasn't raised here. No ma'am.

"My daddy's name was Chance Ayers and my mammy's name was Mary Ayers. So I guess the white folks was named Ayers.

"White folks was good to us. Had plenty to eat, plenty to wear, plenty to drink. That was water. Didn't have no whisky. Might a had some but they didn't give us none.

"Oh, yes ma'am, I got plenty kin folks. Oh, yes ma'am, I wish I was back there but I can't get back. I been here so long I likes Arkansas now.

"My mammy give me away after freedom and I ain't seed her since. She give me to a colored man and I tell you he was a devil untied. He was so mean I run away to a white man's house. But he come and got me and nearly beat me to death. Then I run away again and I ain't seed him since.

"I had a hard time comin' up in this world but I'm livin' yet, somehow or other.

"I didn't work in no field much. I washed and ironed and cleaned up the house for the white folks. Yes ma'am!

"No ma'am, I ain't never been married in my life. I been ba'chin'. I get along so fine and nice without marryin'. I never did care anything 'bout that. I treat the women nice—speak to 'em, but just let 'em pass on by.

"I never went to school in my life. Never learned to read or write. If I had went to school, maybe I'd know more than I know now.

"These young folks comin' on is pretty rough. I don't have nothin' to do with 'em—they is too rough for me. They is a heap wuss than they was in my day—some of 'em.

"I gets along pretty well. The Welfare gives me eight dollars a month."

Interviewer: Samuel S. Taylor
Person interviewed: James Bertrand
1501 Maple Street, Little Rock, Arkansas
Age: 68

JAMES BERTRAND

[HW: "Pateroles" Botlund Father]

"I have heard my father tell about slavery and about the Ku Klux Klan bunch and about the paterole bunch and things like that. I am sixty-eight years old now. Sixty-eight years old! That would be about five years after the War that I was born. That would be about 1870, wouldn't it? I was born in Jefferson County, Arkansas, near Pine Bluff.

"My father's name was Mack Bertrand. My mother's name was Lucretia. Her name before she married was Jackson. My father's owners were named Bertrands. I don't know the name of my mother's owners. I don't know the names of any of my grandparents. My father's owners were farmers.

"I never saw the old plantation they used to live on. My father never told me how it looked. But he told me he was a farmer—that's all. He knew farming. He used to tell me that the slaves worked from sunup till sundown. His overseers were very good to him. They never did whip him. I don't know that he was ever sold. I don't know how he met my mother.

"Out in the field, the man had to pick three hundred pounds of cotton, and the women had to pick two hundred pounds. I used to hear my mother talk about weaving the yarn and making the cloth and making clothes out of the cloth that had been woven. They used to make everything they wore—clothes and socks and shoes.

"I am the youngest child in the bunch and all the older ones are dead. My mother was the mother of about thirteen children. Ten or more of them were born in slavery. My mother worked practically all the time in the house. She was a house worker mostly.

"My father was bothered by the pateroles. You see they wouldn't let you go about if you didn't have a pass. Father would often get out and go 'round to see his friends. The pateroles would catch him and lash him a little and let him go. They never would whip him much. My mother's people were good to her. She never did have any complaint about them.

"For amusement the slaves used to dance and go to balls. Fiddle and dance! I never heard my father speak of any other type of amusement.

"I don't remember what the old man said about freedom coming. Right after the War, he farmed. He stayed right on with his master. He left there before I was born and moved up near Pine Bluff where I was born. The place my father was brought up on was near Pine Bluff too. It was about twenty miles from Pine Bluff.

"I remember hearing him say that the Ku Klux Klan used to come to see us at night. But father was always orderly and they never had no clue against him. He never was whipped by the Ku Klux.

"My father never got any schooling. He never could read or write. He said that they treated him pretty fair though on the farms where he worked after freedom. As far as he could figure, they didn't cheat him. I never had any personal experience with the Ku Klux. I never did do any sharecropping. I am a shoemaker. I learned my trade from my father. My father was a shoemaker as well as a farmer. He used to tell me that he made shoes for the Negroes and for the old master too in slavery times.

"I have lived in Little Rock thirty years. I was born right down here in Pine Bluff like I told you. This is the biggest town—a little bigger than Pine Bluff. I run around on the railroad a great deal. So after a while I just come here to this town and made it my home."

United States. Work Projects Administration

Interviewer: Miss Irene Robertson
Person Interviewed: Alice Biggs
Holly Grove, Ark.
Age: "Bout 70"

ALICE BIGGS

"My mother come from Kentucky and my father from Virginia. That where they born and I born close to Byihalia, Mississippi. My father was Louis Anthony and mama name Charlotte Anthony.

"Grandma and her children was sold in a lump. They wasn't separated. Grandpa was a waiter on the Confederate side. He never come back. He died in Pennsylvania; another man come back reported that. He was a colored waitin' man too. Grandma been dead 49 years now.

"Mama was a wash woman and a cook. They liked her. I don't remember my father; he went off with Anthony. They lived close to Nashville, Tennessee. He never come back. Mama lived at Nashville a while. The master they had at the closin' of the war was good to grandma and mama. It was Barnie Hardy and Old Kiss, all I ever heard her called. They stayed on a while. They liked us. Held run us off if he'd had any bother.

"The Ku Klux never come bout Barnie Hardy's place. He told em at town not to bother his place.

"I never wanted to vote. I don't know how. I am too old to try tricks new as that now.

"Honey, I been workinr in the field all my life. I'm what you call a country nigger. I is a widow—just me an my son in family. Our home is fair. We got two hundred acres of land, one cow and five hogs—pigs and all.

"The present conditions is kind of strange. With us it is just up-and-down-hill times. I ain't had no dealins with the young generation. Course my son would tell you about em, but I can't. He goes out a heap more an I do.

"I don't get no pension. I never signed up. I gets long best I can."

Interviewer: Mrs. Bernice Bowden
Person interviewed: Mandy Billings
3101 W. 14th Highland Add., Pine Bluff, Ark.
Age: 84

MANDY BILLINGS

"Now I was born in 1854. That was in slavery times. That wasn't yistiday was it? Born in Louisiana, in Sparta—that was the county seat.

"Bill Otts was my last owner. You see, how come me sold my mother was my grandfather's baby chile and his owner promised not to separate him nary time again. It was in the time of the Old War. Charles McLaughlin—that was my old master—he was my father and Bill Otts, he bought my mother, and she was sold on that account. Old Master Charles' wife wouldn't 'low her to stay. I'm tellin' it just like they told it to me.

"We stayed with Bill Otts till we was free, and after too. My grandfather had to steal me away. My stepfather had me made over to Bill Otts. You know they didn't have no sheriff in them days—had a provost marshal.

"As near as I can come at it, Miss, I was thirteen or fourteen. I know I was eighteen years and four days old when I married. That was in '74, wasn't it? '72? Well, I knowed I was strikin' it kinda close.

"My white folks lived in town. When they bought my

mother, Miss Katie took me in the house. My mother died durin' of the War—yes ma'am.

"I member when the bloodhounds used to run em and tree em up.

"Yes'm, niggers used to run away in slavery times. Some of em was treated so mean they couldn't help it.

"Yes ma'am, I've seen the Ku Klux. Seen em takin' the niggers out and whip em and kick em around. I'm talkin' bout Ku Klux. I know bout the patrollers too. Ku Klux come since freedom but the patrollers was in slavery times. Had to get a pass. I used to hear the niggers talkin' bout when the patrollers got after em and they was close to old master's field they'd jump over the fence and say, 'I'm at home now, don't you come in here.'

"I farmed in Louisiana after I was married, but since I been here I mostly washed and ironed.

"When I worked for the white folks, I found em a cook cause I didn't like to be bound down so tight of a Sunday.

"I been treated pretty well. Look like the hardest treatment I had was my grandfather's, Jake Nabors. Look like he hated me cause I was white—and I couldn't help it. If he'd a done the right thing by me, he could of sent me to school. He had stepchillun and sent them to school, but he kep' me workin' and plowin'."

Interviewer: Miss Irene Robertson
Person interviewed: Jane Birch, Brinkley, Arkansas
Age: 74

JANE BIRCH

"I was three years old when the Yankees come through. I can't recollect a thing about them. Ma told us children if we don't be quiet the Ku Kluck come take us clean off but I never seed none. When we be working she say if we don't work the grass out pretty soon the Ku Kluck be taking us out whooping us. So many of us she have to scare us up to get us to do right. There was fifteen children, nearly all girls. Ma said she had good white folks. She was Floy Sellers. She belong to Mistress Mary Sellers. She was a widow. Had four boys and a girl. I think we lived in Chester County, South Carolina. I am darky to the bone. Pa was black. All our family is black. My folks come to Arkansas when I was so young I jes' can't tell nothing about it. We farmed. I lived with my husband forty years and never had a child.

"Black folks used to vote more than I believe they do now. The men used to feel big to vote. They voted but I don't know how. No ma'am, reckon I don't vote!

"The times been changing since I was born and they going to keep changing. Times is improving. That is all right.

"I think the young generation is coming down to destruction. You can't believe a word they speak. I think they do get married some. They have a colored preacher and have jes' a witness or so at home. Most of them marry at night. They fuss mongst theirselves and quit sometimes. I don't know much about young folks. You can't believe what they tell you. Some work and some don't work. Some of them will steal."

Interviewer: Miss Irene Robertson
Person interviewed: Beatrice Black, Biscoe. Arkansas
Age: 48 Occupation: Store and "eating joint"

BEATRICE BLACK

"I was born below the city pump here in Biscoe. My husband is a twin and the youngest of thirteen children. His twin brother is living. They are fifty years old today (August 6, 1938). His mother lived back and forth with the twins. She died year before last. She was so good. She was sure good to me. She helped me raise my three children. I misses her till this very day. Her name was Dedonia Black when she died.

"She said master brought her, her father and mother and two sisters, Martha and Ida, from Brownsville, Tennessee at the commencement of the old war to Memphis in a covered ox wagon, and from there on a ship to Cavalry Depot at De Valla Bluff. They was all sold. Her father was sold and had to go to Texas. Her mother was sold and had to go back to Tennessee, and the girls all sold in Arkansas. Master Mann bought my mother-in-law (Dedonia). She was eighteen years old. They sold them off on Cavalry Depot where the ship landed. They put her up to stand on a barrel and auctioned them off at public auction.

"Her father got with the soldiers in Texas and went to war. He enlisted and when the war was over he come on hunt of my mother-in-law. He found her married and had three children. He had some money he made in the war and bought forty acres of land. It was school land (Government land). She raised all her thirteen children there. They brought grandma back out here with them from Tennessee. They all died and buried out here. My mother-in-law was married three times. She had a slavery husband named Nathan Moseby. After he died she married Abe Ware. Then he died. She married Mitchell Black and he died long before she died. She was ninety-two years old when she died and could outdo me till not but a few years ago. Her strength left her all at once. She lived on then a few years.

"She always told me Master Mann's folks was very good to her. She said she never remembered getting a whooping. But then she was the best old thing I ever seen in my life. She was really good.

"One story she tole more than others was: Up at Des Arc country the Yankees come and made them give up their something-to-eat. Took and wasted together. Drunk up their milk and it turning, (blinky—ed.). She'd laugh at that. They kept their groceries in holes in the ground. The Yankees jumped on the colored folks to make them tell where was their provision. Some of them had to tell where some of it was. They was scared. They didn't tell where it all was.

"When they went to Des Arc and the gates was closed they had to wait till next day to get their provisions. They had to start early to get back out of the pickets before they closed."

Name of Interviewer: Beulah Sherwood Hagg
Name of Ex-Slave; Boston Blackwell Age: 98
Residence: 520 Plum, North Little Rock

BOSTON BLACKWELL

Make yourself comfoble, miss. I can't see you much 'cause my eyes, they is dim. My voice, it kinder dim too. I knows my age, good. Old Miss, she told me when I got sold—"Boss, you is 13—borned Christmas. Be sure to tell your new misses and she put you down in her book." My borned name was Pruitt 'cause I got borned on Robert Pruitt's plantation in Georgia,—Franklin County, Georgia. But Blackwell, it my freed name. You see, miss, after my mammy got sold down to Augusta—I wisht I could tell you the man what bought her, I ain't never seed him since,—I was sold to go to Arkansas; Jefferson county, Arkansas. Then was when old Miss telled me I am 13. It was before the Civil War I come here. The onliest auction of slaves I ever seed was in Memphis, coming on to Arkansas. I heerd a girl bid off for $800. She was about fifteen, I reckon. I heerd a woman—a breeding woman, bid off for $1500. They always brought good money. I'm telling you, it was when we was coming from Atlanta.

Do you want to hear how I runned away and jined the Yankees? You know Abraham Lincoln 'claired freedom in '63, first day of January. In October '63, I runned away and went to Pine Bluff to get to the Yankees. I was on the Blackwell plantation south of Pine Bluff in '63. They was building a new house; I wanted to feel some putty in my hand. One early morning I clim a ladder to get a little chunk and the overseer man, he seed me. Here he come, yelling me to get down; he gwine whip me 'cause I'se a thief, he say. He call a slave boy and tell him cut ten willer whips; he gwine wear every one out on me. When he's gone to eat breakfas', I runs to my cabin and tells my sister, "I'se leaving this here place for good." She cry and say, "Overseer man, he kill you." I says, "He kill me anyhow." The young boy what cut the whips—he named Jerry—he come along wif me, and we wade the stream for long piece. Heerd the hounds a-howling, getting ready for to chase after us. Then we hide in dark woods. It was cold, frosty weather. Two days and two nights we traveled. That boy, he so cold and hungry, he want to fall out by the way, but I drug him on. When we gets to the Yankee camp all our troubles was over. We gets all the contraband we could eat. Was they more run-aways there? Oh, Lordy, yessum. Hundreds, I reckon. Yessum, the Yankees feeds all them refugees on contraband. They made me a driver of a team in the quatamasters department. I was always keerful to do everything they telled me. They telled me I was free when I gets to the Yankee camp, but I couldn't go outside much. Yessum, iffen you could get to the Yankee's camp you was free right now.

That old story 'bout 40 acres and a mule, it make me laugh. Yessum, they sure did tell us that, but I never knowed any pusson which got it. The officers telled us we would all get slave pension. That just exactly what they tell. They sure did tell me I would get a passel (parcel) of ground to farm. Nothing ever hatched out of that, neither.

When I got to Pine Bluff I stayed contraband. When the battle come, Captain Manly carried me down to the battle ground and I stay there till fighting was over. I was a soldier that day. No'um, I didn't shoot no gun nor cannon. I carried water from the river for to put out the fire in the cotton bales what made the breas'works. Every time the 'Federates shoot, the cotton, it come on fire; so after the battle, they transfer me back to quartermaster for driver. Captain Dodridge was his name. I served in Little Rock under Captain Haskell. I was swored in for during the war (Boston held up his right hand and repeated the words of allegiance). It was on the corner of Main and Markham street in Little Rock I was swored in. Year of '64. I was 5 feet, 8 inches high. You says did I like living in the army? Yes-sum, it was purty good. Iffen you obeyed them Yankee officers they treated you purty good, but iffen you didn't, they sure went rough on you.

You says you wants to know how I live after soldiers all go away? Well, firstes thing, I work on the railroad. They was just beginning to come here. I digged pits out, going along front of where the tracks was to go. How much I get? I get $1.00 a day. You axes me how it seem to earn money? Lady, I felt like the richess man in the world! I boarded with a white fambly. Always I was a watching for my slave pension to begin coming. 'Fore I left the army my captain, he telled me to file. My file number, it is 1,115,857. After I keeped them papers for so many years, white and black folks bofe telled me it ain't never coming—my slave pension—and I reckon the chilren tored up the papers. Lady, that number for me is filed in Washington. Iffen you go there, see can you get my pension.

After the railroad I went steamboating. First one was

a little one; they call her Fort Smith 'cause she go frum Little Rock to Fort Smith. It was funny, too, her captain was name Smith. Captain Eugene Smith was his name. He was good, but the mate was sure rough. What did I do on that boat? Missy, was you ever on a river boat? Lordy, they's plenty to do. Never is no time for rest. Load, onload, scrub. Just you do whatever you is told to do and do it right now, and you'll keep outen trouble, on a steamboat, or a railroad, or in the army, or wherever you is. That's what I knows.

Yessum, I reckon they was right smart old masters what didn't want to let they slaves go after freedom. They hated to turn them loose. Just let them work on. Heap of them didn't know freedom come. I used to hear tell how the govmint had to send soldiers away down in the far back country to make them turn the slaves loose. I can't tell you how all them free niggers was living; I was too busy looking out for myself. Heaps of them went to farming. They was share croppers.

Yessum, miss, them Ku-Kluxers was turrible,—what they done to people. Oh, God, they was bad. They come sneaking up and runned you outen your house and take everything you had. They was rough on the women and chilren. People all wanted to stay close by where soldiers was. I sure knowed they was my friend.

Lady, lemme tell you the rest about when I runned away. After peace, I got with my sister. She's the onliest of all my people I ever seed again. She telled me she was skeered all that day, she couldn't work, she shake so bad. She heerd overseer man getting ready to chase me and Jerry. He saddle his horse, take his gun and pistol, bofe. He gwine kill me en sight, but Jerry, he say he bring him back, dead er alive, tied to his horse's tail. But he didn't get us, Ha, Ha, Ha. Yankees got us.

Now you wants to know about this voting business. I voted for Genral Grant. Army men come around and registered you before voting time. It wasn't no trouble to vote them days; white and black all voted together. All you had to do was tell who you was vote for and they give you a colored ticket. All the men up had different colored tickets. Iffen you're voting for Grant, you get his color. It was easy. Yes Mam! Gol 'er mighty. They was colored men in office, plenty. Colored legislaturs, and colored circuit clerks, and colored county clerks. They sure was some big officers colored in them times. They was all my friends. This here used to be a good county, but I tell you it sure is tough now. I think it's wrong—exactly wrong that we can't vote now. The Jim Crow lay, it put us out. The Constitution of the United States, it give us the right to vote; it made us citizens, it did.

You just keeps on asking about me, lady. I ain't never been axed about myself in my whole life! Now you wants to know after railroading and steamboating what. They was still work the Yankee army wanted done. The war had been gone for long time. All over every place was bodies buried. They was bringing them to Little Rock to put in Govmint graveyard. They sent me all over the state to help bring them here. Major Forsythe was my quartemaster then. After that was done, they put me to work at St. John's hospital. The work I done there liked to ruin me for life. I cleaned out the water closets. After a while I took down sick from the work—the scent, you know—but I keep on till I get so for gone I can't stay on my feets no more. A misery got me in the chest, right here, and it been with me all through life; it with me now. I filed for a pension on this ailment. I never did get it. The Govmint never took care of me like it did some soldiers. They said I was not a 'listed man; that I was a employed man, so I couldn't get no pension. But I filed, like they told me. I telled you my number, didnft I? 1,115,827, Boston Blackwell. I give my whole time to the Govmint for many years. White and black bofe always telling me I should have a pension. I stood on the battlefield just like other soldiers. My number is in Washington. Major Forsythe was the one what signed it, right in his office. I seed him write it.

Then what did I do? You always asking me that. I was low er long time. When I finally get up I went to farming right here in Pulaski county. Lordy, no, miss, I didn't buy no land. Nothing to buy with. I went share cropping with a white man, Col. Baucum. You asking me what was the shares? Worked on halvers. I done all the work and fed myself. No'um, I wasn't married yit. I took the rheumatiz in my legs, and got short winded. Then I was good for nothing but picking cotton. I kept on with that till my eyes, they got so dim I couldn't see to pick the rows clean. Heap o' times I needed medicine—heap o' times I needed lots of things I never could get. Iffen I could of had some help when I been sick, I mought not be so no account now. My daughter has taked keer of me ever since I not been able to work no more.

I never did live in no town; always been a country nigger. I always worked for white folks, nearly. Never mixed up in big crowds of colored; stayed to myself. I never been arrested in my whole life; I never got jailed for nothing. What else you want to know, Miss?

About these days, and the young folks! Well, I ain't

saying about the young folks; but they—no, I wouldn't say. (He eyed a boy working with a saw.) Well, I will say, they don't believe in hard work. Iffen they can make a living easy, they will. In old days, I was young and didn't have nothing to worry about. These days you have to keep studying where you going to get enough to eat.

United States. Work Projects Administration

Interviewer: Samuel S. Tayler
Person interviewed: Henry Blake
Rear of 1300 Scott Street, Little Rock, Arkansas
Age: 80, or more Occupation: Farming and junk, when able

HENRY BLAKE

[HW: Drove a "Horsepower Gin Wagon"]

"I was born March 16, 1863, they tell me. I was born in Arkansas right down here on Tenth and Spring Streets in Little Rock. That was all woods then. We children had to go in at night. You could hear the wolves and the bears and things. We had to make a big fire at night to keep the wolves and varmints away.

"My father was a skiffman. He used to cross the Arkansas River in a ferry-boat. My father's name was Doc Blake. And my mother's name was Hannah Williams before she married.

"My father's mother's name was Susie somethin'; I done forgot. That is too far back for me. My mother's mother was named Susie—Susie Williams.

"My father's master was named Jim Paty. My father was a slavery man. I was too. I used to drive a horsepower gin wagon in slavery time. That was at Pastoria Just this side of Pine Bluff—about three or four miles this side. Paty had two places-one about four miles from Pine Bluff and the other about four miles from England on the river.

"When I was driving that horsepower gin wagon. I

was about seven or eight years old. There wasn't nothin' hard about it. Just hitch the mules to one another's tail and drive them 'round and 'round. There wasn't no lines. Just hitch them to one another's tail and tell them to git up. You'd pull a lever when you wanted them to stop. The mule wasn't hard to manage.

"We ginned two or three bales of cotton a day. We ginned all the summer. It would be June before we got that cotton all ginned. Cotton brought thirty-five or forty cents a pound then.

"I was treated nicely. My father and mother were too. Others were not treated so well. But you know how Negroes is. They would slip off and go out. If they caught them, he would put them in a log hut they had for a jail. If you wanted to be with a woman, you would have to go to your boss man and ask him and he would let you go.

"My daddy was sold for five hundred dollars—put on the block, up on a stump—they called it a block. Jim Paty sold him. I forget the name of the man he was sold to—Watts, I think it was.

"After slavery we had to get in before night too. If you didn't, Ku Klux would drive you in. They would come and visit you anyway. They had something on that they could pour a lot of water in. They would seem to be drinking the water and it would all be going in this thing. They was gittin' it to water the horses with, and when they got away from you they would stop and give it to the horses. When he got you good and scared he would drive on away. They would whip you if they would catch you out in the night time.

"My daddy had a horse they couldn't catch. It would run right away from you. My daddy trained it so that it would run away from any one who would come near it. He would take me up on that horse and we would sail away. Those Ku Klux couldn't catch him. They never did catch him. They caught many another one and whipped him. My daddy was a pretty mean man. He carried a gun and he had shot two or three men. Those were bad times. I got scared to go out with him. I hated that business. But directly it got over with. It got over with when a lot of the Ku Klux was killed up.

"In slavery time they would raise children just like you would raise colts to a mare or calves to a cow or pigs to a sow. It was just a business It was a bad thing. But it was better than the county farm. They didn't whip you if you worked. Out there at the county farm, they bust you open. They bust you up till you can't work. There's a lot of people down at the state farm at Cummins—that's where the farm is ain't it—that's raw and bloody. They wouldn't let you come down there and write no history. No Lawd! You better not try it. One half the world don't know how the other half lives. I'll tell you one thing, if those Catholics could get control there would be a good time all over this world. The Catholics are good folks.

"That gang that got after you if you let the sun go down while you were out—that's called the Pateroles. Some folks call 'em the Ku Klux. It was all the same old poor white trash. They kept up that business for about ten years after the War. They kept it up till folks began to kill up a lot of 'em. That's the only thing that stopped them. My daddy used to make his own bullets.

"I've forgot who it is that told us that we was free.

Somebody come and told us we're free now. I done forgot who it was.

"Right after the War, my father farmed a while and after that he pulled a skiff. You know Jim Lawson's place. He stayed on it twenty years. He stayed at the Ferguson place about ten years. They're adjoining places. He stayed at the Churchill place. Widow Scott place, the Bojean place. That's all. Have you been down in Argenta to the Roundhouse? Churchill's place runs way down to there. It wasn't nothing but farms in Little Rock then. The river road was the only one there at that time. It would take a day to cone down from Clear Lake with the cotton. You would start 'round about midnight and you would get to Argenta at nine o'clock the next morning. The roads was always bad.

"After freedom, we worked on shares a while. Then we rented. When we worked on shares, we couldn't make nothing—Just overalls and something to eat. Half went to the other man and you would destroy your half if you weren't careful. A man that didn't know how to count would always lose. He might lose anyhow. They didn't give no itemized statement. No, you just had to take their word. They never give you no details. They just say you owe so much. No matter how good account you kept, you had to go by their account and now, Brother, I'm tellin' you the truth about this. It's been that way for a long time. You had to take the white man's work on notes and everything. Anything you wanted, you could git if you were a good hand. You could git anything you wanted as long as you worked. If you didn't make no money, that's all right; they would advance you more. But you better not leave him—you better not try to leave and get caught.

They'd keep you in debt. They were sharp. Christmas come, you could take up twenty dollars in somethin' to eat and much as you wanted in whiskey. You could buy a gallon of whiskey. Anything that kept you a slave because he was always right and you were always wrong if there was difference. If there was an argument, he would get mad and there would be a shooting take place.

"And you know how some Negroes is. Long as they could git somethin', they didn't care. You see, if the white man came out behind, he would feed you, let you have what you wanted. He'd just keep you on, help you get on your feet—that is, if you were a good hand. But if you weren't a good hand, he'd just let you have enough to keep you alive. A good hand could take care of forty or fifty acres of land and would have a large family. A good hand could git clothes, food, whiskey, whenever he wanted it. My father had nine children and took care of them. Not all of them by one wife. He was married twice. He was married to one in slavery time and to another after the War. I was a child of the first one. I got a sister still living down here in Galloway station that is mighty nigh ninety years old. No, she must be a hundred. Her name is Frances Dobbins. When you git ready to go down there, I'll tell you how to find that place jus' like I told you how to fin' this one. Galloway is only 'bout four miles from Rose City.

"I been married twice in my life. My first woman, she died. The second lady, she is still living. We dissolved friendship in 1913. Least-wise, I walked out and give her my home. I used to own a home at twenty-first and Pulaski.

"I belong to the Baptist Church at Wrightsville. I used

to belong to Arch Street. Was a deacon there for about twelve years. But they had too much splittin' and goin' on and I got out. I'll tell you more sometime."

Interviewer's Comment

Henry Blake's age appears in excess of eighty. His idea of seventy-five is based on what someone told him. He is certain that he drove a "Horsepower Gin Wagon" during "slavery times", and that he was seven or eight when he drove it. Even if that were in '65, he would be at least eighty years old—seventy-three years since the War plus seven years of his life. His manner of narration would indicate that he drove earlier.

The interview was held in a dark room, and for the first time in my life I took notes without seeing the paper on which I was writing.

Interviewer: Mary D. Eudgins
Person Interviewed: Miss Adeline Blakeley Age: 87
Home: 101 Rock Street, Fayetteville, Arkansas.

MISS ADELINE BLAKELEY

There is no hint of elision in the speech of Adeline Blakeley, scarcely a trace of vernacular. All of her life her associations have been with white persons. She occupies a position, rare in post-slavery days, of negro servant, confidant and friend. After the death of Mrs. Hudgins, family intimates, wives of physicians, bankers' wives and other Fayetteville dowagers continued periodically to come to see Adeline. They came not in the spirit of Lady Bountifuls condescending to a hireling, but because they wanted to chat with an old time friend.

"Honey, look in the bible to get the date when I was born. We want to have it just right. Yes, here's the place, read it to me. July 10, 1850? Yes, I remember now, that's what they've always told me. I wanted to be sure, though. I was born in Hickman County, Tenn. and was about a year when they brought me to Arkansas. My mother and her people had been bought by Mr. John P. Parks when they were just children—John and Leanna and Martha. I was the first little negro in the Parks kitchen. From the first they made a pet out of me. I was little like a doll and they treated me like a plaything—spoiled me—rotten.

After Mr. Parks came to Arkansas he lived near what is now Prarie Grove, but what do you think it was called then—Hog Eye. Later on they named it Hillingsley for a man who settled there. We were two miles out on the Wire Road, the one the telegraph line came in on, Honey. Almost every conmunity had a 'Wire Road'.

It was the custom to give a girl a slave when she was married. When Miss Parks became Mrs. Blakeley she moved to Fayetteville and chose me to take with her. She said since I was only 5 she could raise me as she wanted me to be. But I must have been a lot of trouble and after she had her baby she had to send me back to her father to grow up a little. For you might say she had two babies to take care of since I was too little to take care of hers. They sent a woman in my place.

Honey, when I got back, I was awful: I had been with the negroes down in the country and said 'hit' and 'hain't' and words like that. Of course all the children in the house took it up from me. Mrs. Blakeley had to teach me to talk right. Your Aunt Nora was born while I was away. I was too little to take full charge of her, but I could sit in a chair and hold her on my lap.

Mrs. Blakeley taught her children at home. Her teaching was almost all they had before they entered the University. When I was little I wanted to learn, learn all I could, but there was a law against teaching a slave to read and write. One woman—she was from the North did it anyway. But when folks can read and write its going to be found out. It was made pretty hard for that woman.

After the war they tried to get me to learn, but I tossed my head and wouldn't let them teach me. I was about 15 and thought I was grown and wouldn't need to know any more. Mary, it sounds funny, but if I had a million dollars

I would give it gladly to be able to read and write letters to my friends.

I remember well when the war started. Mr. Blakeley, he was a cabinet maker and not very well, was not considered strong enough to go. But if the war had kept up much longer they would have called him. Mr. Parks didn't believe in seceding. He held out as long as it was safe to do so. If you didn't go with the popular side they called you 'abolitionist' or maybe 'Submissionist'. But when Arkansas did go over he was loyal. He had two sons and a son-in-law in the Confederate army. One fought at Richmond and one was killed at Gettysburg.

The little Blakeley boy had always liked to play with the American flag. He'd march with it and carry it out on the porch and hang it up. But after the trouble began to brew his mother told him he would have to stay in the house when he played with the flag. Even then somebody saw him and scolded him and said 'Either burn it or wash it.' The child thought they meant it and he tried to wash it. Dyes weren't so good in those days and it ran terribly. It was the awfulest thing you ever saw.

Fayetteville suffered all thru the war. You see we were not very far from the dividing line and both armies were about here a lot. The Federals were in charge most of the time. They had a Post here, set up breast works and fortified the square. The court house was in the middle of it then. It was funny that there wasn't more real fighting about here. There were several battles but they were more like skirmishes—just a few men killed each time. They were terrible just the same. At first they buried the Union soldiers where the Confederate Cemetery is now. The Southerners were placed just anywhere. Later on they moved the Northern caskets over to where the Federal Cemetery is now and they took up the Southern men when they knew where to find them and placed them over on the hill where they are today.

Once an officer came into our home and liked a table he saw, so he took it. Mrs. Blakeley followed his horse as far as she could pleading with him to give it back because her husband had made it. The next day a neighbor returned it. He hod found it in the road and recognized it. The man who stole it had been killed and dropped it as he fell.

Just before the Battle of Prairie Grove the Federal men came thru. Some officers stopped and wanted us to cook for them. Paid us well, too. One man took little Nora on his lap and almost cried. He said she reminded him of his own little girl he'd maybe never see again. He gave her a cute little ivory handled pen knife. He asked Mrs. Blakeley if he couldn't leave his pistols with her until he came back thru Fayetteville. She told him it was asking too much, what would happen to her and her family if they found those weapons in her possession? But he argued that it was only for a few days. She hid them under a tub in the basement and after waiting a year gave them to her brother when he came through. The Yankees met the Southerners at Prairie Grove. The shots sounded just like popcorn from here in Fayetteville. We always thought the man got killed there.

The soldiers camped all around everywhere. Lots of them were in tents and some of the officers were in houses. They didn't burn the college—where Miss Sawyer had taught, you know. The officers used it for their living quarters. They built barracks for the men of upright logs. See that building across the street. It's been lots of things, a livery stable, veterinary barn, apartment house. But it was one of the oldest buildings in Arkansas. They've kept on remodeling it. The Yankees made a commissary out of it. Later on they moved the food up on the square and used it for a hospital. I can remember lots of times seeing the feet of dead men sticking out of the windows.

Your Aunt Nora's mother saved that building from being burned. How did it happen? Well you see both sides were firing buildings—the Confederates to keep the Yankees from getting them, and the other way about. But the Southerners did most of the burning. Mrs. Blakeley's little boy was sick with fever. She and a friend went up, because they feared burnings. They sat there almost all night. Parties of men would come along and they would plead with them. One sat in one doorway and the other in the building next. Mrs. Blakely was a Southerner, the other woman a Northerner. Between them they kept the buildings from being burned: saved their own homes thereby and possibly the life of the little sick boy.

It was like that in Fayetteville. There were so many folks on both sides and they lived so close together that they got to know one another and were friends. Things like this would happen. One day a northern officer came over to our house to talk to his wife who was visiting. He said he would be away all day. He was to go down to Prarie Grove to get 'Old Man Parks, dead or alive'. Not until he was on his way did somebody tell him that he was talking about the father of his wife's hostess. Next day he came over to apologize. Said he never would have made such a cruel remark if he had known. But he didn't find his man. As the officers went in the front door, Mr. Parks went out of the back and the women surrounded him until he got away.

There was another time when the North and South took refuge together. During the war even the little children were taught to listen for bugle calls and know what they meant. We had to know—and how to act when we heard them. One day, I remember we were to have peas for dinner, with ham hock and corn bread. I was hungry that day and everything smelled so good. But just as the peas were part of them out of the pot and in a dish on the table the signal came 'To Arms'. Cannon followed almost immediately. We all ran for the cellar, leaving the food as it was.

The cellar was dug out only a little way down. It had been raining and snowing all day—melted as it fell. It was about noon and the seep water had filled a pool in the middle of the cellar. They placed a tub in the water and it floated like a little boat. They put Nora and a little girl who was visiting her, and me in it. The grown folks clung to the damp sides of the cellar floor and wall. After the worst bombing was over we heard someone upstairs in the house calling. It was the wife of a Northern officer. He had gotten away so fast he had forgotten his pistols. She had tried to follow him, but the shots had frightened her. We called to her to come to the basement. She came, but in trying to climb up the slick sides she slid down and almost into our tub. She looked so funny with her big fat legs that I giggled. Mrs. Blakeley slapped me—it was one of the few times she struck me. I was glad she did, for I would have laughed out. And it didn't do to laugh at Northerners.

It wes night before the fighting was over. An old man who was in the basement with us went upstairs because he heard someone groan. Sure enough a wounded man had dragged himself to our door. He laid the man, almost fainting down before the fireplace. It was all he could do. The man died. When we finally came up there wasn't a pea, nor a bit of ham, not a crum of cornbread. Floaters had cleaned the pot until it shone.

We had a terrible time getting along during those years. I don't believe we could have done it except for the Northern soldiers. You might say the Confederacy was kept up by private subscription, but the Yankees had the whole Federal government back of them. They had good rations which were issued uncooked. They could get them prepared anywhere they liked. We were good cooks so that is the way we got our food—preparing it for soldiers and eating it with them. They had quite a variety and a lot of everything. They were given bacon and coffee and sugar and flour and beans and somthing they called 'mixed vegetables'. Those beans were little and sweet—not like the big ones we have today. The mixed vegetables were liked by lots of folks—I didn't care for them. Everything was ground up together and then dried. You had to soak it like dried peas before cooking.

After the war they came to Mrs. Blakeley, the soldiers did, and accused her of keeping me against my will. I told them that I stayed because I wanted to, the Blakeleys were my people. They let me alone, the whites did, but the negroes didn't like it. They tried to fight me and called me names. There was a well near the square from which everybody got water. Between it and our house was a negro cabin. The little negroes would rock me. I stood it as long as I could. Then I told Mrs. Blakeley. She said to get some rocks in my bucket and if they rocked me to heave back. I was a good shot and they ran. Their mother came to Mrs. Blakeley to complain, but she told her after hearing her thru that I had stood all I could and the only reason I hadn't been seriously hurt was because her children weren't good shots. They never bothered me again.

It was hard after the war. The Federals stayed on for a long time. Fences were down, houses were burned, stock was gone, but we got along somehow. When Nora Blakeley was 14 a lady was teaching a subscription school in the hall across the street—the same hall Mrs. Blakely had saved from burning. She wanted Nora to teach for her. So, child that she was, she went over and pretty soon she was teaching up to the fourth grade. I went over every morning and built a fire for her before she arrived.

That fall she went over to the University, but the next year she had to stay out to earn money. She wanted to finish so badly that we decided to take boarders. They would come to us from way over on the campus. There were always lots more who wanted to stay than we could take. We bought silver and dishes just as we could pay for them, and we added to the house in the summer time. I used to cook their breakfasts and dinners and pack baskets of lunch for them to take over to the Campus. We had lots of interesting people with us. One was Jeff Davis—later he was governor and then senator. He and a Creek Indian boy named Sam Rice were great friends. There were lots of Indians in school at the University then. They didn't have so many Indian schools and tribes would make up money and send a bright boy here.

Ten years after she graduated from the University

Nora married Harvey M. Hudgins. They moved to Hot springs and finally ran a hotel. It burned the night of Washington's birthday in 1895. It was terrible, we saved nothing but the night clothes we were in. Next morning it was worse for we saw small pox flags all over town. Our friends came to our rescue and gave us clothes and we went with friends out into the country to escape the epidemic. There were three or four families in one little house. It was crowded, but we were all friends so it was nice after all.

About ten years before Mr. Hudgins had built a building in Fayetteville. They used the second floor for an Opera House. When we came back here after the fire we took it over to run. Mr. Hudgins had that and all the billboards in town. We saw all the shows. Several years later the twins, Helen and Wade were born. I always went to see the shows and took them with me. Folks watched them more than the shows. I kept them neat and clean and they were so cute.

We saw the circuses too. I remember once Barnum and Bailey were coming to Fort Smith. We were going down. I didn't tell anybody, but I put $45 in my purse. I made money then. Mr. Hudgins got me a cow and I sold milk and butter and kept all I made. Why the first evening dress Helen had and the first long pants Bud (Wade) had I bought. Well, we were going down to Fort Smith, but Bud got sick and we couldn't go. You know, Mary, it seemed so queer. When Helen and I went to California, we all saw the same circus together. Yes, I've been to California with her twice. Whenever the train would stop she would come from the pullman to the coach where the colored persons had to ride to see about me. We went out to visit Sister (Bess Hudgins Clayton) and Bud. While we were there, Barnum and Bailey came to Los Angeles. It seemed so funny. There we were—away out in California—all the children grown up and off to themselves. There we were—all of us—seeing the show we had planned to see way back in Arkansas, years and years before.

You know, Honey, that doll Ann has—she got it for her seventh birthday (Elisabeth Ann Wiggans—daughter of Helen Hudgins Wiggans). It was restrung for her, and was once before for her mother. But it's the same doll Baby Dean (Dean Hudgins) carried out of that fire in Hot Springs in 1895. Everybody loves Ann. She makes the fifth generation I've cared for. When Helen is going out she brings Ann down here or I go up there. It's usually down here tho. Because since we turned the old home into apartments I take care of them, and it's best for me to be here most of the time.

All the people in the apartments are mighty nice to me. Often for days at a time they bring me so much to eat that I don't have to cook for myself. A boy going to the University has a room here and tends to the furnace. He's a nice boy. I like him.

My life's been a full one, Honey, and an interesting one. I can't really say which part of it is best. I can't decide whether it's a better world now or then. I've had lots of hard work, and lots of friends, lots of fun and I've gone lots of places. Life is interesting."

Interviewer: Miss Irene Robertson
Person interviewed: Vera Roy Bobo (Mulatto, almost white)
Holly Grove, Arkansas
Age: 62

VERA ROY BOBO

"My parents come from Macon, Georgia. My mother was Margaret Cobb. Her people were owned by the Cobbs. They reared her. She was a house girl and a seamstress. She sewed for both white and black. She was light color.

"My father was St. Roy Holmes. He was a C.M.E. preacher in Georgia and later in Arkansas. He came on the train to Forrest City, 1885. He crossed the Mississippi River on a ferry boat. Later he preached at Wynne. He was light color.

"I never heard them say very much about slavery. This was their own home.

"My husband's father was the son of a white man also—Randall Bobo. He used to visit us from Bobo, Mississippi. The Bobo a owned that town and were considered rich people. My husband was some darker and was born at Indian Bay, Arkansas. He was William Bobo. I never knew him till two months before I married him. We had a home wedding and a wedding supper in this house."

(This may be continued)

United States. Work Projects Administration

Interviewer: Miss Irene Robertson
Person interviewed: Liddie Boechus, (second interview)
Madison, Arkansas
Age: 73

LIDDIE BOECHUS

"I was born in West Point, Mississippi. My own dear mother's owner was Pool. His wife was Mistress Patty Pool. Old man Pool raised our set. He was an old soldier, I think. He was old when I came to know him.

"My own papa's pa was Smith. After he came back from the Civil War he took back his Smith name. He changed it back from Pool to Smith.

"I was a small child when my own dear mother died. My stepmother had some children of her own, so papa hired me out by the year to nurse for my board and clothes. My stepmother didn't care for me right. White folks raised me.

"I married when I was fifteen years old to a man twenty years old or more. White folks was good to me but I didn't have no sense. I lef' 'em. I married too young. I lived wid him little over twelve years, and I had twelve children by him. Then I married a preacher. We had two more children. My first husband was trifling. I ploughed, hoed, split wood to raise my babies.

"My daughter come from Louisiana to stay with me

last winter when I was sick. I got eight dollars, now I gets six dollars from the Welfare. My daughter here now.

"I went to one white teacher a few days—Miss Perkins. I never got to go enough to learn. I took up reading and writing from my children. I write mighty poor I tell you.

"I used to be a midwife and got ten dollars a case. They won't pay off now. I do a little of that work, but I don't get nothing for it. They have a doctor or won't pay.

"My husband was a good man. He was a preacher. I'm a Baptist.

"I don't know what to think about young folks. Every feller is for his own self. Times is hard with old folks. I had a stroke they said. This new generation ain't got no strength. I think it is because they set around so much. What would a heap of them do? A long day's work in the field would kill some of them. It would! Some folks don't work 'nough to be healthy. I don't know, but though, I really believes education and automobiles is the whole cause."

Interviewer: Miss Irene Robertson
Person interviewed: Maggie (Bunny) Bond, Madison, Arkansas
Age: Well up in 80's

MAGGIE (BUNNY) BOND

"I was born at Magnolia, North Carolina. Lou Nash named me Maggie after my mistress. That was her name. They had a rabbit they called Bunny. It died. They started calling me Bunny. Our old mistress was a Mallory from Virginia. She was the old head of all these at Forrest City. (A big family of people are descendants at Forrest City.)

School During the War

"Mrs. Eddy Williams said to my mother, 'Let her go to school and play with the children.' I was young. I don't know how old I was. I was washed, my hair combed, and clean dresses put on me. I went to school four or five days. I set by different ones. They used slates. It was a log schoolhouse. It had a platform the teacher sat on. They preached in it on Sunday. Where Mt. Vernon Cemetery now stands. The teacher was Mrs. McCallis. She rode horseback from out of the bottoms. The families of children that come there were: Mallorys, Izards, Nashs, Dawsons, Kittrells, and Pruitts.

"There was a big oak tree in front. The boys played on one side, the girls on the other. Cake and pie was a fortune then. If the children had any they would give me part of it. Times was so hard then people had plain victuals every day at school.

"The children tried to learn me at recess under the tree. They used McGuffey's and Blue Back books. One day I said out loud, 'I want to go home.' The children all laughed. One day I went to sleep and the teacher sent me out doors to play. Mrs. McCallis said, 'Bunny, you mus'n't talk out loud in school.' I was nodding one day. The teacher woke me up. She wrapped her long switch across the table. She sent me to play. The house set up on high blocks. I got under it and found some doodle holes. Mrs. McCallis come to the door and said, 'Bunny, don't call so loud. You must keep quiet.' I would say: 'Doodle, doodle, your house on fire. Come get some bread and butter.' They would come up.

"After the War I had a white lady teacher from the North. I went a little bit to colored school but I didn't care about books. I learned to sew for my dolls. The children would give me a doll all along.

"The happiest year of my whole life was the first year of my married life. I hardly had a change of clothes. I had lots of friends. I went to the field with Scott. I pressed cotton with two horses, one going around and the other coming. Scott could go upstairs in the gin and look over at us. We had two young cows. They had to be three years old then before they were any service. I fed hogs. I couldn't cook but I learned. I had been a house girl and nurse.

"I was nursing for Mrs. Pierce at Goodwin. I wanted to go home. She didn't want me to leave. I wouldn't tell her why. She said, 'I speck you going to get married.' She gave me a nice white silk dress. Mrs. Drennand made it. My owner, Miss Leila Nash, lend me one of her chemisette, a corset cover, and a dress had ruffles around the bottom. It was wide. She never married. I borrowed my veil from a colored woman that had used it. Mr. Rollwage (dead now but was a lawyer at Forrest City) gave Scott a tie and white vest and lend him his watch and chain to be married in. They was friends. Miss Leila made my cake. She wanted my gold band ring to go in it. I wouldn't let her have it for that. Not my ring! She put a dime in it. Miss Maggie Barrow and Mrs. Maggie Hatcher made two baskets full of maple biscuits for my wedding. They was the best cake. Made in big layers and cut and iced. Two laundry baskets full to the brim."

She showed us a white cedar three-gallon churn, brass hoops hold the staves in place, fifty-seven years old and a castor with seven cruits patented December 27, 1859. It was a silver castor and was fixed to ring for the meal.

She showed us the place under a cedar tree where there are four unmarked graves—Mr. and Mrs. McMurray and their son and daughter and one niece. The graves are being ploughed over now.

"Mrs. Murray's son gave her five hundred dollars. She hid it. After she died no one knew where to find it."

Scott Bond bought the place. Bunny was fixing the hearth (she showed us the very spot) brick and found a brick. Dora threw it out. The can could never be found and soon Dora went home near Chattanooga, Tennessee. Dora was a Negro servant in the Bond home. It seems the money was in the old can that Bunny found but thought it was just a prop for the brick.

Maggie (Bunny) Bond has given two of her white friends coffins. One was to a man and two years ago one was to a woman, Mrs. Evans' daughter. She wanted to do something, the nicest thing she could do for them, for they had been good to her. People who raised them and had owned them. They gratefully accepted her present. In her life she has given beautiful and expensive wedding preaents to her white friends who raised her and owned her. She told us about giving one and someone else said she gave two. Theo Bond's wife said this about the second one.

The Yankees passed along in front of the Scott Bond home from Hunter, Arkansas to Madison, Arkansas. It was an old military road. The Yankees burnt up Mt. Vernon, Arkansas. Madison was a big town but it overflowed so bad. There were pretty homes at Madison. Levies were not known, so the courthouse was moved to Forrest City. Yankees camped at Madison. A lot of them died there. A cemetery was made in sight of the Scott Bond yard. The markings were white and black letters and the pailings were white with black pointed tips. They were moved to the north. Madison grew to be large because it was on a river.

Interviewer's Comment

Maggie (Bunny) Bond is eight-ninth white.

Interviewer: Thomas Elmore Lucy
Person interviewed: Caroline Bonds
Russellville, Arkansas
Age: 70

CAROLINE BONDS

"What's all dis info'mation you askin' about goin' to be for? Will it help us along any or make times any better? All right, then. My name's Caroline Bonds. I don't know jist exactly when I was born, but I think it was on de twentieth of March about—about—yes, in 1866, in Anderson County, North Carolina.

"So you was a 'Tarheel' too? Bless my soul!

"My old master was named Hubbard, and dat was my name at first. My parents belonged to Marse Hubbard and worked on his big plantation till dey was freed.

"I was too little to remember much about what happened after de War. My folks moved to Arkansas County, in Arkansas, soon after de War and lived down dere a long time.

"I joined de Missionary Baptis' Church when I was fifteen and has belonged to it ever' since.

"No sir, I never got in de habit of votin' and never did vote, never thought it was necessary."

United States. Work Projects Administration

Interviewer: Samuel S. Taylor
Person interviewed: Rev. Frank T. Boone
1410 W. Seventeenth Street, Little Rock, Arkansas
Age: 80

REV. FRANK T. BOONE

[HW: Free Colonies]

"I was born in Nansemond County, Virginia on my father's place near the center of the County. I was born free. We were members of the colonies. You know there were what is known as Free Colonies. They were Negroes that had always been free. The first landing of the Negroes in America, they claimed, formed a colony. The Negro men who came over, it is said, could buy their freedom and a number of them did.

"But I didn't become free that way. My ancestors were a white man and an Indian woman. He was my great-grandfather. None of my family have been slaves as far back as I know.

"There was one set of white people in Virginia called Quakers. Their rule was to free all slaves at the age of twenty-one. So we got some free Negroes under that rule. My mother who was a Negro woman was freed under this rule. My father was always free.

"My grandmother on my father's side owned slaves. The law was that colored people could own slaves but they were not allowed to buy them. I don't know how many slaves my grandmother owned. I didn't know they were slaves until the War was over. I saw the colored people living in the little houses on the place but I didn't know they was slaves.

"One morning my grandmother went down to the quarters and when she came back she said to my aunt, 'Well, the slaves left last night.' And that was the first I knew of their being slaves.

"My father's name was Frank Boone. I was named for him. My mother's name was Phoebe Chalk. I don't know who her mother and father were. She said that her mother died when she was a child. She was raised by Quaker people. I presume that her mother belonged to these Quaker people.

"On our place no grown person was ever whipped. They was just like one family. They called grandmother's house the big house. They farmed. They didn't raise cotton though. They raised corn, peas, wheat, potatoes, and all things for the table. Hogs, cows, and all such like was raised. I never saw a pound of meat or a peck of flour or a bucket of lard or anything like that bought. We rendered our own lard, pickled our own fish, smoked our own meat and cured it, ground our own sausage, ground our own flour and meal from our own wheat and corn we raised on our place, spun and wove our own cloth. The first suit of clothes I ever wore, my mother spun the cotton and wool, wove the cloth and made the clothes. It was a mixed steel gray suit. She dyed the thread so as to get the pattern. One loom carried the black thread through and the other carried the white thread to weave the cloth into the mixed pattern.

"I don't know how large our place was. Maybe it was about a hundred acres. Every one that married out of the family had a home. They called it a free Negro colony. Nothing but Negroes in it.

"My father volunteered and went to the army in 1862. He served with the Yankees. You know Negroes didn't fight in the Confederate armies. They was in the armies, but they were servants. My father enrolled as a soldier. I think it was in Company F. I don't know the regiment or the division. He was a sergeant last time I saw him. I remember that well, I remember the stripes on his arm. He was mustered out in Galveston, Texas, in 1865.

"The house I was born in was a log house, sealed inside. The cracks were chinked with dirt and mud, and it was weather boarded on the outside. You couldn't tell it was a log house. It had two rooms. In them times you didn't cook in the house you lived in. You had a kitchen built off from the house you lived in just like you have servant quarters now. You went across the yard to do your cooking. The smokehouse was off by itself. Milk was off by itself too. The dairy house was where you kept the flour and sugar and preserves and fruit and pickles and all those kind of things. No food was kept in the house. The milk house had shelves all up in it and when you milked the cows the pans and bowls and crocks were put up on the shelves. Where it was possible the milk house was built on a branch or spring where you could get plenty of cold water. You didn't milk in the milk house. You milked in the cow pen right out in the weather. Then you carried it down to the milk house and strained it. It was poured out in vessels. When the cream rose it was skimmed off to churn for butter.

"Feed for the stock was kept in the corn crib. We would call it a barn now. That barn was for corn and oft'times we had overhead a place where we kept fodder. Bins were kept in the barn for wheat and peas.

Slaves on Other Places

"I seen the slaves outside the colonies. I was little and didn't pay any attention to them. Slaves would run away. They had a class of white people known as patrollers. They would catch the slaves and whip them. I never saw that done. I heard them talking about it. I was only a child and never got a chance to see the slaves on the places of other people, but just heard the folks talking about them.

Within the Yankee Lines

"When the War broke out, the free colored people became fearful. There was a great deal of stuff taken away from them by the Confederate soldiers. They moved into the Yankee lines for protection. My family moved also. They lost live stock and feed. They lost only one horse and then they came back home. I can see that old horse right now. He was a sorrel horse, with a spot in his forehead, and his name was John. My father was inside the Yankee lines when he volunteered for the service. I don't know how much he got or anything about it except that I know the Yankees were holding Portsmouth, Norfolk, Hampton Roads, and all that country.

Expectations of the Slaves

"I could hear my mother and uncle talk about what the slaves expected. I know they was expecting to get something. They weren't supposed to be turned out like wild animals like they were. I think it was forty acres and a mule. I am not sure but I know they expected something to be settled on them.

What They Got

"If any of them got anything in Virginia, I don't know anything about it. They might have been some slaves that did get something—just like they was here in Arkansas.

"Old Man Wilfong, when he freed Andy Wilfong in Bradley County, Arkansas, gave Andy plenty. He did get forty acres of land. That is right down here out from Warren. Wilfong owned that land and a heap more when he died. He hasn't been dead more than six or seven years. I pastored him in 1904 and 1905. There were others who expected to get something, but I don't know any others that got it. Land was cheap then. Andy bought land at twenty-five and fifty cents an acre, and sold the timber off of it at the rate of one thousand dollars for each forty acres. He bought hundreds of acres. He owned a section and a section and one-half of land when he was my member. He had seven boys and two girls and he gave them all forty acres apiece when they married. Then he sold the timber off of four forties. Whenever a boy or girl was married he'd give him a house. He'd tell him to go out and pick himself out a place.

"He sold one hundred and sixty acres of timber for

four thousand dollars, but if he had kept it for two years longer, he would have got ten thousand dollars for it. The Bradley Lumber Company went in there and cut the timber all through.

"Wilfong's master's name was Andrew Wilfong, same as Andy's. His master came from Georgia, but he was living in Arkansas when freedom came. Later on Andy bought the farm his master was living on when freedom came. His master was then dead.

Right After the War

"My mother came back home and we went on farming just like we did before, raising stuff to eat. You know I can't remember much that they did before the War but I can remember what they did during the War and after the War,—when they came back home. My folks still own the old place but I have been away from there sixty-one years. A whole generation has been raised up and died since I left.

"I came out with one of my cousins and went to Georgia (Du Pont) following turpentine work. It was turpentine farming. You could cut a hole in the tree known as the box. It will hold a quart. Rosin runs out of that tree into the box. Once a week, they go by and chip a tree to keep the rosin running. Then the dippers dip the rosin out and put it in barrels. Them barrels is hauled to the still. Then it is distilled just like whiskey would be. The evaporation of it makes turpentine; the rosin is barreled and shipped to make glass. The turpentine is barreled and sold. I have dipped thousands of gallons of turpentine.

"I came to South Carolina in 1880 and married. I

stayed there seven years and came to Arkansas in 1888. I came right to North Little Rock and then moved out into the country around Lonoke County,—on a farm. I farmed there for five years. Then I went to pastoring. I started pastoring one year before I quit making cotton. I entered the ministry in 1892 and continued in the active service until November 1937. I put in forty-five years in the active ministry.

Schooling

"I first went to school at a little log school in Suffolk, Virginia. From there I went to Hampton, Virginia. I got my theological training in Shorter College under Dr. T.H. Jackson.

Ku Klux

"I never had any experience with the Ku Klux Klan. I seen white men riding horses and my mother said they was Ku Kluxes, but they never bothered us as I remember. They had two sets of white folks like that. The patrollers were before and during the War and the Ku Klux Klan came after the War. I can't remember how the Ku Klux I saw were dressed. The patrollers I remember. They would just be three or four white men riding in bunches.

Nat Turner Rebellion

"I have heard the 'Nat Turner Rebellion' spoken of, but I don't know what was said. I think the old people called it the 'Nat Turner War.'

Reconstruction Days

"Lawyer Whipper was one of the best criminal lawyers in the state. He was a Negro. The Republican party had the state then and the Negroes were strong. Robert Small was a noted politician and was elected to go to Congress twice. The last time he ran, he was elected but had a hard fight. The election was so close it was contested but Small won out. He was the last nigger congressman. I heard that there were one or two more, but I don't remember them.

"When I first went to South Carolina, them niggers was bad. They organized. They used to have an association known as the Union Laborers, I think. The organization was like the fraternal order. I don't know's they ever had any trouble but they were always in readiness to protect themselves if any conflict arose. It was a secret order carried on just like any other fraternal order. They had distress calls. Every member has an old horn which he blew in time of trouble. I think that sane kind of organization or something like it was active here when I came. The Eagles (a big family of white people in Lonoke County) had a fight with members of it once and some of the Eagles were killed a year or two before I came to this state.

Voting and Political Activities

"I voted in South Carolina, but I wasn't old enough to vote in Georgia. However, I stumped Taliaferro County for Garfield when I was in Georgia. I lived in a little town by the name of McCray. The town I was in, they had never had more than fifteen or twenty Republican votes polled. But I polled between two hundred and three hundred votes. I was one of the regular speakers. The tickets were in my care too. You see, they had tickets in them days and not the long ballots. They didn't have long ballots like they have now. The tickets were sent to me and I took care of them until the election. In the campaign I was regularly employed through the Republican Campaign Committee Managers.

"According to preparation and conditions there were less corruption then than there is now. In them days, they had to learn the tricks. But now they know them. Now you find the man and he already knows what to do.

Songs

"Back in that period, nearly all the songs the Negro sang considerably were the spirituals: 'I'm Going Down to Jordan,' 'Roll Jordan Roll.'"

United States. Work Projects Administration

Interviewer: Samuel S. Taylor
Person interviewed: J.F. Boone
1502 Izard, Little Rock, Arkansas
Age: 66

J.F. BOONE

[HW: A Union Veteran]

"My father's name was Arthur Boone and my mother's name was Eliza Boone, I am goin' to tell you about my father. Now be sure you put down there that this is Arthur Boone's son. I am J.F. Boone, and I am goin' to tell you about my father, Arthur Boone.

"My father's old master was Henry Boone. My mother came from Virginia—north Virginia—and my father came from North Carolina. The Boones bought them. I have heard that my father, Arthur Boone, was bought by the Boones. They wasn't his first masters. I have heard my father say that it was more than a thousand dollars they paid for him.

"He said that they used to put up niggers on the block and auction them off. They auctioned off niggers accordin' to the breed of them. Like they auction off dogs and horses. The better the breed, the more they'd pay. My father was in the first-class rating as a good healthy Negro and those kind sold for good money. I have heard him say that niggers sometimes brought as high as five thousand dollars.

"My father don't know much about his first boss man. But the Boones were very good to them. They got biscuits once a week. The overseer was pretty cruel to them in a way. My father has seen them whipped till they couldn't stand up and then salt and things that hurt poured in their wounds. My father said that he seen that done; I don't know whether it was his boss man or the overseer that done it.

"My father said that they breeded good niggers— stud 'em like horses and cattle. Good healthy man and woman that would breed fast, they would keep stalled up. Wouldn't let them get out and work. Keep them to raise young niggers from. I don't know for certain that my father was used that way or not. I don't suppose he would have told me that, but he was a mighty fine man and he sold for a lot of money. The slaves weren't to blame for that.

"My father said that in about two or three months after the War ended, his young master told them that they were free. They came home from the War about that time. He told them that they could continue living on with them or that they could go to some one else if they wanted to 'cause they were free and there wasn't any more slavery.

"I was born after slavery. Peace was declared in 1865, wasn't it? When the War ended I don't know where my father was living, but I was bred and born in Woodruff near Augusta in Arkansas. All the Booneses were there when I knew anything about it. They owned hundreds and hundreds of acres of ground. I was born on old Captain Boone's farm.

"My father was always a farmer. He farmed till he

died. They were supposed to give him a pension, but he never did get it. They wrote to us once or twice and asked for his number and things like that, but they never did do nothing. You see he fit in the Civil War. Wait a minute. We had his old gun for years. My oldest brother had that gun. He kept that gun and them old blue uniforms with big brass buttons. My old master had a horn he blowed to call the slaves with, and my brother had that too. He kept them things as particular as you would keep victuals.

"Yes, my father fit in the Civil War. I have seen his war clothes as many times as you have hairs on your head I reckon. He had his old sword and all. They had a hard battle down in Mississippi once he told me. Our house got burnt up and we lost his honorable discharge. But he was legally discharged. But he didn't git nothin' for it, and we didn't neither.

"My father was whipped by the pateroles several times. They run him and whipped him. My daddy slipped out many a time. But they never caught him when he slipped out. They never whipped him for slippin' out. That was during the time he was a slave. The slaves wasn't allowed to go from one master to another without a pass. My father said that sometimes, his young master would play a joke on him. My father couldn't read. His young master would give him a pass and the pass would say, 'Whip Arthur Boone's --- and pass him out. When he comes back, whip his --- again and pass him back.' His young master called hisself playin' a joke on him. They wouldn't hit him more than half a dozen licks, but they would make him take his pants down and they would give them to him jus' where the pass said. They wouldn't hurt him much. It was more devilment than anything else. He would say, 'Whut you hittin' me for when I got a pass?' and they would say, 'Yes, you got a pass, but it says whip your ---.' And they would show it to him, and then they would say, 'You'll git the res' when you come back.' My father couldn't read nothin' else, but that's one word he learnt to read right well.

"My father was quite a young man in his day. He died in 1891. He was just fifty-six years old. I'm older now than he was when he died. My occupation when I was well was janitor. I have been sick now for three years and ain't done nothin' in all that time. If it wasn't for my wife, I don't know whut I would do.

"I was born in 1872, on December the eighth, and I am sixty-six years old now. That is, I will be if the Lord lets me live till December the eighth, this year.

"Now whose story are you saying this is? You say this is the story of Arthur Boone, father of J.F. Boone? Well, that's all right; but you better mention that J.F. Boone is Arthur Boone's son. I rent this house from Mr. Lindeman. He has the drug store right there. If anybody comes lookin' for me, I might be moved, but Mr. Lindeman will still be there."

Interviewer's Comment

If you have read this interview hastily and have missed the patroller joke on page three, turn back and read it now. The interviewer considers it the choicest thing in the story.

That and the story of an unpensioned Union veteran and the insistence on the word "son" seemed to me to set this story off as a little out of the ordinary.

Interviewer: Mrs. Annie L. LaCotts
  Person interviewed: Jonas Boone, St, Charles. Arkansas
Age: 86

JONAS BOONE

Most any day in St. Charles you can see an old Negro man coming down the street with a small sack made of bed ticking hanging shot-pouch fashion from his shoulder. This is old Uncle Jonas Boone who by the aid of his heavy cane walks to town and makes the round of his white folks homes to be given some old shoes, clothes, or possibly a mess of greens or some sweet potatoes—in fact whatever he may find.

"Jonas, can you remember anything about the war or slavery time?"

"Yes mam I was a great big boy when the slaves were sot free."

"Do you know how old you are?"

"Yes mam I will be 87 years old on March 15th. I was born in Mississippi at Cornerville. My mother belonged to Mr. L.D. Hewitt's wife. She didn't have many slaves—just my parents and my two uncles and their families. My daddy and two uncles went to the war but our mistress' husband Mr. Hewitt was too old to go. I guess my daddy was killed in de war, for he never come home when my uncles did. We lived here in Arkansas close to St. Charles. Our mistress was good to her slaves but when they were free her husband had got himself drowned in big LaGrue when de water was high all over the bottoms and low ground; he was trying to cross in a boat, what you call a dug out. You know it's a big log scooped out till it floats like a boat. Then after that our mistress wanted to go back to her old home in Mississippi and couldn't take us with her cause she didn't have any money, so we stayed here. My mammy cried days and nights when she knew her mistress was going to leave her here in Arkansas. We moved down on de Schute and worked for Mr. Mack Price. You know he was Mr. Arthur's and Miss Joe's father."

"Jonas, if your owners were Hewitts why is your name Boone?"

"Well you see, miss, my daddy's daddy belonged to Mr. Daniel Boone, Mr. John Boone's and Miss Mary Black's grandpa, and I was named Boone for him, my granddaddy. I been married twice. My last wife owns her home out close to de church west of St. Charles. I haven't been able to work any for over two years but my wife makes us a living. She's 42 or 43 years old and a good worker and a good woman. I've been all de time wanting some of this help other folks been getting but dey won't give me nothing. The woman what goes to your house to see if you needs relief told me I was better off den most folks an' of course I know I'd rather have my wife and home than have to be like lots of dese niggers who's old and can't work and got nothing but what de Government give 'em."

Interviewer: Miss Irene Robertson
Person Interviewed: John Bowdry, Clarendon, Arkansas
Age: 75

JOHN BOWDRY

"I was born at Baldwyn, Mississippi not for from Corinth. When my mother was last seen she was going away with a bunch of Yankees. I don't know what it was. She was a dark woman. Pa was light. I was born in 1865. I was left when I was two or three months old. I never seen no pa. They left me with my uncle what raised me. He was a slave but too young to go to war. His master was named Porter. Master Stevenson had sold him. He liked Porter the best. He took the name of Stanfield Porter at freedom. Porters had a ordinary farm. He wasn't rich. He had a few slaves. Stevenson had a lot of slaves. Grandfather was in Charleston, South Carolina. Him and my uncle corresponded. My uncle learnet to read and write but I guess somebody done his writing for him at the other end.

"My Uncle Stanfield seen a heap of the War. He seen them fight, come by in droves a mile long. They wasted their feed and living too.

"At freedom Master Porter told them about it and he lived on there a few years till I come into recollection. I found out about my pa and mother. They had three sets of children in the house. They was better to them. All of them got better treatment 'en I did. One day I left. I'd been making up my mind to leave. I was thirteen years old. Scared of everything. I walked twenty miles to Middleton, Tennessee. I slept at the state line at some stranger's but at black folks' house. I walked all day two days. I got a job at some white folks good as my parents. His name wae J.D. Palmer. He was a big farmer. I slept in a servant's house and et in his own kitchen. He sont me to school two two-month terms. Four months all I got. I got my board then four months. I got my board and eight dollars a month the other months in the year. He died.

"I come to Forrest City when I was twenty years old.

"I been married. I got a girl lives wid me here. My girl, she married.

"I ain't got no complaint again' the times. My life has been fair. I worked mighty hard."

Slave Narratives

Name of Interviewer: Irene Robertson
Subject: Ex-Slave—History

This information given by: Jack Boyd
Place of Residence: Hazen, Arkansas
Occupation: Light jobs now. AGE: 72

[TR: Information moved from bottom of first page.]

JACK BOYD

[HW: The Boyd Negroes]

Jack Boyd was born a slave. Miss Ester's mother was a Boyd and married a Donnahoo. Miss Ester Donnahoo married Jim Shed. The Boyd's lived in Richmond, Virginia. They sold Jack Boyd's grandmother, grandfather, mother, and father a number of times. One time they were down, in Georgia not far from Atalnta. They were being ill treated. The new master had promised to be good to them so he wasn't and the news had gotten back to Virginia as it had a time or two before so the Boyds sent to Georgia and brought them back and took them back home to Virginia. The Boyds always asked the new masters to be good to them but no one was never so good to them as the Boyds were, and they would buy them back again. When freedom was declared three of the Boyd brothers and Miss Ester's husband Jim Shed, was the last master of Charlie Boyd. Jack's father came to Waco, Texas. They may have been there before for they were "big ranchmen" but that is when Jack Boyds whole family came to Texas. There were thirty six in his family. The families then were large. When Jack grew up to be about ten years old there wasn't anything much at Waco except a butcher shop and a blacksmith shop. Jim Shed alone had 1800 acres of land his own. He used nine cowboys, some white and some black. The first of January every year the cattle was ready to be driven to Kansas City to market. They all rode broncos. It would rain, sometimes hail and sometimes they would get into thunder storms. The cattle would stampede, get lost and have to be found.

They slept in the open plains at night. They had good clothes. They would ride two or three weeks and couldn't get a switch. Finally in about June or July they would get into Kansas City. The white masters were there waiting and bought food and supplies to take back home. They would have started another troop of cowboys with cattle about June and meet them in Kansas City just before Christmas. Jack liked this life except it was a hard life in bad weather. They had a good living and the Masters made "big money." Jack said he always had his own money then. His people are scattered around Waco now, "the Boyd negroes." He hasn't been back since he came to Arkansas when he was about eighteen. He married here and had "raised" a big family. The plains were full of rattle snakes, rabbits, wild cats and lots of other wild animals. They never started out with less than 400 head of cattle. They picked cattle that would travel about together. It would all be grown or about the same age. The worst thing they had to contend with was a lack of water. They had to carry water along and catch rainwater and hunt places to water the cattle. His father's and grandfather's masters names were Gillis, Hawkins, and Sam

Boyd. They were the three who came to Texas and located the ranch at Waco. Jack thinks they have been dead a long time but they have heirs around Waco now. Jack Boyd left Waco in 1881.

United States. Work Projects Administration

STATE—Arkansas
NAME OF WORKER—Bernice Bowden
ADDEESS—1006 Oak Street, Pine Bluff, Arkansas
DATE—November 2, 1938
SUBJECT—Ex-slaves

MAL BOYD

[TR: Repetitive information deleted from subsequent pages.]

Circumstances Of Interview

1. Name and address of informant—Mal Boyd, son of slaves

2. Date and time of interview—November 1, 1938, 9:45 a.m.

3. Place of interview—101 Miller Street

4. Name and address of person, if any, who put you in touch with informant—None. I saw him sitting on porch as I walked along.

5. Name and address of person, if any, accompanying you—None

6. Description of room, house, surroundings, etc.—Frame house. Sat on porch. Yard clean—everything neat. Near foundry on graveled street in suburbs of west Pine Bluff.

Text of Interview

"Papa belonged to Bill Boyd. Papa said he was his father and treated him just like the rest of his children. He said Bill Boyd was an Irishman. I know papa looked kinda like an Irishman—face was red. Mama was about my color. Papa was born in Texas, but he came to Arkansas. I member hearin' him say he saw 'em fight six months in one place, down here at Marks' Mill. He said Bill Boyd had three sons, Urk and Tom and Nat. They was in the Civil War. I heered Tom Boyd say he was in behind a crew of men in the war and a Yankee started shootin' and when he shot down the last one next to Tom, he seen who it was doin' the shootin' and he shot him and saved his life. He was the hind one.

"I've farmed mostly and sawmilled.

"I use to get as high as three and five dollars callin' figgers for the white folks."

Interviewer's Comment

Subscribes to the Daily Graphic and reads of world affairs. Goes to a friend's house and listens to the radio. Lives with daughter and is supported by her. House belongs to a son-in-law. Wore good clothing and was very clean. He hoped that the United States would not become involved in a war.

Personal History of Informant

1. Ancestry—Father, Tol Boyd; Mother, Julia Dangerfield.

2. Place and date of birth—Cleveland County, August 4, 1873

3. Family—Lives with daughter. Has one other daughter. Mother one-half Indian, born in Alabama, he thinks.

4. Places lived in, with dates—Ouachita County, Dallas County. Bradley County, Jefferson County.

5. Education, with dates—Began schooling in 1880 and went until twelve or thirteen.

6. Occupations and accomplishments, with dates—Farmed till 21, public work? Sawmill work.

7. Special skills and interests—None

8. Community and religious activities—Ward Chapel on West Sixth.

9. Description of informant—Gray hair, height 5 ft. 9 in., high cheekbones. Gray hair—practically straight says like father.

10. Other points gained in interview—Says father was part Irish. Belonged to Bill Boyd. Stayed there for years after freedom.

United States. Work Projects Administration

Name of Interviewer: Irene Robertson
Subject: EX-SLAVE—HISTORY—OLD SAYINGS

This information given by: George Braddox
Place of Residence: Hazen, Arkansas
Occupation: Farmer AGE: 80

[TR: Information moved from bottom of first page.]

GEORGE BRADDOX

George Braddox was born a slave but his mother being freed when he was eipht years old they went to themselves—George had one sister and one brother. He doesn't know anything about them but thinks they are dead as he is the youngest of the three. His father's name was Peter Calloway He went with Gus Taylor to the war and never came back to his family. George said he had been to Chicago several times to see his father where he was living. But his mother let her children go by that name. She gave them a name Braddox when they were freed. Calloways lived on a joining plantation to John and Dave Gemes. John Gemes was the old master and Dave the young. George said they were mean to him. He can remember that Gus Taylor wes overseer for the Gemes till he went to war. The Gemes lived in a brick house and the slaves lived in log houses. They had a big farm and raised cotton and corn. The cotton was six feet tall and had big leaves. They had to pull the leaves to let the bowls get the sun to open. They topped the cotton too. They made lots of cotton and corn to an acre. Dave

Gemes had several children when George moved away, their names were Ruben, John, Margaret, Susie and Betty. They went to school at Marshall, Texas.

John Gemes had fine carriages, horses and mules. He had one old slave who just milked and churned. She didn't do anything else. When young calves had to be attended to somebody else had to help her and one man did all the feeding. They had lots of peafowles, ducks, geese and chickens.

They had mixed stock of chickens and guineas—always had a drove of turkeys. Sometimes the turkeys would go off with wild turkeys. There were wild hogs and turkeys in the woods. George never learned to read or write. He remembers they built a school for white children on the Calloway place joining the Gemes place but he thought it was tuition school. George said he thought the Gemes and all his "kin" folks came from Alabama to Texas, but he is not sure but he does know this. Dr. Hazen came from Tennessee to Texas and back to Hazen, Arkansas and settled. His cousin Jane Hodge (colored) was working out near here and he came here to deer hunt and just stayed with them. He said deer was plentiful here. It was not cleared and so close to White Cache, St. Francis and Mississippi rivers.

George said his mother cooked for the Gemes the first he could remember of her. That was all she had time to do. It was five miles to Marshall. They lived in Harrison County and they could buy somethings to eat there if they didn't raise enough. They bought cheese by the cases in round boxes and flour in barrels and sugar in barrels. They had fine clothes for Sunday. After his mother left the Gemes they worked in the field or did anything she could for a living.

George married after he came to Arkansas and bought a farm 140 acres of land 4 miles north of Hazen and a white man, — --- closed a mortgage out on him and took it. He paid $300.00 for a house in town in which he now lives. His son was killed in the World War and he gets his son's insurance every month.

George said when he came to Arkansas it was easy to live if you liked to hunt. Ship the skins and get some money when you couldn't be farming. Could get all the wood you would cut and then clear out land and farm. He hunted 7 or 8 years with Colonel A.F. Yopp and fed Colonel's dogs. He hunted with Mr. Yopp but he didn't think Colonel was a very good man. I gathered from George that he didn't approve of wickedness.

It is bad luck to dig a grave the day before a person is buried, or any time before the day of the burying. Uncle George has dug or helped to dig lots of graves. It is bad luck to the family of the dead person. The grave ought not to be "left open" it is called. He has always heard this and believes it, yet he can't remember when he first heard it.

He thinks there are spirits that direct your life and if you do wrong the evil fates let you be punished. He believes in good and evil spirits. Spirits right here among us. He says there is "bound to be spirits" or "something like 'em."

United States. Work Projects Administration

Interviewer: Miss Irene Robertson
Person interviewed: George Braddox, Hazen, Arkansas
Age: 81

GEORGE BRADDOX

Most of the old songs were religious. I don't remember none much. When the war broke out my papa jess left and went on off with some people and joined the Yankee army. I went to see him since I been at Hazen. He lived in Chicago. Yes mam he's been dead a long time ago. Gus Taylor and Peter Calloway (white) took my papa with them for their helper. He left them and went with the Yankee army soon as he heard what they was fighting about. Peter Calloway lived on a big track of land joining Dave Genes land. It show was a big farm. Peter Calloway owned my papa and Dave Genes my mama. Gus Taylor was Dave Genes overseer. Peter Calloway never come back from the war. My folks come from Alabama with Dave Genes and his son John Genes. I was born in Harrison county, Texas. Gus Taylor was a great big man. He was mean to us all. The Yankees camped there. It was near Marshall. I had some good friends among the Yankees. They kept me posted all time the war went on. Nobody never learnt me nothing. I can cipher a little and count money. I took that up. I learned after I was grown a few things. Just learned it myself. I never went to school a day in my life. The Genes had a brick, big red brick house. They sent their children to schools. They had stock, peafowls, cows, guineas, geese, ducks and chickens, hogs and everything. Old woman on the place just milked and churned. That is all she done.

I never heard of no plantations being divided. They never give us nothing, not nothing. Right after the war was the worse times we ever have had. We ain't had no sich hard times since then. The white folks got all was made. It was best we could do. The Yankees what camped down there told us about the surrender. If the colored folks had started an uprisin the white folks would have set the hounds on us and killed us.

I never heard of the Ku Klux Klan ever being in Texas. Gus Taylor was the ridin boss and he was Ku Klux enough. Everybody was scared not to mind him. He rode over three or four hundred acres of ground. He could beat any fellow under him. I never did see anybody sold. I never was sold. We was glad to be set free. I didn't know what it would be like. It was just like opening the door and lettin the bird fly out. He might starve, or freeze, or be killed pretty soon but he just felt good because he was free. We show did have a hard time getting along right after we was set free. The white folks what had money wouldn't pay nothing much for work. All the slaves was in confusion.

A cousin of mine saw Dr. Hazen down in Texas and they all come back to work his land. They wrote to us about it being so fine for hunting. I always liked to hunt so I rode a pony and come to them. The white folks in Texas told the Yankees what to do after the surrender; get off the land. We didn't never vote there but I voted in Arkansas. Mr. Abel Rinehardt always hope me. I could trust him. I don't vote now. No colored people held office in Texas or here that I heard of.

I got nothing to say bout the way the young generation is doing.

I farmed around Hazen nearly ever since the Civil War. I saved $300 and bought this here house. My son was killed in the World War and I get his insurance every month. I hunted with Colonel Yapp and fed his dogs. He never paid me a cent for taking care of the dogs. His widow never as much as give me a dog. She never give me nothing!

I'm too old to worry bout the present conditions. They ain't gettin no better. I sees dot.

United States. Work Projects Administration

Interviewer: Bernice Bowden
Person Interviewed: Edward Bradley
115 South Plum Street, Pine Bluff, Arkansas
Age: 70

EDWARD BRADLEY

"I was seventy years old this last past June, the sixth day. Lots of people say I don't look that old but I'm sure seventy and I've done a lot of hard work in my day. One thing, I've taken good care of myself. I never did lose much sleep.

"I farmed forty years of my life. Been in this State thirty-seven years. I was born in Hardin County, Tennessee. I disremember what age I was when I left Tennessee.

"My mother was named Mary Bradley and my father was named Hilliard Bradley. They originated in Alabama and was sold there, and they was free when they come to Tennessee.

"Bradley was the last man owned 'em. I think Beaumont sold 'em to Bradley. That's the way I always heered 'em talk. I think they claimed their owners was pretty good to 'em. I know I heered my father say he never did get a whippin' from either one of 'em.

"Of course my mother wasn't a Bradley fore she married, she was a Murphy.

"I had one brother four years older than I was. He was

my half-brother and I had a whole brother was two years older than I.

"First place I lived in Arkansas was near Blytheville. I lived there four years. I was married and farmin' for myself.

"I went from Hardin County, Tennessee to Blytheville, Arkansas by land. Drove a team and two cows. I think we was on the road four days. My wife went by train. You know that was too wearisome for her to go by land.

"I had been runnin a five-horse crop in Tennessee and I carried three boys that I used to work with me.

"The last year I was there I cleared $1660.44. I never will forget it. I made a hundred and ten bales of cotton and left 2000 pounds of seed cotton in the field cause I was goin' to move.

"My folks was sick all the time. Wasn't any canals in that country, and my wife had malaria every year.

"After I got my crop finished I'd get out and log. I was raised in a poor county and you take a man like that, he's always a good worker. I rented the land—365 acres and I had seven families workin for me. I was responsible for everything. I told 'em that last year that if I cleared over a $1000, I'd give 'em ten dollars a piece. And I give it to 'em too. You see they was under my jurisdiction.

"Next place I lived was Forrest City. They all went with me. Had to charter a car to move 'em. It was loaded too.

"I had 55 hogs, 17 head of cattle, 13 head of mules and

horses. And I had killed 1500 pounds of hogs. You see besides my family I had two-month-hands—worked by the month.

"I own a home in Forrest City now. I'm goin back right after Christmas. My children had it fixed up. Had the waterworks and electric lights put in.

"Two of my daughters married big school teachers. One handles a big school in Augusta and the other in Forrest City. One of 'em is in the Smith-Hughes work too.

"I've done something no other man has done. I've educated four of my brothers and sisters after my father died and four of my wife's brothers and sisters and one adopted boy and my own six children—fifteen in all. A man said to me once, "Why any man that's done that much for education ought to get a pension from the educator people."

"I never went to school six months in my life but I can read and write. I'm not extra good in spelling—that's my hindrance, but I can figger very well.

"We always got our children started 'fore they went to school and then I could help 'em in school till they got to United States money.

"Another thing I always would do, I would buy these block A, B, C's. Everyone learned their A, B, C's fore they went to school.

"I reckon I'm a self-made man in a lot of things. I learnt my own self how to blacksmith. I worked for a man for nothin' just so I could learn and after that for about a year I was the best plow sharpener. And then I learned how to carpenter.

"My mother was awful good on head countin' and she learnt me when I was a little fellow. My oldest brother use to help me. We'd sit by the fire, so you see you might say I got a fireside education.

"When I left Forrest City I moved to England and made one crop and moved to Baucum and made one crop and then I moved on the Sheridan Pike three miles the other side of Dew Drop. I got the oil fever. They was sellin' land under that headin'. Sold it to the colored folks and lots o' these Bohemians. They sho is fine people to live by—so accommodatin'.

"Then I came here to Pine Bluff in 1921. I hauled wood for two years. Then I put in my application at the Cotton Belt Shops. That was in 1923 and I worked there fifteen years. I retired from the shops this year and took a half pension. I think I'll get about fifteen dollars a month. That's my thoughts.

"I have two daughters in Camden. One teaches school and one operates a beauty parlor.

"All six of my children finished high school and three graduated from college.

"I think the younger generation is livin' too fast. I know one thing, they has done—they 'bout wore out the old folks. Old folks educate 'em and can't accumulate anything.

"They don't settle much now till they marry. Seems like the young folks don't have much accommodation.

"I'll tell you another thing, the children aren't carryin' out things like they use to. I think when us old folks plays out this world is goin' to be in a bad shape.

"I belong out here to the Catholic Church—the oldest church in the world. I use to belong to the Methodist Church, but they got along so bad I got tired, so I went to the Catholic. I like it out there—everthing so quiet and nice."

Name of Interviewer: Mrs. Bernice Bowden
Person interviewed: Rachel Bradley. 1103 State Street, Pine Bluff, Arkansas
Age: 107?

RACHEL BRADLEY

Upon arriving at the humble unpainted home of Rachel Bradley I found her sitting in the doorway on a typical split-oak bottomed chair watching the traffic of State Street, one of our busiest streets out of the high rent district. It is a mixture of white and Negro stores and homes.

After asking her name to be sure I was really talking to Rachel Bradley, I said I had been told she was a former slave. "Yes'm, I used to be a slave." She smiled broadly displaying nearly a full set of teeth. She is of a cheerful, happy disposition and seemed glad to answer my questions. As to her age, she said she was "a little girl on the floor whan the stars fell." I looked this up at the public library and found that falling stars or showers of meteors occur in cycles of thirty-three years. One such display was recorded in 1833 and another in 1866. So if Rachel Bradley is really 107 years old, she was born in 1830. It is a question in my mind whether or not she could have remembered falling stars at the age of three, but on the other hand if she was "a little girl on the floor" in 1866 she would be only somewhere between seventy-five and eighty years of age.

Her master and mistress were Mitchell and Elizabeth Simmons and they had two sons and two daughters. They lived on a plantation about twelve miles from Farmersville, Louisiana.

Rachel was a house girl and her mother was the cook. Besides doing house work, she was nursemaid and as she grew older did her mistress' sewing and could also weave and knit. From the way she smiled and rolled her eyes I could see that this was the happiest time of her life. "My white folks was so good to me. I sat right down to the same table after they was thru."

While a child in the home of her white folks she played with her mistress' children. In her own words "My mistress give us a task to do and when we got it done, we went to our playhouse in the yard."

When the war came along, her master was too old to go but his two sons went and both lived through the war.

Questioned about the Yankees during the war she said, "I seen right smart of the Yankees. I seen the 'Calvary' go by. They didn't bother my white folks none."

Rachel said the ABC's for me but cannot read or write. She said her mistress' children wanted to teach her but she would rather play so grew up in ignorance.

After the war Rachel's white folks moved to Texas and Rachel went to live with her mistress' married daughter Martha. For her work she was paid six dollars a month. She was not given any money by her former owners after being freed, but was paid for her work. Later on Rachel went to work in the field making a crop with her brother, turning it over to the owner of the land for groceries and other supplies and when the cotton was weighed "de white folks taken out part of our half. I knowed they done it but we couldn't do nothin bout it."

Rachel had four husbands and eleven children. Her second husband abandoned her, taking the three oldest and leaving five with her. One boy and one girl were old enough to help their mother in the field and one stayed in the house with the babies, so she managed to make a living working by the day for the white people.

The only clash with the Ku Klux Klan was when they came to get an army gun her husband had bought.

Being a woman, Rachel did not know much about politics during the Reconstruction period. She had heard the words "Democrat," "Radical" and "Republican" and that was about all she remembered.

Concerning the younger generation Rachel said: "I don't know what goin' come of 'em. The most of 'em is on the beat" (trying to get all they can from others).

After moving to Arkansas, she made a living working in the field by the day and as she grew older, washing and ironing, sewing, housecleaning and cooking.

Her long association with white people shows in her speech which is quite plain with only a few typical Negro expressions, such as the following:

"She died this last gone Sattiday and I hope (help) shroud her."

"When white lady find baby, I used to go hep draw the breas'."

"Heap a people."

"Bawn."

The Welfare Department gives Rachel $8.00 a month. She pays $2.00 a month for two rooms with no drinking water. With the help of her white friends she manages to exist and says she is "pendin on the Lord" to help her get along.

She sang for me in a quavering voice the following songs reminiscent of the war:

> "Homespun dresses plain I know.
> And the hat palmetto too.
> Hurrah! Hurrah!
> We cheer for the South we love so dear,
> We cheer for the homespun dresses
> The Southern ladies wear!"

> "Who is Price a fightin'?
> He is a fightin', I do know.
> I think it is old Curtis.
> I hear the cannons roa'"

Interviewer: Miss Irene Robertson
Person interviewed: Elizabeth Brannon, Biscoe, Arkansas
(Packed to move somewhere else)
Age: 40 plus

ELIZABETH BRANNON

"I was born in Helena, Arkansas. Grandma raised me mostly. She was born up in Virginia. Her name was Mariah Bell.

"Grandmother was sold more than once. When she was small she and her mother were sold together to different buyers. The morning she was sold she could see her mother crying through the crowd, and the last she ever seen her mother she was crying and waving to her. She never could forget that. We all used to sit around her and we would all be crying with her when she told that so many, many times. Grandmother said she was five years old then and was sold to a doctor in Virginia. He made a house girl of her and learned her to be a midwife.

"She told us about a time when the stars fell or a time about like it. Her master got scared in Virginia. His niece killed herself 'cause she thought the world was coming to on end. Mama of the baby was walking, crying and praying. Grandmama had the baby. She said it was a terrible morning.

"When grandmama was sold away from her own mother she took the new master's cook for her mother. I live to see her. Her name was Charity Walker. She was awful old. Grandmama didn't remember if her mother had other children or not. She was the youngest.

"Grandmama was sold again. Her second master wasn't good as her doctor master. He didn't feed them good, didn't feed the children good neither. He told his slaves to steal. Grandmama had two children there. She was pregnant again. Grandpa stole a shoat. She craved meat. Meat was scarce then and the War was on. Grandpa had it cut up and put away. Grandmama had the oldest baby in the box under her bed and the youngest child asleep in her bed. She was frying the meat. She seen the overseer across the field stepping that way. Grandpa left and grandmama put the skillet of meat in the bed with the baby and threw a big roll of cotton in the fire. The overseer come in and looked around, asked what he smelled burning. She told him it was a sack of motes (cotton lumps). Grandpa was Jim Bell. His master learnet him to steal and lie. He got better after freedom.

"Grandmama never would let us have pockets in our aprons and dresses. Said it was a temptation for us to learn to steal. She thought that was awful and to lie too.

"Grandmama and grandpa and mama and her sister, the baby, died. Come with soldiers from Virginia to Helena, Arkansas on a big boat. They nursed soldiers in the hospital in the last of the War. Grandpapa died in 1895. He had heart trouble. He was seventy-five years old then. Grandmama died in 1913. She was awful, awful old. Grandmama said they put her off on College and Perry streets but that wasn't the names of the streets then. She wore a baggin dress and brogan shoes. Brass-toed shoes and brass eyelets. She would take grease and soot and make shoe polish for them. We all wore that dress and the shoes at times. I wore them to Peabody School in Helena and the children made so mich fun of their cry (squeaking) till I begged them to get me some better looking shoes for cold rainy spells of weather. I wore the dress. It was strong nearly as leather.

"When she was sold the last time she got a marble box and it had a small lock and key. It was square and thick, size of four men's shoe boxes. When she come to Arkansas she brought it filled with rice on the boat. She kept her valuable papers in it. Our house burned and the shoes and box both got away from me. Her oldest girl died after the surrender and was never married. Never had children.

"On College and Perry streets the hospital was cleared away and grandpa bought the spot. It has had two houses rot down of his own on it. It has been graded down and a big brick house stands there now.

"She used to tell how when meat was so scarce she'd be cooking. She'd wipe her girls' faces with the dishrag. One of them would lick her lips. Make other children hungry for meat to see them so greasy. They hadn't had any meat.

"Grandmama told me her doctor master bought them shoes for her, and I think they gave her the marble box. The children teased me so much grandmama bought me some limber sole shoes.

"Auntie was good they said and mama was mean so they said. Auntie died after surrender. We'd tell grandmama she ought to put the skillet on mama. She said the good Lord took care of her baby that time. Mama would get so mad. She would whoop us for saying she ought to put the hot skillet on her.

"Grandmama was a midwife with black and white for forty-five years in Helena. She worked for Joe Horner, Mr. Leifer, Mrs. E.M. Allen. Mama had seven children, and grandmama raised Will Marshal (colored). He works at D.T. Hargraves & Sons store now in Helena. He started a delivery boy but now he is their main repair man.

"Grandmama was a strong woman. Mama worked out at some places I told you. Grandmama worked. Grandmama always had a pretty flower yard. She did love pretty flowers.

"Mama minded grandmama like one of us. She was a good woman. None of us, not even the boys, ever had pockets in our clothes. Grandmama made them for us. She taught us not to lie and steal. She thought it was the worse thing you could do. She was loved and respected by white and black till she died down at Helena in 1913. They are all buried down there."

Interviewer: Miss Irene Robertson
Person interviewed: Mack Brantley, Brinkley, Arkansas
Age: 80

MACK BRANTLEY

"I was born in Dallas County close to Selma, Alabama. My mother's owners was Miss Mary Ann Roscoe and her husband was Master Ephriam Roscoe. They had a good size gin and farm. We would gather 'round and tell ha'nt tales till we would be scared to go home in the dark. The wind would turn the old-fashioned screw and make a noise like packing cotton. We older children would run and make out we thought it was the spirits. We knowed better but the little children was afraid.

"My parents was Lucindy Roscoe. My pa belong to Warren Brantley. His name was Silica Brantley.

"I was a stole chile. Ma had a husband the master give her and had children. My pa lived on a joining farm. She wasn't supposen to have children by my pa. That is why I'm called Mack Brantley now. Mama died and Green Roscoe, my older brother, took me to Howell's so they would raise me. They was all kin. I was six months old when ma died. My sister nursed me but Miss Mary Ann Roscoe suckled me wid Miss Minnie. When Miss Minnie got grown and married she went to Mobile, Alabama to live. Later Brother Silica give me to Master Henry Harrell. They sent me to school. I never went to colored school.

We went to Blunt Springs three months every year in the summer time. When we come home one year Mr. Hankton was gone and he never come back. He was my only teacher. The white population didn't like him and they finally got him away.

"They was good white people. I had a pallet in the room and in the morning I took it up and put it away in a little room. I slept in the house till I was good and grown. I made fires for them in the winter time. Mr. Walter died three years ago. He was their son. He had a big store there. Miss Carrie married Charlie Hooper. He courted her five years. I bring her a letter and she tore it up before she read it. He kept coming. He lived in Kentucky. The last I heard they lived in Birmingham. Miss Kitty Avery Harrell was my mistress at freedom and after, and after boss died. I had four children when I left. If Mr. Walter was living I'd go to him now. Mr. Hooper would cuss. Old boss didn't cuss. I never liked Mr. Hooper's ways. Old boss was kinder. All my sisters dead. I reckon I got two brothers. Charles Roscoe was where boss left him. He was grown when I was a child. Jack Roscoe lives at Forrest, Mississippi. Brother Silica Roscoe had a wife and children when freedom come on. He left that wife and got married to another one and went off to Mississippi. Preachers quit their slavery wives and children and married other wives. It wasn't right. No ma'am, it wasn't right. Awful lot of it was done. Then is when I got took to my Miss Kitty. After freedom is right.

"I tole you I was a stole chile. I never seen my own pa but a few times. He lived on a joining farm. Ma had a husband her master give her the first time they had been at a big log rolling and come up for dinner. They put the planks out and the dinner on it. They kept saying, 'Mack, shake hands with your papa.' He was standing off to one side. It was sorter shame. They kept on. I was little. I went over there. He shook hands with me. I said, 'Hi, papa! Give me a nickel.' He reached in his pocket and give me a nickel. Then they stopped teasing me. He went off on Alabama River eighteen miles from us to Caholba, Alabama. I never seen him much more. Ma had been dead then several years.

"Green, my brother, took me to Miss Mary Ann Roscoe when mama died. She was my ma's owner. I stayed there till Green died. A whole lot of boys was standing around and bet Green he couldn't tote that barrel of molasses a certain piece. They helped it up and was to help him put it down and give him five dollars. That was late in the ebenin'. He let the barrel down and a ball as big as a goose egg of blood come out of his mouth. The next day he died. Master got Dr. Blevins quick as he could ride there. He was mad as he could be. Dr. Blevins said it weighed eight hundred pounds. It was a hogshead of molasses. Green was much of a man. He was a giant. Dr. Blevins said they had killed a good man. Green was good and so strong. I never could forget it. Green was my standby.

"The Yankees burnt Boss Henry's father's fine house, his gin, his grist mill, and fifty or sixty bales of cotton and took several fine horses. They took him out in his shirt tail and beat him, and whooped his wife, trying to make them tell where the money was. He told her to tell. He had it buried in a pot in the garden. They went and dug it up. Forty thousand dollars in gold and silver. Out they lit then. I seen that. He lived to be eighty and she lived to be seventy-eight years old. He had owned seven or eight or ten miles of road land at Howell Crossroads. Road land is like highway land, it is more costly. He had Henry and Finas married and moved off. Miss Melia was his daughter and her husband and the overseer was there but they couldn't save the money. I waited on Misa Melia when she got sick and died. She was fine a woman as ever I seen. Every colored person on the place knowed where the pot was buried. Some of them planted it. They wouldn't tell. We could hear the battles at Selma, Alabama. It was a roar and like an earthquake.

"Freedom—I was a little boy. I cried to go with the bigger children. They had to tote water. One day I heard somebody crying over 'cross a ditch and fence covered with vines and small trees. I heard, 'Do pray master.' I run hid under the house. I was snoring when they found me. I heard somebody say, 'Slave day is over.' That is all I ever knowed about freedom. The way I knowed, a Yankee. We was in the road piling up sand and a lot of blue coats on horses was coming. We got out of the road and went to tell our white folks. They said, 'Get out of their way, they are Yankees.'

"When I left Alabama I went to Mississippi. I worked my way on a steamboat. I had been trained to do whatever I was commanded. The man, my boss, said, 'Mack, get the rope behind the boiler and tie it to the stob and 'dead man'. I tied it to the stob and I was looking for a dead man. He showed me what it was. Then I tied it. I went to Vicksburg then. I had got mixed up with a woman and run off.

"I been married once in my life. I had eighteen children. Nine lived. I got a boy here and a girl in Pine Bluff. My son's wife is mean to me. I don't want to stay here.

If I can get my pension started, I want to live with my daughter.

"I used to vote Republican. They claimed it made times better for my race. I found out better. I don't vote now. Wilson was good as Mr. Roosevelt, I think. I voted about eight years ago, I reckon. I didn't vote for Mr. Roosevelt.

"I wish I was young and had the chance this generation has got. Times is better every way for a good man unless he is unable to work like I am now. (This old man tends his garden, a large nice one—ed.) My son supports me now."

United States. Work Projects Administration

Interviewer: Samuel S. Taylor
Person interviewed: Ellen Brass
1427 W. Eighth Street, Little Rock, Arkansas
Age: About 82

ELLEN BRASS

[HW: White Folks want Niggers]

"I was born in Alabama in Green County. I was about four years old when I came from there; so I don't know much about it. I growed up in Catahoula, Louisiana. My mother's name was Caroline Butler and my father's name was Lee Butler. One of my father's brothers was named Sam Butler. I used to be a Butler myself, but I married. My father and mother were both slaves. They never did any slave work.

Father Free Raised

"My father was free raised. The white folks raised him. I don't know how he became free. All that I know is that he was raised right in the house with the white folks and was free. His mother and father were both slaves. I was quite small at the time and didn't know much. They bought us like cattle and carried us from place to place.

Slave Houses

"The slaves lived in log cabins with one room. I don't know what kind of house the white folks lived in. They, the colored folks, ate corn bread, wheat bread (they raised wheat in those times), pickled pork. They made the flour right on the plantation. George Harris, a white man, was the one who brought me out of Louisiana into this State. We traveled in wagons in those days. George Harris owned us in Louisiana.

Slave Sales

"We were sold from George Harris to Ben Hickinbottom. They bought us then like cattle. I don't know whether it was a auction sale or a private sale. I am telling it as near as I know it, and I am telling the truth. Hickinbottom brought us to Catahoula Parish in Louisiana. Did I say Harris brought us? Well, Hickinbottom brought us to Louisiana. I don't know why they went from one place to the other like that. The soldiers were bad about freeing the slaves. From Catahoula Parish, Hickinbottom carried us to Alexandria, Louisiana, and in Alexandria, we was set free.

How Freedom Came

"According to my remembrance the Yankees come around and told the people they was free. I was in Alexandria, Louisiana. They told the colored folks they was free and to go and take what they wanted from the white folks. They had us all out in the yard dancing and playing. They sang the song:

> 'They hung Jeff Davis on a sour apple tree
> While we all go marching on.'

It wasn't the white folks on the plantation that told

us we was free. It was the soldiers their selves that came around and told us. We called 'em Yankees.

Right After the War

"Right after the War, my folks farmed—raised cotton and corn. My mother had died before I left Alabama. They claimed I was four years old when my mother died in Alabama. My father died after freedom.

Occupation

"My first occupation was farming—you know, field work. Sometimes I used to work around the white people too—clean house and like that.

Random Opinions

"The white folks ain't got no reason to mistreat the colored people. They need us all the time. They don't want no food unless a nigger cooks it. They want niggers to do all their washing and ironing. They want niggers to do their sweeping and cleaning and everything around their houses. The niggers handle everything they wears and hands them everything they eat and drink. Ain't nobody can get closer to a white person than a colored person. If we'd a wanted to kill 'em, they'd a all done been dead. They ain't no reason for white people mistreating colored people."

United States. Work Projects Administration

Interviewer: Miss Irene Robertson
Person interviewed: Alice Bratton, Wheatley, Arkansas
Age: 56

ALICE BRATTON

"I was born a few miles from Martin, Tennessee. Mama was born in Virginia. She and her sister was carried off from the Witherspoon place and sold. She was Betty and her sister was named Addie.

"Their mama had died and some folks said they would raise them and then they sold them. She said they never did know who it was that carried them off in a big carriage. They brought them to Nashville, Tennessee and sold them under a big oak tree. They was tied with a hame string to a hitching ring. Addie wanted to set down and couldn't. She said, 'Betty, wouldn't our mama cry if she could see us off like this?' Mama said they both cried and cried and when the man come to look at them he said he would buy them. They felt better and quit crying. He was such a kind looking young man.

"They lived out from Nashville a piece then. He took them home with him, on a plank across the wagon bed. He was Master Davy Fuller. He had a young wife and a little baby. Her name was Mistress Maude and the baby was Carrie. She was proud of Betty and Addie. They told her their mama died. Mama said she was good to them. She died the year of the surrender and Master Davy took them all to his mother's and his papa put them out to live with a family that worked on his place.

"They went to see Carrie and played with her till Addie married and mama come close to Martin to live with them. Addie took consumption and died, then mama married Frank Bane and he died and I was born.

"My pa was a white man. He was a bachelor, had a little store, and he overcome mama. She never did marry no more. I was her only child. I don't remember the man but mama told me how she got tripped up and nearly died and for me never to let nobody trip me up that way. I sorter recollect the store. It burned down one night. We lived around over there till I was sixteen years old. We moved to a few miles of Corinth, Mississippi on a farm. Mr. Cat Madford was the manager. I got married. I married Will Bratton. We had a home wedding on Sunday evening. It was cold and freezing and the freeze lasted over a week. Will Bratton was black as night. I had one little boy. After mama died Will Bratton went off with another woman. He come back but the place was mine. Mama left it to me. I wouldn't let him stay there. I let him go on where he pleased.

"Times been growing slacker for a long time. People live slack. Young folks coming on slacker and slacker every day. Don't know how to do, don't want to know. They get by better 'en I did. I work in the field and I can't hardly get by. I see folks do nothing all the time. Seem like they happy. Times is hard for some, easy for some. I want to live in the country like I is 'cause I belongs there. I can work and be satisfied! I did own my home. I reckon I still do. I got a little cow and some chickens."

Interviewer: Samuel S. Taylor
Person interviewed: Frank Briles
817 Cross Street, Little Rock, Arkansas
Age: About 82 or 83

FRANK BRILES

[HW: Gives up the Ghost]

"I was born right here in Arkansas. My father's name was Moses Briles. My mother's name was Judy Briles. Her name before she was married I don't know. They belonged to the Briles. I don't know their first name either.

"My father was under slavery. He chopped cotton and plowed and scraped cotton. That is where I got my part from. He would carry two rows along at once. I was little and couldn't take care of a row by myself. I was born down there along the time of the War, and my father didn't live long afterwards. He died when they was settin' them all free. He was a choppin' for the boss man and they would set them up on blocks and sell them. I don't know who the man was that did the selling, but they tell me they would sell them and buy them.

"I am sick now. My head looks like it's goin' to bust open.

"I have heard them tell about the pateroles. I didn't know them but I heard about them. Them and the Ku Klux was about the same thing. Neither one of them never did bother my folks. It was just like we now, nobody was 'round us and there wasn't no one to bother you at all at Briles' plantation. Briles' plantation I can't remember exactly where it was. It was way down in the west part of Arkansas. Yes, I was born way back south—east—way back. I don't know what the name of the place was but it was in Arkansas. I know that. I don't know nothing about that. My father and mother came from Virginia, they said. My father used to drive cattle there, my mother said. I don't know nothin' except what they told me.

"I learnt a little some thing from my folks. I think of more things every time I talk to somebody. I know one thing. The woman that bossed me, she died. That was about—Lord I was a little bitty of a fellow, didn't know nothin' then. She made clothes for me. She kept me in the house all the time. She was a white woman. I know when they was setting them free. I was goin' down to get a drink of water. My father said. 'Stop, you'll be drowned.' And I said, 'What must I do?' And he said, 'Go back and set down till I come back.' I don't know what my father was doing or where he was going. There was a man—I don't know who—he come 'round and said, 'You're all free.' My mama said, 'Thank God for that. Thank God for that.' That is all I know about that.

"When I got old enough to work they put me in the woods splitting rails and plowing. When I grew up I scraped cotton and worked on the farm. That is where my father would come and say, 'Now, son, if anybody asks you how you feel, tell them the truth.'

"I went to school one session and then the man give down. He got sick and couldn't carry it no longer. His pupils were catching up with him I reckon. It was time to get sick or somethin'.

"I never did marry. I was promised to marry a woman and she died. So I said, 'Well, I will give up the ghost. I won't marry at all.'

"I ain't able to do no work now 'cept a little pittling here and there. I get a pension. It's been cut a whole lot."

United States. Work Projects Administration

Interviewer: Mrs. Bernice Bowden
Person interviewed: Mary Ann Brooks
James Addition, Pine Bluff, Arkansas
Age: 90

MARY ANN BROOKS

"I was born here in Arkansas. Durin' the war we went to Texas and stayed one year and six months.

"My old master was old Dr. Brewster. He bought me when I was a girl eight yeers old. Took me in for a debt. He had a drug store. I was a nurse girl in the house. Stayed in the house all my life.

"I stayed here till Dr. Brewster—Dr. Arthur Brewster was his name—stayed here till he carried me to his brother-in-law Dr. Asa Brunson. Stayed there awhile, then the war started and he carrled us all to Texas.

"I seen some Yankeee after we come back to Arkansas. I wes scared of em.

"I don't knew nothln' bout the war. I wasn't in it. I was livin' but we was in Texas.

"The Ku Klux got after us twice when we was goin' to Texas. We had six wagons, a cart, and a carriage. Old Dr. Brunson rode in the carriage. He'd go ahead and pilot the way. We got lost twice. When we come to Red River it was up and we had to camp there three weeks till the water fell.

"We took some sheep and some cows so we could kill meat on the way. I member we forded Saline River. Dr. Brunson carried us there and stayed till he hired us out.

"After the war ceasted he come after us. Told as we didn't belong to him no more—said we was free as he was. Yankees sent him after us. All the folks come back—all but one famlly.

"I had tolerable good owners. Miss Fanny Brewster good to me.

"Old master got drunk so much. Come home sometimes muddy as a hog. All his chillun was girls. I nursed all the girls but one.

"I was a mighty dancer when I was young—danced all night long. Paddyrollers run us home from dancin' one night.

"I member one song we used to sing:

> 'Hop light lady
> Cake was all dough—
> Never mind the weather,
> So the wind don't blow.'

"How many chillun I have? Les see—count em up. Ida, Willie, Clara—had six.

"Some of the young folks nowadays pretty rough. Some of em do right and some don't.

"Never did go to school. Coulda went but papa died and had to go to work.

"I thinks over old times sometimes by myself. Didn't

know what freedom was till we was free and didn't hardly know then.

"Well, it's been a long time. All the Brewsters and the Bransons dead and I'm still here—blind. Been blind eight years."

United States. Work Projects Administration

Waters Brooks
1814 Pulaski Street, Little Rock, Ark.
Retired railroad worker, No. Pac. 75

[TR: Information moved from bottom of each page.]

WATERS BROOKS

[HW: A Railroad Work History]

I was only three years old when peace (1865) was declared. I was born in 1862. Peace was declared in 1865. I remember seeing plenty of men that they said the white folks never whipped. I remember seeing plenty of men that they said bought their own freedom.

I remember a woman that they said fought with the overseer for a whole day and stripped him naked as the day he was born. She was Nancy Ward. Her owner was named Billie Ward. He had an overseer named Roper. Her husband ran away from the white folks and stayed three years. He was in the Bayou in a boat and the bottom dropped out of it. He climbed a tree and hollered for someone to tel his master to come and get him if he wanted him.

FATHER

My father's master was John T. Williams. He went into the army—the rebel army—and taken my father with him. I don't know how long my father stayed in the army but I was only 6 months old when he died. He had some kind of stomach trouble and died a natural death.

MOTHER

My mother and father both belonged to Joe Ward at first but Ward died and his widow married Williams. My mother told me and not only told me but showed me knots across her shoulder where they whipped her from seven in the morning until nine at night. She went into the smoke house to get some meat and they closed in on her and shut the door and strung her up by her hands (her arms were crossed and a rope run from her wrists to the hook in the ceiling on which meat was hung). There were three of them. One would whip until he was tired, and then the other would take it up.

Some years after she got that whipping, her master's child was down to the bayou playing in the water. She told the child to stop playing in the water, and it did not. Instead it threw dirt into the water that had the bluing in it. Then she took the child and threw it into the Bayou. Some way or other the child managed to scramble out. When the child's aunt herd it from the child, she questioned my mother and asked her if she did it. My mother told her "Yes". Then she said. "Well what do you want to own it for? Don't you know if they find it out they will kill you?"

HOW FREEDOM CAME

My mother said that an old white man came through the quarters one morning and said that they were all free—that they could go away or stay where they were or do what they wanted to. If you will go there, I can send you to an old man eighty-six years old who was in General Sherman's army. He came from Mississippi. I don't know where he was a slave. But he can tell you when peace was declared aad what they said and everything.

WHAT THE SLAVES EXPECTED

The slaves were not expecting much but they were expecting more than they got. I am not telling you anything I read in history but I have heard that there was a bounty in the treasury for the ex-slaves, and them alone. And some reason or other they did not pay it off, but the time was coming when they would pay it off. And every man or woman living that was born a slave would benefit from it. They say that Abraham Lincoln principally was killed because he was going to pay this money to the ex-slaves end before they would permit it they killed him. Old man White who lives out in the west part of town was an agent for some Senator who was in Washington, and he charged a dime and took your name and age and the place where you lived.

KU KLUX KLAN

They called the K.K.K. "White Cape". Right there in my neighborhood, there was a colered man who hadn't long come in. The colored man was late coming into the lot to get the mule for the white man and woman he was working for. The white man hit him. The Negro knocked the white man down and was going to kill him when the white man begged him off, telling him that he wouldn't let anybody else hurt him. He (the Negro) went on off and never came back. That night there were two hundred White Caps looking for him but they didn't find him.

Another man got into an argument. They went to work and it started to rain. The Negro thought that they would stop working because of the rain; so he started home. The man he was working for met him and asked him where he was going. When he told him he started to hit him with the butt end of the gun he was wearing. The Negro knocked his gun up, took it away from him, and drawed down and started to kill him when another Negro knocked the gun up, and saved the white man's life. But the Nigger might as well have killed him because that night seventy-five masked men hunted him. He was hid away by his friends until he got a chance to get away. This man was named Matthew Collins.

There was another case. This was a political one. The colored man wanted to run for representative of some kind. He had been stump speaking. He lived on a white man's place, and the owner came to him and told him he had better get away because a mob was coming after him (not just K.K.K.). He told his wife to go away and stay with his brother but she wouldn't. He hid himself in a trunk and his wife was under the floor with his two children. The white men fired into the house and that didn't do anything, so they throwed a ball of fire into the house and burned his wife and children. Then he rose up and came out of the trunk and hollered, "Look out I'm coming", and he fired a load of buck shot and tore one man nearly in two and ran away in the confusion. The next day he went to the man on whose place he lived, but he told him he couldn't do anything about it.

Another man by the name of Bob Sawyer had a farm

near my home and another farm down near Maginty's place. He worked the ????[TR: Illegible] Niggers from one farm to the other.

His boy would ride in front with a rifle and he would be in the rear with a big gun swinging down from his hip. There wae one Nigger who got out and went down to Alexandria (Louisiana). He wrote to the officers and they caught the Nigger and put him into the stocks and brought him back, and the man hadn't done a thing but run away. After that they worked him with a chain holding his legs together so that he could only make short steps.

They had an old white man who worked there and they treated him so mean he ran away and left his wife. They treated the poor whites about as bad as they treated the colored.

If Bob met a Negro carrying cotton to the Gin, he would ask "Whose cotton is that?", and if the Nigger said it was some white man's, he would let him alone. But if he said. "Mine", Bob would tell him to take it to some Gin where he wanted it taken. He was the kind of man that if you seen him first, you wouldn't meet him.

One night he slipped up on a Nigger man that had left his place and killed him as he sat at supper. I had an aunt with five or six children who worker with him. He married my young Mistress after I was freed.

I saw him do this. The white folks had a funeral at the church down there one Sunday. He came along and young Billie Ward (white man) was sitting in a buggy driving with his wife. When he saw Billie, he jumped down out of his buggy and horse-whipped him until he ran away. All the while, Sawyer's mother-in-law was sitting in his buggy calling out, "Shoot him, Bob, shoot him." this was because Billie and another man had done some talk about Bob.

OCCUPATIONS

I came to Brinkley, Arkansas, March 4, 1900, and have been in Arkansas ever since. Why I came, the postmaster where I was rented farm on which I was farming. In March he put hands in my field to pick my cotton. All that was in the field was mine. I knew that I couldn't do anything about it so I left. A couple of years before that I rented five acres of land from him for three dollars as acre (verbal agreement) sowed it down in cotton. It done so well I made five bales of cotton on it. He saw the prospects were so good that he went to the man who furnished me supplies and told him that I had agreed to do my work on a third and fourth (one-third of the seed and one-fourth of the cotton to go to the owner). He get this although if he had stuck to the agreement he would not have gotten but fifteen dollars. So he dealt me a blow there, but I got over it.

Before this I had bought a piece of timber land in Moorehouse parish (Louisiana) and was expecting to get the money to finish paying for it from my cotton. The cost was $100.00. So when he put hands in my field, it made me mad, and I left. (Brooks would have lost most of his cotton if the hands had picked it.)

At Brinkley, I farmed on halves with Will Carter, one of the richest men in Monroe County (Arkansas). I done

$17.50 worth of work for Carter and he paid me for it. Then he turned around and charged me up with it. When we came to settle up, we couldn't settle. So finally, he said, "Figures don't lie." and I said, "No, figures don't lie but men do." When I sed that I stepped out and didn't get scared until I was half way home. But nobody did anything. He sent for me but I wouldn't go back because I knew what he was doing.

After that I went to Wheatley, Arkansas, about five miles west of Brinkley. I made a crop for Goldberg. Jake Readus was Goldberg's agent. The folks had told the white folks I wasn't no account, so I couldn't get nothing only just a little fat meat and bread, and I got as naked as a jaybird. About the last part of August, when I had done laid by and everything. Jake Readus came by and told me what the Niggers had said and said he knowed it was a lie because I had the best crop on the place.

When Goldberg went to pay me off, he told Dr. Beauregard to come and get his money. I said. "You give me my money; I pay my own debts. You have nothing to do with it." When I said that you could have heard a pin drop. But he gave it to me. Then I called the Doctor and gave him his money and he receipted me. I never stayed there but one year.

I moved then down to Napel[TR: Possibly Kapel] Slough on Dr. West's place. I wanted to rent but Dr. West wouldn't advance me anything unless he took a mortgage on my place; so I wouldn't stay there. I chartered a car and took my things back to Brinkley at a cost of ten dollars. I stayed around Brinkley all the winter.

While I was at Wheatley, there was a man by the name

of Will Smith who married the daughter of Dr. Paster, druggist at Brinkley. Now Jim Smith, poor white trash, attempted to assault Will Thomas' daughter. Negro girl. When Thomas heard it, he hunted Jim with a Winchester. When that got out, Deputy Sheriff arrested Will and they said that he was chained when he was brought to trial. He got away from them somehow and went to Jonesboro. I took my horse and rid seven or eight miles to carry his clothes. Another Nigger who had promised to make a crop when he left had the blood beat out of his back because he didn't do it.

The winter, I worked at the Gin and Black Saw Mills. That spring I pulls up and goes to Brises. That was in the year 1903. I made a crop with old man Wiley Wormley one of the biggest Niggers there. I fell short. George Walker furnished what I had.

Then I left and went back to Brinkley and worked at the Sawmill again. That was in 1904. I went to Jonesboro. I had just money enough to go to Jonesboro, and I had a couple of dollars over. I had never been out before that; so I spent that and didn't get any work. I stayed there three days and nights and didn't get anything to eat. Lived in a box car. Then I went to work with the Cotton Belt.

My boarding mistress decided to go up to fifteen dollars for board. I told her I couldn't pay her fifteen dollars for that month, but would begin next month. She wouldn't have that and got the officers to look for my money so I caught the train and went back to Brinkley and worked on the railroad again from the Cotton Belt to the Rock Island.

I was getting along all right and I done my job, but

when the foreman wanted me to work on the roof and I told him if that was all he had for me to do he could pay me off because that was off the ground and I was fraid of falling. He said that I was a good hand and that he hated to lose me.

In March, 4, 1907, I came here (Little Rock) and at first rolled concrete in Niemeyer's at $1.50 a day where the other men were getting from two to two and a half dollars. They quit for more wages and I had to quit with them. Then I worked around till May 24 when I was hired at the Mountain Shops as Engine wiper for about six or eight months, then painted flues for three or four months, then was wood hauler for about thirteen or more years, then took care of the situation with shavings and oil, then stayed in wash room six or seven years until I was retired. I had control of the ice house, too.

IDEAS ABOUT THE PRESENT

Young people are just going back to old Ante-Bellum days. They are going to destruction. They got a way of their own and you can't tell them anything. They don't educate anything but their heads. The heart isn't educated and if my heart is black as my hat, can I do anything for God? The old people are not getting a square deal. Some of them are being moved.

SCHOOLING

I did not get much schooling. Between the time I was old enough to go to school and the time I went to the field, I got a little. I would go to school from July to September, and also about six weeks in January.

They had public school taught by some of the people. I went to a white man once. An old white woman taught there before him. I went to a Negro woman, Old Lady Abbie Lindsay. She lives here now down on State Street. She is about ninety years old. I went to Jube Williams (white), Current Lewis, Abbie Lindsay, and A.G. Mertin. They didn't paas you by grades then. I got through the fourth reader. If you got through, they would go back and carry you through again. They had the old Blue Back Speller. I got ready for the fifth reader but I quit. I had just begun to cipher, in arithmetic, but I had to quit because they couldn't spare me out of the field. In fact they put me into the field when I was eight years old, but I managed to go to school until I was about twelve years old or something like that. I never got a year's schooling all put together. My mother was a widow and had five or six children, none of them able or big enough to work but my oldest sister. She raised five of us.

If I had done as she told me, I might have been a good scholar. But I played around and went off with the other children. I learnt way afterwards when I was grown how to write my name. I could work addition and I could work some in multiplication, but I couldn't work division and couldn't work subtraction. Come around any time, specially on Sunday afternoons.

Name of Interviewer: Velma Sample
Subject: NEGRO LORE—THE STORY OF CASIE JONES BROWN

CASIE JONES BROWN

Casie Jones Brown was a dearly loved Negro servant. He was known for his loving kindness toward children, both black and white. Lots of the white children would say, "Casie sure is smart" because Casie was a funny and witty old darkie. Casie has a log house close to his master, Mr. Brown. They live on what is called the Brown Plantation. The yard had large old cedars planted all around it. They were planted almost a century ago. The plantation is about six miles from Paragould, [TR: possibly Baragould] Arkansas, where the hills are almost mountains. There have been four generations living in the old house. They have the big sand stone fireplaces. Casie has a spiritual power that makes him see and hear things. He says that sometimes he can hear sweet voices somewhere in his fireplace. In the winter time he does all of his cooking in a big black kettle with three legs on it, or a big iron skillet. And when he first settled there he did not have a stove to cook on except the fireplace. He says the singing that comes from somewhere about the fireplace is God having his angels entertain him in his lonely hours. Casie is 91 years old and has been in that settlement as long as he can remember.

The little white boys and girls like to be entertained by Casie. He tells them stories about the bear and peter rabbit. Also he has subjects for them to ask questions about and he answers them in a clever way. He was kind enough to let me see the list and the answers. He cannot write but he has little kids to write them for him. He cannot read, but they appoint one to read for him, and he has looked at the list so much that he has it memorized.

Casie, what does hat mean or use hat for a subject. "De price ob your hat ain't de medjer ob your brain."

Coat—"Ef your coat tail catch afire don't wait till you kin see de blaze 'fo' you put it out."

Graveyard—"De graveyard is de cheapes' boardin' house."

Mules—"Dar's a fam'ly coolness 'twix' de mule an' de single-tree."

Mad—"It pesters a man dreadful when he git mad an' don' know who to cuss."

Crop—"Buyin' on credit is robbin' next 'er's crop."

Christmas—"Christmas without holiday is like a candle without a wick."

Crawfish—"De crawfish in a hurry look like he tryin' to git dar yastiddy."

Lean houn'—"Lean houn' lead de pack when de rabbit in sight."

Snow Flakes—"Little flakes make de deepes' snow."

Whitewash—"Knot in de plank will show froo de whitewash."

Yardstick—"A short yardstick is a po' thing to fight de debbul wid."

Cotton—"Dirt sho de quickes' on de cleanes' cotton."

Candy—"De candy-pullin' din call louder dan de log-rollin'."

Apple—"De bes' apple float on de top o' 'ligion heaps de half-bushel."

Hoe—"De steel hoe dat laughs at de iron one is like de man dat is shamed of his grand-daddy."

Mule—"A mule kin tote so much goodness in his face dat he don't hab none lef' for his hind legs."

Walks—"Some grabble walks may lead to de jail."

Cow bell—"De cow bell can't keep a secret."

Tree—"Ripe apples make de tree look taller."

Rose—"De red rose don't brag in de dark."

Billy-goat—"De billy-goat gits in his hardes' licks when he looks like he gwine to back out of de fight."

Good luck—"Tis hard for de bes' an' smartes' fokes in de wul' to git 'long widout a little tech o' good luck."

Blind horse—"Blind horse knows when de trough empty."

Wagon—"De noise of de wheels don't medjer de load in de wagon."

Hot—"Las' 'ear's hot spell cools off mighty fast."

Hole—"Little hole in your pocket is wusser'n a big one at de knee."

Tim o' day—"Appetite don't regerlate de time o' day."

Quagmire—"De quagmire don't hang out no sign."

Needle—"One pusson kin th'ead a needle better than two."

Pen—"De pint o' de pin is de easier in' to find."

Turnip—"De green top don't medjer de price o' de turnip."

Dog—"Muzzle on de yard dog unlocks de smokehouse."

EQUAL TO THE EMERGENCY

Hebe: "Unc Isrul, mammy says, hoocume de milk so watery on top in de mornin'."

Patriarch: "Tell you' mammy dat's de bes' sort o' milk, dat's de dew on it, de cows been layin' in de dew."

Hebe: "An' she tell me to ax you what meck it so blue."

Patriarch: "You ax your mammy what meck she so black."

Here are some of Casie's little rhymes that he entertained the neighbor children with:

Look at dat possum in dat holler log. He hidin' he know dis nigger eat possum laik a hog.

Hear dat hoot owl in dat tree. Dat old hoot owl gwine hoot right out at yew.

Rabbit, rabbit, do you know; I can track you in de snow.

One young man lingered at the gate after a long visit, but a lots ob sweethearts do det. His lady love started to cry. He said, "Dear, don't cry; I will come to see you again." But she cried on. "Oh, darling don't cry so; I will come back again, I sure will." Still she cried. At last he said: "Love, did I not tell you that I would soon come again to see you?" And through her tears she replied: "Yes, but I am afraid you will never go; that is what is the matter with me. We must all go."

Uncle Joshua was once asked a great question. It was: "If you had to be blown up which would you choose, to be blown up on the railroad or the steamboat?" "Well," said Uncle Joshua, "I don't want to be blowed up no way; but if I had to be blowed up I would rather be blowed up on de railroad, because, you see, if you is blowed up on de railroad, dar you is, but if you is blowed up on de steamboat, whar is you?"

Casie tells me of some of his superstitions:

If you are the first person a cat looks at after he has licked hisself, you are going to be married.

If you put a kitten under the cover of your bed and leave it until it crawls out by itself, it will never leave home.

If you walk through a place where a horse wallows, you will have a headache.

If a woodpecker raps on the house, someone is going to die.

If an owl screeches, turn the pocket of your apron inside out, tie a knot in your apron string, and he will stop.

If a rabbit runs across the road in front of you, to the left, it is a sign of bad luck; if it goes to the right, it is a sign of good luck.

If you cut a child's finger nails before it is a year old, it will steal when it grows up.

If you put your hand on the head of a dead man, you will never worry about him; he will never haunt you, and you will never fear death.

If the pictures are not turned toward the wall after a death, some other member of the family will die.

If you see a dead man in the mirror, you will be unlucky the rest of your life.

Name of Interviewer: Velma Sample
Subject: Slavery Days

ELCIE BROWN

The Attack The Yankees Made On Johnnie Reaves Place Given By Aunt Elcie Brown

Aunt Elcie Brown (a negro girl age nine years old) was living in the clay hills of Arkansas close to Centerville, and Clinton in Amid County on Johnnie Reeves Place. Johnnie Reeves was old and had a son named Henry L. Reeves who was married. Young Reeves got the news that they were to be attacked by the Yankees at a certain time and he took his family and all the best stock such as horses, cattle, and sheep to a cave in a bluff which was hid from the spy-glasses of the Yankees, by woods all around it. Johnnie Reeves was left to be attacked by the soldiers. He was blind and almost paralyzed. He had to eat dried beef shaved real fine and the negro children fed him. They ate as much of it as he did. Aunt Elcie and her brother fed him most of the time. They would get on each side of him and lead him for a walk most every day. The natives thought they would bluff the soldiers and cut the bridge into and thought that the soldiers would be unable to cross Beavers Creek, but the Yankees was prepared. They had made a long bridge for the soldiers to come marching right over. This bridge was just a mile from Reeves farm. Then the soldiers came they were so many that they could not all come up the big road but part of them came over the hill by the sheeps spring and through the pasture.

All the negroes came out of their shacks and watched them march toward their houses. Elcie and her brother got scared and ran in the house, crawled in bed and thought they were hid, as they had scrutched down in the middle of the bed with the door locked. But the soldiers bursted in and moved the bed from the corner. One stood over the bed and laughed, then asked the other man to look, then threw the covers off of them. He first took her brother by one arm and one leg and stood him on his feet, patted his head and told him not to be afraid, that they would not hurt them. Then took Elcie and stood her up. He reached in a bag lined with fur which was strapped on them and gave them both a stick of candy. Elcie says she thinks that is why she has always liked stick candy. She also says that that day has stood out to her and she can see everything just like it was yesterday. All the negro homes were close together and the soldiers raided them in small bunches. They were kind to the negro children. Wnen they started to the big house where Johnnie Reeves lived all the negro children followed them. When they entered the house Mr. Reeves was sitting by the side of the fire-place and every one that passed him kicked him brutely. They ransacked the place all over and when they got up stairs they kicked out all the window pains and tore off all the window-shutters. They took all the things they wanted out of the house, such as silver-ware, and jewelry. The smoke-house, milk-house and store-house was three separate buildings in a row. The first one they entered was the milk-house. It had seven shelves of milk, cream and butter in it. There was eleven crocks of sweet milk larger than a waterbucket. They had forty gallons of butter milk, and over three gallons of butter in a large flat crock. They also had over five gallons of cream. The Yankee soldiers ate all the butter and cream and set the milk in the yard and ask the negro kids to finish the milk.

They drank it like pigs without a cup, just stuck their heads down and drank like pigs. When they were full the balance of the milk was so dirty it looked like pigs had been in it.

The soldiers entered the next building which was the store-room where they stored rice, flour, sugar, coffee, and such like, and they took what they wanted, then destroyed the rest. Mr. Reeves had just been to town and bought a hogshead of sugar and they took it out and burst it and invited the negro children to help themselves. Elcie says that when the kids all got full there was not a half bushel left. The last raid was the smoke-house where stuffed sausage was hanging by the hundred and hams by the dozens. They didn't leave a thing, took lard and everything. It took over two wagons to hold everything. Then they crossed over to the next place owned by Bill Gunley.

*****

Dr. Levy tells me of his father being partial to the southerners although he lived in Evansville, Indiana, and fought as a Yankee. He was accused of being partial and they would turn over his wagons and cause him trouble. He had fine wagons and sometimes when he would be turning his wagons back up after them being turned over to contrary him, he would curse Gen. Grant and call him that G.D. Old Tobacco spitter. Although Henry Levy seldom did swear as he was French, sometimes they would make him mad and he would do so.

Interviewer: Samuel S. Taylor
Person interviewed: F. H. Brown
701 Hickory Street, North Little Rock, Arkansas
Age: 75

F. H. BROWN

[HW: Builds Church and School]

"I was born in Marion County, Mississippi. Columbus is the county-seat. My father's name was Hazard Brown, and my mother's name was Willie Brown. She was a Rankin before she married. My mother was born in Lawrence County, Mississippi, and married father there. My father was born in Tangipahoa Parish, Louisiana. I was born in three feet of the line in Louisiana. I was born in the old slave quarters. The house was just across the line between Mississippi and Louisiana. The lower room was in Louisiana and the other was in Mississippi. There was a three foot hall between the rooms. It was a matter of convenience that I was born in Mississippi. I might have been just as well born in Louisiana. The house was in both states.

"My father's master was Black Bill Warren. Black Bill was just a title they give him. I think that his name was Joe Warren, but they nicknamed him Black Bill, and everybody called him that. My mother belonged to the Rankinses.

"My mother's mother was named Dolly Ware. My father's mother was named Maria. Their papa's father was named Thomas, and I forget my mother's father's name. I know it but I forget it just now. I haven't thought over it for a long time.

"My father when he died was eighty-five years old. He was treated pretty good in slavery time. He did farm work. His mars had about ninety slaves, that is, counting children and all. When I was a boy, I was in those quarters and saw them. I went back there and though it was some time afterward, taught in them. And later on, I preached in them, since I have been a preacher, of course. I have a cousin there now. He is about a hundred years old. He belongs to the Methodist Episcopal Church.

"My father lived to see freedom. He has been dead more than twelve years. He died at my home.

"He was so close to the fighting that he could hear the guns and the firing. When they was freed, some white people told him, 'You are just as free as we are.' I was born after the Emancipation proclamation. The proclamation was issued in September and I was born in October. It didn't become effective till January first. So I was born a slave any way you take it.

"The farm my father worked on was on the Pearl River. It was very fertile. It was in Mississippi. A very big road runs beside the farm. The road is called the Big Road. The nigger quarters were across the road on the south side.

"My mother's folks treated her nicely too. Mr. Rankins didn't have any slaves but Mrs. Rankins had some. Her people gave them to her. My grandma who belonged to her had twenty-six children. She got her start off of the slaves her parents gave her, and finally she had about seventy-five. She ran a farm. My mother's work was house woman. She worked in the house. Her mistress was good to her. The overseer couldn't whip the niggers, except in her presence, so that she could see that it wasn't brutal. She didn't allow the women to be whipped at all. When an overseer got rough, she would fire him. Slaves would run away sometimes and stay in the woods if they thought that they would get a whipping for it. But she would send word for them to come on back and they wouldn't be whipped. And she would keep her word about it. The slaves on her place were treated so good that they were called free niggers by the other white people. When they were whipped, they would go to the woods.

"I have heard them speak of the pateroles often. They had to get a pass and then the pateroles wouldn't bother them. They would whip you and beat you if you didn't have a pass. Slavery was an awful low thing. It was a bad system. You had to get a pass to go to see your wife. If you didn't have that pass, they would whip you. The pateroles carried on their work for a good while after slavery was over, and the Civil War had ended.

"I was pretty good when I was a boy. So I never had any trouble then. I was right smart size when I saw the Ku Klux. They would whip men and women that weren't married and were living together. On the first day of January, they would whip men and boys that didn't have a job. They kept the Negroes from voting. They would whip them. They put up notices, 'No niggers to come out to the polls tomorrow.' They would run them off of government land which they had homesteaded. Sometimes they would just persuade them not to vote. A Negro like my father, they would say to him, 'Now, Brown, you are too good to get messed up. Them other niggers 'round here ain't worth nothing, but you are, and we don't want to see you get hurt. So you stay 'way from the polls tomorrow.' And tomorrow, my father would stay away, under the circumstances. They had to depend on the white people for counsel. They didn't know what to do themselves. The other niggers they would threaten them and tell them if they came out they would kill them.

"Right after the war, we farmed on shares. When we made our last share-crop, father farmed on Senator Bilbo's mother's farm on the State line. I nursed Senator Bilbo when he was a baby. Theoda Bilbo. He is the one who says Negroes should be sent to Africa. Then there wouldn't be nobody here to raise people like him. He fell into the mill pond one day and I pulled him out and kept him from drowning. If it weren't for that, he wouldn't be here to say, 'Send all the Negroes to Africa.' If I'd see him right now, he'd give me ten dollars.

"Mrs. Bilbo's first husband was a Crane. He killed himself. He didn't intend to. It was in a horse race. The horse ran away with him and killed him. Then Theoda's father married her. He was a poor man. He married that widow and got up in the world. They had a gin mill, and a grist mill, and a sawmill. They got business from everybody. That was Theoda's daddy—old man Bilbo.

"In 1870, we stayed on Elisha McGhee's farm. We called him Elisha but his name was Elijah. I began to remember them. The next year, we farmed for old man William Bilbo. But we didn't get along so well there because daddy wouldn't let anybody beat him out of anything that was his. That was Theoda's gran'daddy. Then we went to (Mississippi) Miss Crane's. The next year she married Theoda Bilbo's daddy and in 1874, my daddy moved up on his own place at Hurricane Creek. There he built a church and built a school, and I went to the school on our own place. He stayed there till 1880. In 1880, we moved to Holly Springs. That was right after the yellow fever epidemic. I went to school there at Shaw University. I stayed in that school a good while. It's called Rust College now. It's named after the Secretary of the Freedman's Aid Society. Rust was the greatest donor and they named the school after him. I went to the state school in my last year because they would give you a lifetime certificate when you finished there. I mean a lifetime teaching certificate for Mississippi. I finished the course and got the certificate. There is the diploma up there on the wall. J.H. Henderson was the principal and he was one of my teachers too. Henderson was a wonderful man. You know he died out here in the county hospital sometime ago. Sometime I'll tell you all about him. He was a remarkable man. He taught there behind Highgate, a Northern man. I'll tell you all about him sometime.

"I farmed with my father in the early part of my life. When I went to Holly Springs in 1881, I worked for Dr. T.J. Malone, a banker there, and a big farmer—President of the Holly Springs Bank. I worked for him mornings and evenings and slept at home of nights. I would work in vacation times too at whatever I could find to do till I got about able to teach. When I first commenced to teach, I taught in several counties—Lincoln, Simpson, Pike, Marion (the place I went to school), and Copiah. I built the school at Lawrence County. I organized the Folsom High School there. It was named after President Cleveland's wife. I taught there nine years. I married there. My wife's name was Narcissa Davis. She was a teacher and graduated from the same school I did. She lived in Calhoun County. She died in 1896, in Conway.

"I taught school at Conway in Faulkner County, and joined the ministry as a local preacher, in 1896. I moved from there to White County and taught in Searcy one term. Taught at Beebe ten years. Married again in 1898—Annie Day. I taught at Beebe and lived in White County. Then I bought me a home at Higginson, and went into the ministry solely. I left Higginson and taught and pastored seven years at Des Arc. I know practically everybody in Des Arc. I was thinking today about writing Brick Williams. He is the son of old man Williams, the one you know I think. Then I come to what is called Sixteen Section three miles from Galloway and taught there seven years and pastored. I presided too as Elder some of those years—North Little Rock District. Then I went back and pastored there and taught at West Point, Arkansas four years. Then I pastored at Prescott and was on the Magnolia District as Presiding Elder two years. Then I presided over the North Little Rock District again. Pastored St. Luke Circuit in southwest part of Arkansas below Washington. Then I built a church at Jonesboro. I pastored twenty-nine years altogether, built five churches, and have been responsible for five hundred conversions.

"I think the prospects of the country and the race are good. I don't see much dark days ahead. It is just a new era. You are doing something right now I never saw done before in my life. Even when they had the census, I didn't see any colored people taking it.

"I don't get any assistance in the form of money from the government. I have been trying to get it but I can't. Looks like they cut off a lot of them and can't reach it. Won't let me teach school. Say I am too old for WPA teaching. Superannuate me in the church, and say I'm too old to preach, and still I haven't gotten anything from my church since last January. I get some commodities from the state. I belong to the C.M.E. Church. I have lived in this community twenty-five years."

Interviewer's Comment

Hanging on the wall was the old man's diploma from the Mississippi State Normal School for colored persons. It was dated May 30, 1888, and it bore the signatures of J.R. Preston, State Superintendent; E.D. Miller, County Superintendent (both members of the Board of Directors); J.H. Henderson, Principal; Narcissa Hill and Maria Rabb, faculty members.

United States. Work Projects Administration

Interviewer: Mrs. Bernice Bowden
Person interviewed: George Brown
Route 4; Box 159, Pine Bluff, Arkansas
Age: 84

GEORGE BROWN

"Yes'm, I was born in slavery times. I was born in 1854. How old does that leave me?

"No ma'am, I wasn't born in Arkansas, born in Alabama.

"Jim Hart was my white folks. Good to me? I'd rather let that alone. Plenty to eat? I'll have to let that alone too. I used to say my old missis was 'Hell a mile.' Her name was Sarah. She was a Williams but she married Jim Hart. They had about a hundred and seventy head, little and big together.

"Me? I was a servant at the house. I didn't do any field work till after surrender.

"Some women was pretty mean and old miss was one of 'em.

"You'll get the truth now—I ain't told you half.

"We lived in Marengo County. The Tombigbee River divided it and Sumter County. The War didn't get down that far. It just got as far as Mobile.

"Oh yes'm, I knowed they was a war gwine on. I'd be

waitin' on the table and I'd hear the white folks talkin'. I couldn't keep all I heard.

"I know I heard 'em say General Grant went up in a balloon and counted all the horses and mules they had in Vicksburg.

"I seen them gunboats gwine down the Tombigbee River. And I seen a string of cotton bales as long as from here to there floatin' down the river to Mobile. I reckon they was gettin' it away from the Yankees. You see we was a hundred and fifty miles north of Mobile.

"I wish you'd a caught me with my mind runnin' that way. I could open your eyes.

"They had a overseer named Sothern. One Sunday my mammy slipped off and went to church. Some of 'em told Sothern and he told Miss Sarah. And she had mammy called out and they had a strop 'bout as wide as any hand and had holes in it, and they started whippin' her. I was runnin' around there with my shirt tail full of bricks and I was chunkin' 'em at that overseer. He would a caught me and whipped me too but Tom Kelly—that was old miss' son-in-law—said, 'A calf loves the cow,' so he wouldn't let old miss whip me.

"I come away from Alabama in '75. I lived in Tallulah, Louisiana eight years and the rest of the time I been here in Arkansas.

"I've farmed most of the time. I owned one farm, forty-nine acres, but my boy got into trouble and I had to sell it.

"Then I've been a engineer in sawmills and at gins. I used to be a round man—I could work any place.

"Me? Vote? No, I never did believe in votin'. I couldn't see no sense in it. They was mobbin' and killin' too much for George Brown. I was a preacher—Baptist. I was a ordained preacher. I could marry 'em. Oh Lord, I ain't preached in a long time. I got so I couldn't stand on my feet.

"I been in the Church of God sixty-one years. Never been in any lawsuit or anything like that in my life. I always tried to keep out of trouble.

"I 'member one time I come nearest to gettin' drowned in the Tombigbee River. We boys was in washin' and we got to divin' and I div where it was too deep. When I come up, look like a world of water. A boy in a skiff come and broke right to me. I reckon I was unconscious, I didn't know what. But them boys wasn't unconscious.

"I think the younger generation is mighty bad. There's some exceptions but the general run is bad. I've seen the time you could go to a white man and he would help you but these young white folks, they turn from you."

United States. Work Projects Administration

Interviewer: Bernice Bowden
Person interviewed: J.N. Brown
3500 West 7th Ave.
Pine Bluff, Ark.
Age: 79
Occupation: Sells peanuts from wagon

J.N. BROWN

"Yes'm, I was livin' in slavery times—musta been—I was born in 1858, near Natchez, Mississippi—in town.

"Old Daniel Virdin was my first master. I can halfway remember him. Oh Lord, I remember that shootin'. Used to clap my hands—called it foolishness. We kids didn't know no better.

"I was in Camden, Arkansas when we was freed. Colored folks in them days was sold and run. My father was in Camden when we got free—he was sold. My mother was sold too.

"I heared em say they had a good master and mistis. Man what bought em was named Brown. They runned us to Texas durin' the war and then come back here to Camden.

"I never went to school. I was the oldest chile my father had out a sixteen and I had to work. We had a kinda hard time. I stayed in Camden till I was eighteen and then I runned off from my folks and went to Texas. Times was so tight in Arkansas, and a cattleman come there and said they'd give me twenty-five dollars a month in Texas. I thought that would beat just something to eat. I been workin' for the white folks and just gettin' a little grub and not makin' any money.

"In Texas I worked for some good white folks. John Worth Bennet was the man who owned the ranch. I stayed there seven years and saved my money. I was just nacherly a good nigger. That was in Hopkins County, Texas.

"I've got a good memory. That's all I got to study bout is how to take care of the situation. I was livin' there in that country in 1882, fore the Spanish-American War.

"I come back here to Arkansas in 1900. My father was named Nelson Brown. He preached. My mother's name was Sally Brown.

"Long in that time we tried to vote but we didn't know 'zactly what we was doin. I think I voted once or twice, but if a man can't read or write and have to have somebody make out his ticket, he don't know what he's votin', so I just quit tryin' to vote.

"Now about this younger generation, you've asked me a question it's hard for me to answer. With all these nineteenth century niggers, the more education they got, the bigger crooks they is.

"We colored people are livin' under the law, but we don't make no laws. You take a one-armed man and he can't do what a two-armed man can. The colored man in the south is a one-armed man, but of course the colored man can't get along without the white folks. But I've lived in this world long enough to know what the cause is—I know why the colored man is a one-armed man."

Interviewer: Mrs. Bernice Bowden
Person interviewed: Lewis Brown
708 Oak Street, Pine Bluff, Arkansas
Age: 83

LEWIS BROWN

"Yes'm my name is Brown—Lewis Brown. Yes'm I lived durin' slavery times. I was born in 1854.

"I been workin' this mornin'. I been diggin' up the ground to bed up some onions. No I don't work every day. Sometimes I feel ailin'—don't feel like doin' nothin'.

"I wasn't big enough to 'member 'bout the war. All I 'member is seein' the soldiers retirin' from the war. They come by my old master's plantation. The Yankees was in front—they was the horsebackers. Then come the wagons and then the southern soldiers comin' along in droves.

"I was born in Arkansas. My mother and father belonged to Dr. Jordan. He was the biggest slaveholder in Arkansas. He was called the 'Nigger Ruler'. If the overseer couldn't make a slave behave, the old doctor went out with a gun and shot him. When the slaves on other plantations couldn't be ruled, they was sold to Dr. Jordan and he ruled 'em or killed 'em.

"I don't 'member much else 'bout my old master but I 'member my old mistress. The last crop she made before freedom, she had two plantations with overseers on 'em and on one plantation they didn't 'low no kind a slave 'cept South Carlinans. But on the other plantation the slaves come from different places.

"After the war we went to Texas and I 'member my old mistress come down there to get her old colored folks to come back to Arkansas. Lots of 'em went back with her. She called herself givin' 'em a home. I don't know what she paid—I never heard a breath of that but she hoped 'em to get back. I didn't go—I stayed in Texas and growed up and married there and then come back to Arkansas in 1882.

"Oh yes'm—the Ku Klux was plentiful after peace. They went about robbin' people.

"Some of the colored folks thought they was better off when they was slaves. They was the ones that had good masters. Some of the masters didn't 'low the overseers to 'buke the slaves and some wouldn't have overseers.

"I never did vote for no President, just for home officers. I don't know what to say 'bout not letting the colored folks vote now. They have to pay taxes and 'spenses and I think they ought to have something to say 'bout things.

"'How did you lose your arm?' It was shot off. I got into a argument with a fellow what owed me twenty-four dollars. He decided to pay me off that way. That was when I was 'bout seventy. He's dead now.

"I think the people is more wickeder now. The devil got more chances than he used to have and the people can't do right if they want to."

"I was born in 1854 and 'co'se I wasn't big enough to work much in slavery times, but one thing I did do and that was to tote watermelons for the overseer and pile 'em on the porch.

"I 'member he said if we dropped one and broke it, we'd have to stop right there and eat the whole thing. I know I broke one on purpose so I could eat it and I 'member he made me scrape the rind and drink the juice. I know I eat till I was tired of that watermelon.

"And then there was a lake old master told us to stay out of. If he caught you in it, he'd take you by the shirt collar and your heels and throw you back in.

"I know he nearly drowned me once."

"In them days, folks raised one another's chillun. If a child was at your house and misbehaved, you whipped him and sent him home and his mother give him another whippin'.

"And you better not 'spute your parents!"

STATE—Arkansas
NAME OF WORKER—Samuel S. Taylor
ADDRESS—Little Rock, Arkansas
DATE—December, 1938
SUBJECT—Ex-slave

[TR: Repetitive information deleted from subsequent pages.]

LEWIS BROWN

Circumstances of Interview

1. Name and address of informant—Lewis Brown, 2100 Pulaski Street, Little Rock

2. Date and time of interview--

3. Place of interview—2100 Pulaski Street, Little Hock, Arkansas

4. Name and address of person, if any, who put you in touch with informant--

5. Name and address of person, if any, accompanying you--

6. Description of room, house, surroundings, etc.--

Personal History of Informant

NAME AND ADDRESS OF INFORMANT—Lewis Brown, 2100 Pulaski Street, Little Rock.

1. Ancestry—father, Lewis Bronson; mother, Millie Bronson.

2. Place and date of birth—Born April 14, 1855 in Kemper County, Mississippi.

3. Family—Five children.

4. Places lived in, with dates—Lived in Mississippi until the eighties, then moved to Helena, Arkansas. Moved from Helena to Little Rock.

5. Education, with dates--

6. Occupations and accomplishments, with dates—Farming.

7. Special skills and interests--

8. Community and religious activities—Belongs to Baptist Church.

9. Description of informant--

10. Other points gained in interview—Facts concerning child life, status of colored girls, patrollers, marriage and sex relationships, churches and amusements.

Text of Interview (Unedited)

"I was born in 1855, April 14, in Kemper County, Mississippi, close to Meridian. I drove gin wagons in the time of the war in a horse-power gin. I carried matches and candles down to weigh cotton with in slavery times.

"They had to pick cotton till dark. They had to tote their weight hundred pounds, two pounds, whatever it was down to the weighing place and they had to weigh it. Whatever you lacked of having your weight, you would get a lick for. On down till they called us out for the war, that was the way it was. They were goin' to give my brother fifty lashes but they come and took him to the army, and they didn't git to whip him.

"My father was Lewis Bronson. He come from South Carolina. My mother was stole. The speculators stole her and they brought her to Kemper County, Mississippi, and sold her. My mother's name was Millie. My father's owner was Elijah McCoy. Old Elijah McCoy was the owner, but they didn't take his name. They went back to the old standard mark after the surrender. They went back to the people where they come from, and they changed their names—they changed off of them old names. McCoys was my masters, but my father went back to the name of the people way back over in there in South Carolina, where he come from. I don't know nothin' bout them. He was the father of nine children. He had two wives. One of them he had nine by, and the other one he had none by. So he went back to the one he had the nine children by.

Early Life

"I was ten years old when war was ended. I had to carry matches and candles to the cotton pickers. It would be too dark for them to weigh up. They couldn't see. They had tasks and they would be picking till late to git their tasks done. Matches and candles come from the big house, and I had to bring it down to them. That was two years before the war.

"I wasn't big enough to do nothing else, only drive

to the gin. I drove horse-power to the gin.—drove mules to the gin. I would drive the cows out to the pasture too. The milk women would milk them. Lawd, I could not do no milking. I was too small. The milk women would milk them and I would drive the cows one way and the calves another so that they couldn't mix. And at night I would go git them and they would milk them again. The milk women milked them. What would I know bout milkin.

"I never did any playin', 'cept plain marbles and goin' in swimmin'.

Schooling

"The white girls and boys learned us our A-B-C's after the war. They had a free school in Kemper County there. My children I learnt them myself or had it done. You couldn't hardly ever find one in Kemper Country that could spell and go on. They didn't have no time for that. Some few of them learned their A-B-C's before the war. But that is all. They learned what they learned after the war in the free government schools mostly. They would not do nothin' to you if they caught you learnin' in slave time. Sometimes the white children would teach you your A-B-C's.

Status of Colored Girls

"They had mighty mean ways in that country. They would catch young colored girls and whip them and make them do what they wanted. There wasn't but one mean one on our place. He was ordered to go to war and he didn't; so they pressed him. He was the one that promised my brother a whipping. He left like this morning and come back a week from today dead. The rest of them was pretty good. The mean one was Elijah.

Master's Sons

"Old man McCoy had four sons; Elijah, that was the mean one, Redder, Nelson, Clay.

Patrollers

"Sometimes the pateroles would do the devil with you if they caught you out without a pass. You could go anywhere you pleased if you had a pass. But if you didn't have a pass, they'd give you the devil.

Marriage and Sex Relationships

"You could have one wife over here and another one over there if you wanted to. My daddy had two women. And he quit the one that didn't have no children. People weren't no more 'n dogs them days,—weren't as much as dogs.

Mother and Father's Work

"In slavery time, my father worked at the field. Plowed and hoed and made cotton and corn—what else was he goin' to do. My mother was a cook.

Sustenance

"My master fed us and clothed us and give us something to eat. Some of them was hell a mile. Some of them was all kinds of ways. Our people was good. One of them was mean.

Father's Brother

"My father's brother belonged to Elijah. I had an auntie over in there too. I don't know what become of them all. They were all in Kemper county, Mississippi.

Churches

"The white people had churches in slavery times just like they have now. The white people would have service one a month. But like these street cars. White people would be at the front and colored would fill up back. They'll quit that after a while. Sometimes they would have church in the morning for the white folks and church in the evening for the colored. They would baptize you just like they would anybody else.

"I'll tell you what was done in slave time. They'd sing and pray. The white folks would take you to the creek and baptize you like anybody else.

"Sometimes the slaves would be off and have prayer meetings of their own—nothing but colored people there. They soon got out uh that.

"Sometimes they would turn a tub or pot down. That would be when they were making a lot of fuss and didn't want to bother nobody. The white people wouldn't be against the meeting. But they wouldn't want to be disturbed. If you wanted to sing at night and didn't want nobody to hear it, you could just take an old wash pot and turn it down—leave a little space for the air, and nobody could hear it.

Amusement

"The grown folks didn't have much amusement in slavery times. They had banjo, fiddle, melodian, and things like that. There wasn't no baseball in those days. I never seed none. They could dance all they wanted to their way. They danced the dotillions and the waltzes and breakdown steps, all such as that. Pick banjo! U-umph! They would give corn huskins; they would go and shuck corn and shuck so much. Get through shucking, they would give you dinner. Sometimes big rich white people would give dances out in the yard and look at their way of dancing, and doing. Violin players would be colored.

"Have cotton picking too sometimes at night, moonshiney nights. That's when they'd give the cotton pickings. Say you didn't have many hands, then they'd go and send you one hand from this place and one from that place. And so on. Your friends would do all that for you. Between 'em they'd git up a big bunch of hands. Then they'd give the cotton picking, and git your field clared up. They'd give you something to eat and whiskey to drink.

How Freedom Came

"Notice was given to my father that he was free. White people in that country give it to him. I don't know what they said to my father. Then the last gun was fired. I don't know where peace was declared. Notice come how that everybody was free. Told my daddy, 'You're just as free as I am.' Some went back to their daddy's name. Some went back to their master's name. My daddy went back to his old master's name.

Right after the War

"First year after the war, they planted a crop. Didn't raise no cotton during the war, from the time the war started till it ended, they didn't raise no cotton.

"After the war, they give the colored people corn and cotton, one-third and one-fourth. They would haul a load of it up during the war I mean, during the time before the war, and give it to the colored people.

"They had two crops. No cotton in the time of the war, nothing but corn and peas and potatoes and so on. All that went to the white people. But they divided it. They give all so much round. Had a bin for the white and a bin for the colored. The next year they commenced with the third and fourth business—third of the cotton and fourth of the corn. You could have all the peanuts you wanted. You could sell your corn but they would only give you fifty cents for it—fifty cents a bushel.

"My father farmed and sharecropped for a while after the war. He changed from his master's place the second year and went on another place. He farmed all his life. He raised all his children and got wore out and pore. He died in Kemper County, Mississippi. All his children and everything was raised there.

Life Since the War

"I came to Arkansas in the eighties. Come to Helena. I did carpenter and farm work in Helena. I made three crops, one for Phil Maddox, two with Miss Hobbs. I come from Helena here.

"I married in Mississippi in Roland Forks, sixty miles this side of Vicksburg. I had two boys and three girls. Two girls died in Helena. One died in Roland Forks before I come to Helena. Nary one of the boys didn't die.

"I don't do no work now. This rheumatism's got me down. I call that age. If I could work, I couldn't git nothing worth while. These niggers here won't pay you nothing they promise you. My boy's got me to feed as long as I live now. I did a batch of work for the colored people round here in the spring of the year and I ain't got no money for it yit.

"I belong to the Mount Zion Baptist Church; I reckon I do. I got down sick so I couldn't go and I don't know whether they turned me OUT OR NO. I tell you, people don't care nothin about you when you get old or stricken down. They pretend they do, but they don't. My mind is good and I got just as much ambition as I ever had. But I don't have the strength.

"I haven't got but a few more days to lag round in this world. When you get old and stricken, nobody cares, children nor nobody else."

Interviewer: Miss Bailie C. Miller
Person interviewed: Mag Brown, Clarksville, Arkansas
Age: 85

MAG BROWN

"I was born in North Carolina and come South with my white folks. They was trying to git out of the war and run right into it. My mother died when I was a baby. I don't remember my mother no more than you do. I left my white folks. When I was 14 years old, we lived out in the country. They was willing to keep me but after the war they was so poor. The girls told me if I could come to town and find work I had better do it. Two of them come nearly to town with me. They told me I was free to come to town and live with the colored folks. I didn't know what it meant to be free. I was just as free as I wanted to be with my white folks. When I got to town I stayed with your aunt awhile then she sent me down to stay with your grandma. A white girl who lived with them, like one of the family, learned me how to cook and iron. I knew how to wash.

"I don't know anything about the present generation. I ain't been able to git out for the last year or two. I think I broke my foot, for I had to go on crutches a long time.

"The white folks always sung but I don't know what they sung. I didn't pay no tention to it then."

United States. Work Projects Administration

Interviewer: Miss Irene Robertson
Person interviewed: Mary Brown, Clarendon, Arkansas
Age: Born in 1860

MARY BROWN

"Mama was born in slavery but never sold. Grandma and her husband was sold and brung eleven children to Crystal Springs. They was sold to Mr. Munkilwell. I was born there. Grandma was born in Virginia. Her back was cut all to pieces where she had been beat by her master. Both of them was whooped. He was a hostler and blacksmith.

"When grandma was a young woman she didn't have no children, so her master thought sure she was barren. He sold her to Taylors. Here come 'long eleven children. Taylor sold them. After freedom she had another. He was her onliest boy. That was so funny to hear her tell it. I never could forgit it long as I ever know a thing. Grandma's baby child was seventy-four years old, 'cepting that boy what was a stole child. She died not long ago at Carpendale, Mississippi. I got the letter two weeks ago. But she had been dead a while 'fore they writ to me. Her name was Aunt Miny. She didn't have no children.

"Grandma said the first time she was sold—the first day of July—they put her in a trader yard in Virginia. She was crying and says, 'Take me back to my mama.' An old woman said, 'You are up to be sold.'

"Aunt Helen, her sister, was taking her husband

something in the field. They fooled her away from her five little children. Grandma said she never was seen no more. She was much older than grandma. Grandma stayed with her slavery husband till he died.

"Since freedom some people tried to steal my mama. She was a fast runner and could dance. They wanted to make money out of her. They would bet on her races. At Lernet School they took about thirty-six children off in wagons. Never could get trace of them. Never seen nor heard of a one of them again. That was in this state at Lernet School years ago but since freedom.

"I was born during the War soon after Master Munkilwell took mama over. He didn't ever buy her. Mama died young but grandma lived to be over a hundred years old. She told me all I know about real olden times.

"I just looks on in 'mazement at this young generation. They is happy all right. Times not hard for them glib and well as they seems. Times have changed a sight since I was born in this world and still changing. Sometimes it seems like they are all right. Ag'in times is tough on old folks like me. This is all in the Bible—about the times and folks changing."

Interviewer: Miss Irene Robertson
Person interviewed: Mattie Brown. Helena. Arkansas
Age: 75

MATTIE BROWN

"I heard mother say time and ag'in I was a year and two months old the year of the surrender. I was born in Montgomery, Alabama. Mother was a milker and a house woman. Father died when I was a baby. Mother never married. There was three of us to raise. I'm the youngest.

"Sister was the regular little nurse girl for mother's mistress. I don't recollect her name. The baby was sickly and fretful. My sister set and rocked that baby all night long in a homemade cradle. Mother said she'd nod and go on. Mother thought she was too young to have to do that way. Mother stole her away the first year of the Civil War and let her go with some acquaintances of hers. They was colored folks. Mother said she had good owners. They was so good it didn't seem like slavery. The plantation belong to the woman. He was a preacher. He rode a circuit and was gone. They had a colored overseer or foreman like. She wanted a overseer just to be said she had one but he never agreed to it. He was a good man.

"Mother said over in sight on a joining farm the overseers whooped somebody every day and more than that sometimes. She said some of the white men overseers was cruel.

"Mother quilted for people and washed and ironed to raise us. After freedom mother sent for my sister. I don't recollect this but mother said when she heard of freedom she took me in her arms and left. The first I can recollect she was cooking for soldiers at the camps at Montgomery, Alabama. They had several cooks. We lived in our own house and mother washed and ironed for them some too. They paid her well for her work.

"I recollect some of the good eating. We had big white rice and big soda crackers and the best meat I ever et. It was pickled pork. It was preserved in brine and shipped to the soldiers in hogheads (barrels). We lived there till mother died and I can recollect that much. When mother died we had a hard time. I look back now and don't see how we made it through. We washed and ironed mostly and had a mighty little bit to eat and nearly nothing to wear. It was hard times for us three children. I was the baby child. My brother hired out when he could. We stuck together till we all married off."

Interviewer: Miss Irene Robertson
Person Interviewed: Molly Brown
Age: 90 or over Brinkley, Ark.

MOLLY BROWN

One morning early I (Irene Robertson) got off the bus and started up Main Street. I hadn't gone far before I noticed a small form of a woman. She wore men's heavy shoes, an old dark dress and a large fringed woolen shawl; the fringe was well gone and the shawl, once black, was now brown with age. I passed her and looked back into her face. I saw she was a Negro, dark brown. Her face was small with unusually nice features for a woman of her race. She carried a slick, knotted, heavy walking stick—a very nice-looking one. On the other arm was a rectangular split basket with wires run through for a handle and wrapped with a dirty white rag to keep the wire from cutting into her hand or arm.

I stopped and said, "Auntie, could you direct me to Molly Brown's house?"

"I'm her," she replied.

"Well, I want to go home with you."

"What you want to go out there for?"

"I want you to tell me about times when you were a girl," I said.

"I'm not going home yet. I got to get somethin' for dinner."

"Well, you go ahead and I'll follow along."

"Very well," she said.

I window shopped outside, and I noticed she had a box of candy, but it was a 25¢ box and had been opened, so I thought it may be nearly anything just put in the box. The next store she went into was a nice-looking meat market and grocery combined, I followed in behind her. A nice-looking middle-aged man gave her a bundle that was large enough to hold a 50¢ meat roast. It was neatly tied, and the wrapping paper was white, I observed. She thanked him. She turned to me and said, "Give me a nickel."

I said, "I don't have one." Then I said teasingly, "Why you think I have a nickel?"

She said, "You look like it."

I opened my purse and gave her a dime. She went over to the bread and picked up a loaf or two, feeling it. The same man said, "Let that alone."

The old woman slowly went on out. I was amazed at his scolding. Then he said to me, "She begs up and down this street every day, cold or hot, rain or shine, and I have to watch her from the time she enters that door till she leaves. I give her scrap meat," he added.

"How old is she?"

"She was about fifty years old sixty years ago when she came to Brinkley. She is close to a hundred years.

People say she has been here since soon after the town started." He remarked, "She won't spend that dime you gave her."

"Well, I will go tell her what to buy with it," I replied.

I hurried out lest I loose her. She had gained time on me and was crossing the Cotton Belt Ry. tracks. I caught up with her before she went into a small country grocery store on #70 highway. She had passed several Negro stores, restaurants, etc, "I want a nickel's worth of meal, please, sir."

I said, "Auntie, buy a dime's worth of meal."

"I don't want but a nickel's worth." The man handed it to her to put in the basket. "Give me a piece candy." The merchant gave her a nice hard stick. She broke it half in to and offered me a piece.

I said, "No, thank you, Auntie." She really wanted me to have it, but I refused it.

She blowed her nose on her soiled old white underskirt. She wormed and went on out.

I asked the merchant "How old is she?"

"Bless her heart, I expect she is ninety years old or more. I give her some hard candy every time she comes in here. I give her a lot of things. She spends her money with me."

Then I asked if she drew an Old Age Pension.

He said, "I think she does, but that is about 30¢ and

it runs out before she gets another one. She begs a great deal."

I lagged behind. The way she made her way across the Broadway of America made me scringe. I crossed and caught up with her as she turned off to a path between a garage and blacksmith shop.

I said, "Auntie, let me take your basket." She refused me. I said, "May I carry your meal or your meat?"

"I don't know you." she said shortly.

A jolly man at the side of the garage heard me. I said, "I'm all right, am I not" to the man.

He said, "Aunt Molly, let her help you home. She is all right. I'm sure."

I followed the path ahead of her. When we turned off across a grassy mesa the old woman said, "Here," and handed over her basket. I carried it. When we got to her house across a section of hay land at least a mile from town, she said, "Push that door open and go to the fire."

An old Negro man, not her husband and no relation, got a very respectable rocking chair for me. He had a good fire in the fireplace. The old woman sat on a tall footstool. She was so cold.

She said, "Bring me some water, please."

A young yellow boy stepped out and gave her a cup of water. She drank it all. She put the meat bones and scrap meat on the coals in an iron pot in some water. She had the boy scald the meal, sprinkle salt in it and add a little cold water to it. He put it in an iron pan and put a heavy iron lid over it. The kettle was iron. The boy set it aside and put the bread on hot embers. She sat down and said, "I'm hungry."

I said, "Auntie, what have you in that box?"

She reached to her basket, untied some coins from the corner of the soiled rag—three pennies and a nickel. She untied her ragged hose—she wore two pairs—tied above the knee with a string, and slipped the money to the foot and in her heavy shoes. It looked safe. Then the old Negro man came in with an armfull of scrub wood and placed it by the fireplace on the floor.

He said, "The Government sent me here to live and take care of Aunt Molly. She been sick. I build her fires, and me and that boy wait on her."

I asked, "Is the boy kin".

He said, "No'm, she's all alone."

He went away and the boy went away. The old woman called them and offered them candy. She had twelve hard pieces of whitish, stale chocolate candy in the box. The boy refused and went away, but the old man took three pieces. I observed it well, when she passed it to me, for worms. I refused it. It seemed free from bugs though. She ate greedily and the old man went away.

We were alone and she was warm. She talked freely till the old Negro man returned at one o'clock for dinner. Notwithstanding the fact the meal hadn't been sifted and the meat not washed, it looked so brown and nice in two pones and the meat smelled so good I left hurriedly before I weakened, for I was getting hungry from the aroma.

"I was born at Edgefield County, South Carolina, and lived there till after I married."

"Did you have a wedding?"

"I sure did."

"Tell me about it."

"I married at home, at night, had a supper, had a nice dance."

"You did?"

"I did."

"Did a colored man marry you?"

"Colored preacher—Jim Woods."

"Did he say the ceremony?"

"He read it out of a little book."

"Did you have a nice supper?"

"Course I did! White folks helped fix my weddin' supper. Had turkey, chickens, baked shoat, pies and cake—a table piled up full. Mama helped cook it. It was all cooked on fireplace."

"How were you dressed?"

"Dressed like folks dressed to marry."

"How was that?"

"I wore three or four starched underskirts trimmed in ruffles and a white dress over em. I wore a long lacy vail of net."

"Did you go away?"

"I lived close to my ma and always lived close bout her. I was called a first class lady then."

"You were."

"My parents name Tempy Harris and Albert Harris. She was a cook. He was a farmer. They had five children. The reason I come to Arkansas was cause brother Albert and Caroline come here and kept writin' for us to come. My folks belong to the Harrises. I don't know nothin' bout em—been too long—and I never fooled round their houses. Some my folks belong to the Joneses. They kinfolks of the Harrises.

"No, I never saw no one sold nor hung neither.

"Remember grandpa. His daddy was a white man. His wife was a black woman. Mama was a brown woman like I is.

"I ain't had narry child. My mother died here in this house. Way me an my husband paid for the house, he farmed for Jim Black and Mr. Gunn. I cooked for Jim Woodfin. Then I run a roomin' house till four years ago. Four years ago I went to South Carolina to see my auntie. Her name Julia. They all had more 'n I had. She'd dead now. All of em dead bout it. She was a light woman—Julia. Her pa was a white man; her ma a light woman. Julia considered wealthy.

"I don't know nothin' bout freedom. I seen the soldiers. I seen both kinds. The white folks was good to us. We stayed on. Then we went to Albany, Georgia. We lived there a long time—lived in Florida a long time, then come here.

"The Joneses and Harrises had two or three families all I know. They didn't have no big sight of land. They was good to us. I picked up chips, put em in the boxes. Picked em up in my dress, course; I fetched up water. We had rocked wells and springs, too. We lived with man named Holman in Georgia. We farmed. I used to be called a smart woman, till I done got not able. My grandpa was a white man; mama's pa.

"What I been doin' from 1864-1937? What ain't I done! Farmin', I told you. Buildin' fences was common. Feedin' hogs, milkin' cows, churnin'. We raised hogs and cows and kept somethin' to eat at home. I knit sox. I spin. I never weaved. Folks wore clothes then. They don't wear none now. Pieced quilts. Could I sew? Course I did! Got a machine there now. (pointed to an old one.)

"I never seen no Ku Klux. I hid if they was about. I sure did hear bout em. They didn't never come on our place.

"I told you I never knowed when freedom come on.

"I went to school in South Carolina. I went a little four or five years. I could read, spell, cipher on a slate. Course I learned to write. Course I got whoopins; got a heap o' whoopins. People tended to childern then. What kind books did we have? I read and spelled out of the Blue Back Speller. We had numbers on our slates. The teacher set us copies. We wrote with soapstone. Some teachers white and some colored.

"Well, course I got a Bible. (disgusted at the question). I go to church and preachin' every Sunday. Yes. ma'am, now.

"I don't study votin'. I don't vote. (disgusted). I reckon my husband and pa did vote. I ain't voted.

"Course I go to town. I go to keep from gettin' hungry.

"Me and this old man get demodities and I get some money.

"I told you I don't bother young folks business. I thought I told you I don't. If I young I could raise somethin' at home that the reason I go hungry. I give down. I know I do get hungry.

"One thing I didn't tell you. I made tallow candles when I was a young woman.

"I don't know nothin' bout that Civil War."

Interviewer: Miss Irene Robertson
Person interviewed: Peter Brown. Helena, Arkansas
Age: 86

PETER BROWN

"I was born on the Woodlawn place. It was owned by David and Ann Hunt. I was born a slave boy. Master Hunt had two sons and one girl. Bigy and Dunbar was the boys' names. Annie was the girl's name.

"My parents' names was Jane and William Brown. Papa said he was a little shirt tail boy when the stars fell. Grandma Sofa and Grandpa Peter Bane lived on the same place. I'm named after him. My papa come from Tennessee to Mississippi. I never heard ma say where she come from.

"My remembrance of slavery is not at tall favorable. I heard the master and overseers whooping the slaves b'fore day. They had stakes fixed in the ground and tied them down on their stomachs stretched out and they beat them with a bull whoop (cowhide woven). They would break the blisters on them with white oak paddles that had holes in it so it would suck. They be saying, 'Oh pray, master.' He'd say, 'Better pray fer yourself.' I heard that going on when I was a child morning after morning. I wasn't big enough to go to the field. I didn't have a hard time then. Ma had to work when she wasn't able. Pa stole her out and one night a small panther smelled them and come on a log up over where they slept in a canebrake. Pa killed it with a bowie knife. Ma had a baby out there in the canebrake. Pa had stole her out. They went back and they never made her work no more. She was a fast breeder; she had three sets of twins. They told him if he would stay out of the woods they wouldn't make her work no more, take care of her children. They prized fast breeders. They would come to see her and bring her things then. She had ten children, three pairs of twins. Jonas and Sofa, Peter and Alice, Isaac and Jacob.

"When I was fifteen years old, mother said, 'Peter, you are fifteen years old today; you was born March 1, 1852.' She told me that two or three times and I kept up wid it. I am glad I did; she died right after that.

"Ma and pa et dinner, well as could be. Took cholera, was dead at twelve o'clock that night. It was on Monday. Ike and Jake took it. They got over it. I waited on the little things. One of them said, 'Peter, I'm hungry.' I broiled some meat, made a ash cake and put the meat in where I split the ash cake. He et it and went to sleep. He started mending. Sister come and got the children and took them to Lake Providence. I fell in the hands then of some cruel people. They had a doctor named Dr. Coleman come to see ma and pa. He said, 'Don't eat no fruit, no vegetables.' He said, 'Eat meat and bread.' I et green plums and peaches like a boy fifteen years old then would do. I never did have cholera. A boy fifteen years old didn't know as much as boys do now that age. The master died b'fore the cholera disease come on. We had moved from the hill place to a place in the bottoms. It was on the same place. None of his family hod cholera but neighbors had it. We buried ma and pa on the neighbor's place. We had kin folks on the Harris place. While we was at the graveyard word come to dig two or three more graves.

"Master's house was set on fire, the smokehouse emptied, the gin burned and the cotton. The mules was drove out of the lot. That turned me ag'in' the Yankees. We helped raise that meat they stole. They left us to starve and fed their fat selves on what was our living. I do not believe in parts of slavery. That whooping was cruel, but I know that the white man helped the slave in ways. The slaves was worked too hard. Men was no better than they are now.

"My owner had two fine black horses name Night and Shade. Clem was a white driver. We lived close to Fiat where they had horse races. He told Clem to get Night ready to win some money. He told Clem not to let nobody have their hand on the horse. Clem slept in the stable with the horse. They had three horses on the track. They made three rounds. Night lost three times, but on Friday Night come in and won the money. He made two or three thousand dollars and paid Clem. I never heard how much.

Freedom

"Some men come to our house searching for arms. We had a chest. They threw things winding. Said it was freedom. We didn't think much of such freedom. Had to take it. We didn't have no arms in the house. We never seen free times and didn't know what to look for nohow. We never felt times as good. We moved to the bottoms and I lost my parents.

"I fell in the hands of some mean people. They worked me on the frozen ground barefooted. My feet frostbit. I wore a shirt dress and a britches leg cap on my head and ears. I had no shoes, no underwear. I slept on a bed made in the corner of a room called a bunk. It had bagging over straw and I covered with bagging. Aunt July (Julie) and Uncle Mass Harris come for me. Sister brought my horse pa left for me. They took me from, them folks to stay at Mr. W.C. Winters. He was good to me. He give me fifty dollars and fed me and my horse. He give me good clothes and a house in his yard. I was hungry. He fattened me and my horse both.

"They broke the Ku Klux up by putting grapevines across the roads. I know about that? I never seen one of them in my life.

"Election days years gone by was big times. I did vote. I voted regular a long time. The last President I voted for was Wilson.

"I farmed and worked on steamboats on the Mississippi River. I was what they called rousterbout. I loaded and unloaded freight, I worked on the Choctaw, Jane White, Kate Adams, and other little boats a few days at a time. Kate Adams burnt at Moons Landing. I stopped off here at Helena for Christmas. Some people got drowned and some burned to death. The mud clerk got lost. He went in and got two bags of silver money, put them in his pockets. The stave plank broke and he went down and never come up. He was at the shore nearly but nobody knew he had that silver in his pockets. He never come up and he drowned. People seen him go in but the others swum out. He never come up. They missed him and found him dead and the two bags of silver. I was due to be on there but I wanted to spend Christmas with grandma and my wife. The Choctaw carried ten thousand bales of cotton at times. I worked at the oil mill sixteen or seventeen years. I night watched on the transfer twenty-two years. I come to Helena when I was thirty years old. I'm eighty-six now. The worst thing I ever done was drink whiskey some. I done quit it. I have asthma. The doctors say whiskey is bad on that disease. I don't tetch it now.

"I think the present generation is crazy. I wish I had the chance they have now. The present times is getting better. I ask the Lord to spare me to be one hundred years old. I'm strong in the faith. I pray every day. He will open the way. The times have changed in my life."

United States. Work Projects Administration

Interviewer: Miss Irene Robertson
Person interviewed: William Brown, Hazen, Arkansas
Age: 67

WILLIAM BROWN

I was born in Virginia but I was born after slavery. I heard my folks talk a heap about oldern times. The way I come here was Dr. Hill brought bout 75 families down to Mississippi to work on farms. I come to Deer Creek close to Sunflower, Mississippi. I lived there 11 years and I drifted to Arkansas.

I don't remember if they was in any uprisings or not. If they was any rebellion cept the big rebellion I don't recall it. My whole families was in de heat of the war.

My mother and father's owner was John Smith. I recollects hearin them talk bout him well as if it was yesterday—we worked on McFowell place close to Petersburg, Virginia when I was little. Then I worked for Miss Bessie and Mr. John Stewart last fore I come with Dr. Hill. I had lived up there but he come and settled down in Mississippi.

The first place I worked on in Arkansas was the John Reeds bout 3 miles from Danville. I stayed there 3 years. My folks stayed on there but I rambled to Little Rock. I worked with Mr. L.C. Merrill. I milked cows and cut grass, fed cows. He has a automobile company in Little Rock now. I farmed bout all my life. Now I don't own nothing.

I stays at my daughters. I been married twice. Both my wives dead.

The times change so much I don't know whether they any better or not. The black race ain't never had nuthin—some few gets a little headway once in a while.

I used to vote some—didn't care nuthin bout it much. Never seed no good come of it. Heap of them vote tickets like somebody tell em or don't know how dey vote.

The young generations better off than the old folks now. The things change so fast I don't know how they will get by.

Interviewer: Samuel S. Taylor
Person interviewed: William Brown
409 W. Twenty-Fifth Street
North Little Rock, Arkansas
Age: 78

WILLIAM BROWN

[HW: U.S. Dictatorship Predicted]

"I was born in Arkansas in Cross County at the foot of Crowley's Ridge on the east side of the Ridge and just about twelve miles from Old Wittsburg, on May 3, 1861. I got the date from my mother. She kept dates by the old family Bible. I don't know where she got her learning. She had a knowledge of reading. I am about her sixth child. She was the mother of thirteen.

"My mother's master was named Bill Neely. Her mistress was named Mag Neely.

"My mother was one of the leading plow hands on Bill Neely's farm. She had a old mule named Jane. When the Yankees would come down, Bill Neely and all his friends would leave home. They would leave when they would hear the cannon, because they said that meant the Yankees were coming. When Neely went away, he would carry my mother to do his cooking.

"She would leave the children there and carry just the baby when she went. Old Aunt Malinda—she wasn't our aunt; she was just an old lady we called Aunt Malinda who cooked for the kitchen—would cook for us while she was gone. When the Yankees had passed through, my mother and the master would all come back.

"My original name was not Brown. It was Pope. I became Brown after the War was over. I moved on the old Barnes' farm. When the soldiers were mustered out in the end of the War, a lot of soldiers worked on that place. Peter Brown, an old colored soldier mustered out from Memphis, met my mother, courted her, and married her. All the other children that were born to her were called Brown, and the people called her Brown, and just called all the other children Brown too, including me. And I just let it go that way. But my father was named Harrison Pope. He died in the Confederate army out there somewheres around Little Rock. He had violated some of the military laws, and they put him in that thing they had to punish them by, and when they taken him out, he contracted pneumonia and died. I don't know where he is buried. I would to God I did! You know when these Southern armies went along they carried colored stevedores to do the work for them.

Patrollers

"I was a little fellow in the time of the pateroles. If the slaves wanted to go out anywhere, they had to get a pass and they had to be back at a certain time. If they didn't get back, it would be some kind of punishment. The pateroles was a mighty bad thing. If they caught you when you were out without a pass, they would whip you unmercifully, and if you were out too late they would whip you. Wherever colored people had a gathering, them pateroles would be there looking on to see if they could find anybody without a pass. If they did find anybody that couldn't show a pass, they would take him right out and whip him then and there.

Ku Klux

"I know the Ku Klux must have been in use before the War because I remember the business when I was a little bit of a fellow. They had a place out there on Crowley's Ridge they used to meet at. They tried to make the impression that they would be old Confederate soldiers that had been killed in the battle of Shiloh, and they used to ride down from the Ridge hollering, 'Oh! Lordy, Lordy, Lordy!' They would have on those old uniforms and would call for water. And they would have some way of pouring the water down in a bag or something underneath their uniforms so that it would look like they could drink four or five gallons.

"One night when they come galloping down on their horses hollering 'Oh! Lordy, Lordy' like they used to, some Yankee soldiers stationed nearby tied ropes across the road and killed about twenty-five of the horses and broke legs and arms of about ten or fifteen. They never used the ridge any more after that.

Parents

"My father's master was Shep Pope and his wife was named Julia Pope. I can't remember where my father was born but my mother was born in Tuscaloosa County, Alabama. I don't know the names of my grandfather and grandmother on either side.

Slave Houses

"The old slave house was a log house built out of hewed logs. The logs were scalped on each side to give it the appearance of a box house. And they said the logs would fit together better, too. They would chink up the cracks with grass and dirt—what they called 'dob'. That is what they called chinking to keep the wind and rain out.

"I was born in a one-room hut with a clapboard room on one side for the kitchen and storeroom. They would go out in the woods and split out the clapboards. My mother had eight of we children in that room at one time.

Furniture

"As to furniture, well, we had benches for chairs. They were made out of punching four holes in a board and putting sticks in there for legs. That is what we sat on. Tables generally were nailed up with two legs out and with the wall to support the other side. The beds were made in a corner with one leg out and the two walls supporting the other sides. They called that bed the 'Georgia Horse'. We had an old cupboard made up in a corner.

Food

"Food was generally kept in the old cupboard my mother had. When she had too much for the cupboard, she put it in an old chist.

Right After the War

"My mother had eight children to feed. After the emancipation she had to hustle for all of them. She would go up to work—pick cotton, pull corn, or what not, and when she came home at night she had on old dog she called 'Coldy'. She would go out and say, 'Coldy, Coldy, put him up.' And a little later, we would hear Coldy bark and she would go out and Coldy would have something treed. And she would take whatever he had-'possum, coon, or what not-and she would cook it, and we would have it for breakfast the next morning.

"Mother used to go out on neighboring farms and they would give her the scraps when they killed hogs and so on. One night she was coming home with some meat when she was attacked by wolves. Old Coldy was along and a little yellow dog. The dogs fought the wolves and while they were fighting, she slipped home. Next morning old Coldy showed up cut almost in two where the wolves had bitten him. We bandaged him up and took care of him. And he lived for two or more years. The little yellow dog never did show up no more. Mother said that the wolves must have killed and eaten him.

Schooling

"I put in about one month schooling when I was a boy about six or seven years old. Then I moved into St. Francis County and went two weeks to a subscription school a few miles below Forrest City. Later I went back and took the examination in Cross County and passed it, and taught for a year. I got the bulk of my education by lamp light reading. I have done some studying in other places—three years in Shorter College where I got the degreee of B.D. and D.D. at the age of fifty-five. I have preached for fifty-seven years and actually pastored for forty-four years. I followed farming in my early days. When I first married my wife, we farmed there for ten or twelve years before I entered the ministry. I have been married fifty-seven years.

Marriage

"I was married January 15, 1882. I am now in the fifty-seventh year of marriage. My wife was named Mary Ellen Stubbs. She was from Baldwyn, Mississippi. They moved from Mississippi about the winter of 1880 and they made one crop in Arkansas before we married. They stopped in our county and attended our church. I met her in that way. The most remarkable thing was that during the time I was acquainted with her our pastor became incapacitated and I took charge of the church. I ran a revival and she was converted during the revival. But she joined the C.M.E. Church. I belong to the A.M.E.

Slave Sales

"I remember my mother carrying the children from the Bill Neely place to the Pope place. That Saturday evening after we got there, there came along some slave traders. They had with them as I remember some ten or twelve boys and girls and some old folks that were able to work. They had them chained. I asked my mother what they were going to do with them and she said they were carrying them to Louisiana to work on a cane farm. One boy cried a lot. The next morning they put those slaves in the road and drove them down to Wittsbarg the same as you would drive a drove of cattle, Wittsburg was where they caught the boat to go down to Louisiana. That was the best mode of travel in those days.

Opinions

"In a few words, my opinion of the present is that our existence as Democrats and Republicans is about played out.

"If Mr. Roosevelt is elected for a third term, I think we will go into a dictatorship just as Russia, Germany, and Italy have already done. I think we are nearer to that now than we heve ever been before. I do not think that Mr. Roosevelt will become a dictator, but I do believe that his being elected a third time will cause some one else to become dictator. My opinion is that he is neither Democrat nor Republican.

"Our young people are advancing from a literary point of view, but I claim that they are losing out along moral lines. I don't believe that we value morals as well as the people did years ago who didn't know so much. I believe that the whole nation, white and black, is losing moral stamina. They do not think it is bad to kill a man, take another man's wife or rob a bank, or anything else. They desecrate the churches by carrying anything into the church. There is no sacred place now. Carnivals and everything else are carried to the church.

"If Mr. Roosevelt is not reelected again, the country is going to have one of the bloodiest wars it has ever had because we have so many European doctrines coming into the United States. I have been living seventy-eight years, and I never thought that I would live to see the day when the government would reach out and take hold of things like it has done—the WPA, the FERA, and the RFC, and other work going on today. We are headed for communism and we are going to get in a bloody war. There are hundreds of men going 'round who believe in communism but who don't want it to be known now."

Interviewer: Miss Irene Robertson
Person interviewed: Maggie Broyles. Forrest City. Arkansas
Age: About 80?

MAGGIE BROYLES

"I was born in Decatur, Tennessee. Mother was sold on the block at public auction in St. Louis. Master Bob Young bought a boy and a girl. My father was a full-blood Irishman. His name was Lassiter. She didn't have no more children by him. He was hired help on Bob Young's place.

"Bob Young had one thousand five hundred acres of land. He had several farms. Little Hill and Creek farms. They had a rock walk from the kitchen to the house. I slept in a little trunnel bed under my mother's mistress' bed. The bed was corded and had a crank. They used no slats in them days. We called Master Bob Young's wife Miss Nippy; her name was Par/nel/i/py. They was good old people. His boys was rough. They drunk and wasted the property.

"The white folks had feather beds and the slaves had grass beds. We'd pull grass and cure it. It made a'good bed. Miss Nippy learnt us to work. I know how to do near 'bout anything now. She kept an ash hopper dripping all the time. We made all our soap and lye hominy by the washpots full. Mother cooked and washed and kept house. She took the lead wid the house-work. Miss Nippy ride off when she got ready. Mother went right on wid the work. I took care of the chickens and took the cows to the pasture. I helped to wash clothes. I stood on a block to turn meat. We had a brick stove and a grill to fry meat on. We had good clothes and good to eat. After I was grown I'd go back to see Miss Nippy. She raised me. She say, 'I thought so much of your mama. I love you. I hope you live a long time.' Mama had a hard time and Miss Nippy knowd all about it.

"After Bob Young bought mother he went back and bought Aunt Sarah. They growed up together. They could dance with a glass of water on their heads and never spill a drap.

"Ma said when she married they had a corn shucking and a big dinner four o'clock in the morning. Her name was Luiza. She had two children by him. Aunt Jane on Welches place took him away from her. He quit mother cold to go wid her. After freedom she married Ben Pitts. The way she married at the corn shucking, they jumped over the broom back'ards and Master Bob Young 'nounced it. She was killed no time after freedom, but she had had six children. Miss Nippy kept me. She was good to me and trained me to read. We all never left after freedom. I never left till I was good and grown.

"I always thought Master Bob Young buried his money during the War. Children wasn't allowed to watch and ask questions. I was standing in the chimney corner and seen him bury a box of something in the flower garden. I was in Miss Nippy's room. I never did know if it was money or what. He had a old yaller dog followed him all the time. Truman was a speckled dog set about on the front porch to bark.

"Sam, the boy that was bought when I was in St. Louis, was hard to control. Bob Young beat him. He died. They said he killed him. They buried him in the white folks' cemetery.

"They celebrated Christmas visiting and big parties. We would have eggnog and ten or fifteen cakes. Master Bob Young was a consumptive. He had it thirty-five years. They all died out with it. They kept a big ten or fifteen gallon demijohn with willow woven around the bottom full of whiskey, all the time upstairs. They kept the door locked.

"I stole miny ah drink. Find the door unlocked. I got too much one time. It made me sick. I thought I had a chill. She thought I been upstairs. They was particular with the children, both black and white then. They put the children to bed by sundown and they would set around the fire and talk. She raised Elnora and the baby Altona after mother got killed. She give them good clothes and good to eat. Their papa took the boy. He left after mother got killed. We took a pride in the place like it was our own. We didn't know but what it was our very own.

"We had a acre in garden. We raised everything. We had three or four thousand pounds of meat and three cribs of corn. I ketched it when I left them. I made thirty-three crops in my life. My children all grown and gone. My son-in-law died. He had dropsy eight months. He had a dead liver. I've wanted since he died. I've had a hard time since he died. He was a worker and so good to us all.

"Mother worked with a white woman. Mother was full-blood Indian herself. The woman's husband got to dealing with his daughter. She had three babies in all. They said they put them up in the ceiling, up in a loft. This old man got mad with Bob Young and burnt his gin. Mother seen him slipping around. They ask her but she wouldn't tell on him, for she didn't see him set it on fire. They measured the tracks. He got scared mother would tell on him. One night a colored man on the place come over. Her husband was gone somewhere and hadn't got home. She was cooking supper. They heard somebody but thought it was a pig come around. Hogs run out all time. The step was a big limestone rock. She opened the door and put the hot lid of the skillet on it to cool. Stood it up sideways. Then they heard a noise at that door. It was pegged. So she went along with the cooking. It wasn't late. He found a crack at the side of the stick and dirt chimney, put the muzzle of the gun in there and shot her through her heart. The man flew. She struggled to the edge of the bed and fell. The children was asleep and I was afraid to move. The moon come up. I couldn't get her on the bed. I put a pillow under her head and a quilt over her, but I didn't think she was dead. The baby cried in the night. I was so scared I put the eight-months-old baby down under there to nurse. It nursed. She was dead then, I think now. When four o'clock come it was daylight. The little brother said, 'I know what's the matter, our mama's dead.' I went up to Mr. Bob Young's. He brought the coroners. I was so young I was afraid they was going to take us to jail. I asked little brother what they said they was going to do. He said, 'They are going to bury mama in a heep (deep) hole. They set out after her husband and chased him clear off. They thought he shot her by him not coming home that night and her cooking supper for him.

"This white man left and went to Texas. His wife said the best woman in Decatur had been killed. They put him on the gallows for killing his daughter's babies, three of them and put them in the loft. He told how he killed mother. He had murdered four. He was afraid mother would tell about him. She knowd so much. She didn't tell. Indians don't tell. She was with his girl when the first baby was born, but she thought it died and she thought the girl come home visiting, so his wife said she had told her to keep her from telling. It was a bad disgrace. His wife was a good, humble, kind woman.

"Master Bob Young sent for Ben Pitts after they'd run him off, and he let him have his pick of us. He took the boy and lived on the place. Her other husband come and got his two children. Miss Nippy took our baby girl and the other little girl. I was raised up at her house, so she kept me on. Kept us all till we married off.

"I'd feel foolish to go try to vote. I'm too old now.

"I don't get help from the government yet. We are having a hard time to scratch around and not go hungry."

United States. Work Projects Administration

Interviewer: Miss Irene Robertson
Person interviewed: Ida Bryant, Hazea. Arkansas
(Very very black Negro woman)
Age: 61

IDA BRYANT

"My mother was Hulda Williams. Grandpa was Jack Williams. Her mistress was a widow woman in slavery times. They lived in Louisiana. I was born close to Bastrop in Morehouse Parish. My father died when I was ten years old. He was old. I was a child. Things look different to you then you know. Grandpa was Hansen Terry, grandma Aggie Terry. They called pa Major Terry but he belong to Bill Talbot. Hansen Terry was a free man. He molded his own money. He died in South Carolina. Pa come from Edgefield, South Carolina to Alabama. Stayed there awhile then come on to Louisiana. He slipped off from his master. Between South Carolina and Louisiana he walked forty miles. He rode all the other time. My folks always farmed.

"Times have been getting some better all along since I was a chile. Times is a heap better now than I ever seen in my life. The young men depends on their wives to cook and make a living. They don't work much—none of em. We old niggers doin' the wash in' and the young women doin' cookin' and easy jobs. None of the men ain't workin' to do no good! A few months in the year ain't no workin'.

"I get commodities. I owns this house now. I bout paid it out. I washes three washin's a week. The rest of the time I pieces up quilts for myself. I need cover."

Interviewer: Miss Irene Robertson
Person interviewed: Belle Buntin, Marianne, Arkansas
Age: Up in 80's

BELLE BUNTIN

"I never was sold. I was born in Oakland, Mississippi. My master said he wanted all he raised. He never sold one. He bought my mother in Lexington County. She was a field hand. Our owners was Master Johnson Buntin and Mistress Sue Buntin. They had two children—Bob and Fannie. He had a big plantation and four families of slaves. Charlotte was the cook. Myra worked at the house and in the field. He had seven little colored boys and two little colored girls. I spent most of my time up at the house playing with Bob and Fannie. When mistress whooped one she whooped all three. She would whoop us for stealing her riding horse out. We would bridle it and all three ride and ride. We got several whoopings about that.

"I have seen colored folks sold at Oakland. They had a block and nigger traders come. One trader would go and see a fine baby. He keep on till he got it. I've seen them take babies from the mother's arm and if the mother dare cry, they would git a beatin'. They look like they bust over their grief.

"If you was out after seven o'clock the patrollers git you. They would beat and take you home. Some masters say to them, 'You done right,' and some say, 'You bring my hands home; I'll whoop them myself.'

"The patrollers caught one of Gaddises women and whooped her awful for coming to town on Sunday. I never did know why she went to town that way.

"That selling was awful and crowds come to see how they sell. They acted like it was a picnic. Some women was always there, come with their husbands. Some women sold slaves and some bought them.

"I never did see none sell naked. I seen men took from their wives and mothers and children. Let me tell you they didn't have no squalling around or they would get took off and a beating.

"Master Alex Buntin was Dr. Buntin. He said, 'I worked like one of my slaves and bought my slaves with what I made and I am not going to have them 'bused by the patrollers. George and Kit and Johnson was his cousins. Kit wasn't so good to his slaves.

"It was my job to brush the flies off the table. I had a fly brush. I would eat out of Bob's and Fannie's plates. Miss Sue say, 'Bell, I'm going to whoop you.' I say, 'Miss Sue, please don't, I'm hungry too.' She say, 'You stop playing and eat first next time.' Then she'd put some more on their plates. We sat on a bench at the table. We et the same the white folks did all cooked up together.

"One time Dr. Buntin got awful mad. The dogs found some whiskey in a cave one of his slaves had hid there. They would steal and hide it in a cave. He got a beating and they washed it in salt water to keep them from getting sore and stiff.

"Some folks kept dogs trained to hunt runaway niggers. They was fat, and you better not hit one or hurt it if it did bite or you would git a awful beating.

"Master Alex was a legislator. He had to leave when the Yankees come through. They killed all the legislators. I loved him. He run a store and we three children went to the store to see him nearly every day. He took us all three on his knees at the some time. I loved him. When he was gone, I said, 'Miss Sue, where is Master Alex?' She say, 'Maybe he be back pretty soon.' While he was gone they had a battle in a little skirt of woods close by. We hung to Miss Sue's skirt tail. I seen the Yankees run by on horses and some walking. Mr. Jordan, a southern soldier, was shot in his ribs. Mr. Buford was shot in his knee. Some of the other southern soldiers drug them up to our house. Miss Sue nursed them. I think they got well and went home.

"Three days before Master Alex left they sent all the stock off and put the turkeys and geese under the house, and chickens too. It was dark so they kept pretty quiet. When the Yankees got there they stripped the smokehouse. We had a lots of meat and they busted the storehouse open and strowed (strewed) meat and flour all along the road. They hired Mammy (Charlotte) to cook a big meal for them. She told the man she was 'fraid Miss Sue whoop her. He said, 'Whooping time near 'bout out.' He asked her 'bout some chickens but she wasn't goin' to tell him 'cause it was her living too for them to waste up. They never found the geese, turkeys, and chickens. They rambled all through the house looking for Master Alex and went through every drawer and closet upstairs and down. It was scandalous. They had Miss Sue walking and crying and us three children clinging to her skirt tail scared to death and crying too. When they left, the big lieutenant rode off ahead on a fine gray horse. They come back when we just got the table sot and et every crumb of our dinner. They was a lively gang. I hate 'em. I was hungry. Rations was scarce. They wasted the best we had. Master Alex hod three stores and he kept the middle one.

Freedom

"Mistress told all Master Alex's slaves they had been freed. The men all left. My mother left and took me. I got mad and went back and lived there till I married. Master Alex come back after two weeks. My mother soon died after the surrender. She died at Batesville, Mississippi. Lots of the slaves died. Their change of living killed lots of 'em. My father lived on Sam Bronoy's (Branough's) place. Master Alex wanted to buy him but he took him on to Texas before I was born. I never did see him.

"I been farming, cooking, wash and iron along. I been in Arkansas twelve or fourteen years.

"How am I supported? I'm not much supported. My boy don't have work much of the time. I don't get the pension. I trusts in the Lord. I belong to New Bethel Baptist Church down here.

"Times—I don't know what to think. My race is the under folks and I don't never say nothing to harm 'em. I'm one of 'em. Times is hardest in my life. I have to sit. I can't walk a step—creeping paralysis."

Interviewer: Miss Irene Robertson
Parson interviewed: Jeff Burgess, Clarendon, Arkansas
Age: Born in 1664 or 1865, forgot which

JEFF BURGESS

"I was born in Granville, Texas. My master was Strathers Burgess and mistress Polly Burgess. My master died 'fore I was born. He died on the way to Texas, trying to save his slaves. Keep them from leaving him and from going into the war. They didn't want to fight. His son was killed in the war. My folks didn't know they was free till three years after the war was over. They come back to Caloche Bay, the old home place. There was a bureau at De Valls Bluff. They had to let the slaves go and they was citizens then. My folks wasn't very anxious to leave the white owners because times was so funny and they didn't have nowhere to go. The courts was torn up powerful here in Arkansas.

"Heap of meanness going on right after the war. One man tell you do this and another man say you better not do that you sho get in trouble. It was hard to go straight. They said our master was a good man but awful rough wid his slaves and the hands overseeing too. Guess he was rough wid his family too.

"Times is hard with me, I gits $10 pension every month. I got no home now. I got me three hogs. I lives three miles from here (Clarendon).

"If I wasn't so old and no account I'd think the times

the best ever. It's bad when you get old. I jess sees the young folks. I don't know much about them. Seems lack they talk a lot of foolish chat to me. I got a lot and a half in town. They tore down my house and toted it off for fire wood. It was rented. Then they moved out and wouldn't pay no rent. They kept doing that way. I never had a farm of my own.

"I was good with a saw and axe. I cleared land and farmed. Once I worked on the railroad they was building. I drove pile mostly. Farming is the best job and the best place to make a living. I found out that myself."

Interviewer: Bernice Bowden
Person interviewed: Norman Burkes
    2305 West Eleventh Street, Pine Bluff, Arkansas
Age: 78

NORMAN BURKES

"I didn't quite make slavery. Me and freedom came here together.

"I was born in Union County, Arkansas. My mother was born in Virginia and my father was an Alabamian.

"I've heered 'em say how they done in slavery times. Whupped 'em and worked 'em and didn't feed 'em much. Said they'd average about three pounds of meat a week and a peck of meal, a half gallon of molasses. That was allowed the hands for a week. No sugar and no coffee. And they'd issue flour on Saturday so they could have Sunday morning biscuits.

"My father was sold to Virginia and he and my mother was married there and they moved with their white people here to Arkansas.

"They called their owner old Master. Yes'm, I can remember him. Many times as he whipped me I ought to remember him. I never will forget that old man. They claimed he was pretty good to 'em. He didn't whup 'em much, I don't think.

"If my mother was livin' she could tell you everything

about Virginia. She was one hundred and two when she died. My folks is long livers.

"My oldest brother was sold in Virginia and shipped down into Texas about ten years before I was born and I ain't never seen him.

"They sold wives from their husbands and children from their parents and they couldn't help it. Just like this war business. Come and draft 'em and they couldn't help it.

"I think the way things is now, they're goin to build up another war."

Extra Comment

I was interviewing this man on the front porch and at this point, he got up and went into the house, so the interview was ended as far as he was concerned.

Interviewer: Miss Irene Robertaon
Person interviewed: Will Burks, Sr.
Pine City, Ark.—5 mi. from Holly Grove
Age: 75

WILL BURKS, SR.

"My parents names was Katherine Hill and Bill Burks. They had five boys and three girls. Their owners fur as I knows was Frank and Polly Burks. They had a heap of slaves. They was good white folks. My folks stayed on two or three years. They was both field hands. They had to go to the house and Master Frank Burks told em they was free. In 1880 Judge Scott paid their way and I come wid them to Forrest City. There was a crowd. He bought em out here to farm. We come Christmas 1880. I never will forgit that. It was jes different in a new country and left some of our folks an all that.

"I was born close to Columbia, Tennessee. I used to see the soldiers pass long the big road, both sides. Seem lack theyd be in strings a mile long. I never heard much bout the war. They wouldn't let white nor black children set round and hear what they was talkin' bout. Why they send em off to play—build playhouses outer rocks and hay, leaves, any little thing they throw way we take it to play house. White children played together then cause it was a long ways between white folks house, and colored children raised up wid em. I don't see none that now.

"One thing I done a long time was stay at the toll gate. They had a heap of em when I was a boy. The fences was rock or rail and big old wooden gates round and on it marked, "Toll Gate." I'd open and shut the gate. Walkers go free. Horseback riders—fifteen cents. Buggies—twenty-five cents. Wagons—fifty cents. The state broke that up and made new roads. Some they changed a little and used. After that I stand 'bout on roads through fields—short ways folks went but where the farmers had to keep closed up on count of the crops. I open and shut the gate. They'd throw me a nickel. That was first money I made—stayin' at toll gates about Columbia, Tennessee.

"Ku Klux come to our house and took my papa off wid em. Mama was cryin', she told us children they was goiner hurt him. I recollect all bout it. They thought my papa knowed about some man bein' killed. My papa died wid knots on his neck where they hung him up wid ropes. It hurt him all his life after that. It made him sick what all they done to him tryin' to make him tell who killed somebody. He was laid up a long time. I recollect that. When they found out papa didn't know nothin' bout it, they said they was sorry they done him so mean.

"I vote a Republican ticket lack my papa till I cluded it not the party, it is the man that rules right. I voted fur Mr. Roosevelt. I know he is. (A Democrat) I know'd it when I voted for him. Times is tough but they was worse 'fo he got elected. Things you buy gets higher and higher that makes it bad. We got two hogs, one cow, few chickens and a home. I owns my home for a fact. My wife is 73. I am purty nigh 75 years old. What make it hard on us, we is bout wore out.

"I been farmin' and carpenterin' all my life. Last years

I been farmin' wid Mr. L.M. Osborne at Osborne. We work forty acres and made 57 bales. I had a team and he had a team. So I worked it on halves. That was long time ago. In 1929 I believe. Best farmin' I ever done. We got twenty cents pound."

United States. Work Projects Administration

Interviewer: Mrs. Annie L. LaCotts
 Person interviewed: Adeline Burris, DeWitt, Arkansas
 Age; 91

ADELINE BURRIS

Adeline Burris is a little old white-haired wrinkled-faced mulatto or yellow Negro woman who says she was old enough to be working in the fields when the war began. According to her story she must have been about 14 then, which would make her at least 90 years old now. She looks as though she might be a hundred. She is stooped and very feeble but can get around some days by the help of a stout walking stick; at other times she cannot leave her bed for days at a time. She owns nothing and is living in the home of her daughter-in-law who is kind to her and cares for her as best she can. She says she was born in Murry County, Tennessee. Columbia was the county seat. When asked if she was born during slavery time she said, "Yes, honey, my mammy was one of de slaves what belonged to Mr. Billie and Miss Liza Renfroe. Lord bless her heart she was good to my mammy and her chillun! I had two little brothers, twins, and when dey come to dis world I can remember how our old mistress would come every day to see about dem and my mammy. She'd bring things to eat, clothes for the babies and everything else. Yes sir! My mother didn't want for anything as long as she stayed with Miss Liza, not even after de Negroes was freed. When I was a little girl I was give to my young mistress, and I stayed with her till my folks was coning to Arkansas and I come too."

"Why did your folks move to Arkansas?"

"Well, you see we heard this was a good country and there was a white man come there to get a lot of niggers to farm for him down on the river and we come with him. He brought a lot of families on a big boat called a flatboat. We were days and nights floating down the river. We landed at St. Charles. I married in about two years and haven't ever lived anywhere else but Arkansas County and I've always been around good white folks. I'd been cold and hungry a lot of times if it wasn't for some of dese blessed white folkes' chillen; dey comes to see me and brings me things to eat and clothes too, sometimes."

"How many tines did you marry, Aunt Add.?"

"Just one time; and I just had four chillen, twins, two times. One child died out of each sit—just left me and Becky and Bob. Bob and Dover, his wife, couldn't get along but I think most of it's his fault, for Dover's just as good to me as she can be. My own child couldn't be better to me den she is.

"I don't know, honey, but looks to me like niggers was better off in dem days den they are now. I know dey was if dey had good white folks like we did. Dey didn't have to worry about rent, clothes, nor sumpin to eat. Dat was there for them. All they had to do was work and do right. Course I guess our master might not of been so good and kind ef we had been mean and lazy, but you know none of us ever got a whippin' in our life.

"Honey, come back to see Aunt Add. sometime. I likes to talk to you."

United States. Work Projects Administration

Interviewer: Samuel S. Taylor
Person interviewed: Jennie Butler
3012 Short Main Street, Little Rock, Arkansas
Age: Between 103 and 107

JENNIE BUTLER

[HW: Nurses ? ? ?][TR: Illegible]

"I was born February 10, 1831 in Richmond, Virginia. I was a nurse raised by our white folks in the house with the Adamses. Sue Stanley (white and Indian) was my godmother, or 'nursemother' they called em then. She was a sister-in-law to Jay Goold's wife. She married an Adams. I wasn't raised a little nigger child like they is in the South. I was raised like people. I wasn't no bastard. My father was Henry Crittenden, an Indian full blooded Creek. He was named after his father, Henry Crittenden. My mother's name was Louisa Virginia. Her parents were the Gibsons, same nationality as her husband. My 'nursemother' was a white woman, but she had English and Indian blood in her. My mother and father were married to each other just like young people are nowadays. None of my people were slaves and none of them owned any slaves.

House

"In Richmond, they lived in a little log cabin. Before I had so much trouble I could tell you all about it, but I never forget that little log cabin. That is near Oak Grove where Lincoln and Garfield and Nat Turner met and talked about slavery.

Furniture

"We had oak furniture. We had a tall bed with a looking glass in the back of it, long bolsters, long pillow cases just like we used to make long infant dresses. There were four rooms in the cabin. It was in the city. The kitchen was a little off from the house. You reached it by going through a little portico.

Food

"We ate bananas, oranges, hazelnuts, apples, fruit for every month in the year for breakfast, batter cakes, egg bread. The mornings we had egg bread we had flesh. For dinner and supper we had milk and butter and some kind of sweetness, and bread, of course. We had a boiled dinner. We raised everything-even peanuts.

Clothes

"We made everything we wore. Raised and made the cloth and the leather, and the clothes and the shoes.

Contacts with Slaves and Slave Owners

"I don't know nothin' about slavery. I didn't have nothin' to do with them folks. We picked em up on our way in our travels and they had been treated like dogs and hadn't been told they were free. We'd tell em they was free and let em go.

Leaving Richmond

"All I can tell you is that we come on down and never stopped until we got to Memphis, and we tarried there twenty-five years. We came through Louisiana and Georgia on our way out here and picked up many slaves who didn't know they was free. They was using these little boats when we came out here. In Louisiana and Georgia when we came out here, they weren't thinkin' bout telling the niggers they were free. And they weren't in Clarksville either. We landed in Little Rock and made it our headquarters.

Occupations

"Christian work has been the banner of my life-labor work, giving messages about the Bible, teaching. Mostly they kept me riding—I mean with the doctors. When we were riding, the doctors didn't go in a mother's room; he sent the rider in. They call em nurses now and handle them indifferently. The doctor jus' stopped in the parlor and made his money jus' sitting there and we women did all the work. In 1912, I gave up my riding license. It was too rough for me in Arkansas. And then they wouldn't allow me anything either.

"Now I have a poor way of making a living because they have taken away everything from me. I prays and lives by the Bible. I can't get nothin' from my husband's endowment. He was an old soldier in the Civil War on the Confederate side and I used to get $30 a month from Pine Bluff. He was freed there. Wilson was President at the time I put in for an increase for him in the days of his sickness. He was down sick thirty years and only got $30 a month. The pension was increased to $60 for about one year. He died in 1917, March 10, and was in his ninetieth year or more from what he told me. The picture shows it too.

Voting

"Paying my taxes was the votin' I ever done. They never could get me to gee nor haw. There wasn't any use voting when you can see what's on the future before you. I never had many colored friends. None that voted. And very few Indians and just a few others. And them that stood by me all the while, they're sleeping.

Thoughts of Young People

"Don't know nothin' bout these young folks today. Don't nothin' spoil a duck but his bill. I have had a hard time. I am heavy and I'm jus' walkin' bout. A little talk with Jesus is all I have. I'll fall on my knees and I'll walk as Jesus says. My heart's bleeding. I know I'm not no more welcome than a dog.

"I pays for this little shack and when you come to see me, you might as well come to that kitchen door. I ain't going to use no deceit with nobody. I'll show you the hole I have to go in."

Interviewer's Comment

I understand that Sister Butler gets a pension of $5 a month. Although her voice is vigorous, her mental powers are somewhat weak. She cannot remember the details of anything at all.

She evidently had heard something about Nat Turner, but it would be hard to tell what. The Nat Turner Rebellion, so called, a fanatical affair which was as much opposed by the Negroes as by the whites, took place in Southampton County, Virginia, in August and September 1831, the same year in which Jennie Butler claims birth. She would naturally hear something about it, but she does not remember what.

She had a newspaper clipping undated and minus the reading matter showing her husband's picture, and another showing herself, February 10, 1938, The Arkansas Democrat.

United States. Work Projects Administration

Interviewer: Mrs. Bernice Bowden
Person interviewed: E.L. Byrd
618 N. Cedar, Pine Bluff, Arkansas
Age: 76

E.L. BYRD

"I was born in 1862. I just can remember the Yankees. They come through there and got horses and money and anything else they wanted. To my reasoning that's the reason the North has got more now. They got all the money they could find. And they took one fellow belonged to the same man I did.

"My owner's name was Jack Byrd. We stayed with him about a year and then we farmed for ourselves.

"I never went to school much.

"My mother was a widow woman and I had to work. That was in South Carolina.

"I come to Arkansas in 1890. I didn't marry till I was about thirty-seven. I got one child living. That's my daughter; I live with her. She's a bookkeeper for Perry's Undertaking Company.

"When I come to Arkansas I stopped down here in Ashley County. I farmed till I come to Pine Bluff. I been here forty years. I worked at the stave mills. I just worked for three different firms in forty years.

"I used to own this place, but I had to let it go on account of taxes. Then my daughter bought it in.

"I been tryin' to get a pension but don't look like I'm go in' to get it.

"I have to stay here with these children while my daughter works. It takes all she makes to keep things goin'."

Interviewer: Miss Irene Robertson.
Person interviewed: Emmett Augasta Byrd, Marianna, Arkansas
Age: 83

EMMETT AUGASTA BYRD

"I was born in Washington County, Missouri. I'm eighty-three years old. Mother's owner was William Byrd. He got killed in a dispute over a horse. A horse trader shot him. His name was Cal Dony. [TR: There is a mark that may be a line over the 'o' or a tilde over the 'n'.] Father's owner was Byrd too. Mother was Miss Harriett Byrd's cook. Yes, I knowed her very well. I was nine years old when I was stole.

"Me and my older brother was both stole. His name was Hugh Byrd. We was just out. It was in September. A gang out stealing horses stole us. It was when Price made his last raid to Missouri. It was some of the soldiers from his gang. We was playing about. They overtook us and let us ride, then they wouldn't let us git off. They would shot us if we had. In a few days we was so far off. We cried and worried a heap.

"It was eighteen years before I see my mother. The old snag I was riding give out and they was leading so they changed me. I cried two or three days. They didn't pay my crying no 'tention. They had a string of nigger men and boys, no women, far as from me 'cross to that bank. I judge it is three hundred yards over there.

"After the battle of Big Blue River my man got killed

and another man had charge of me and somebody else went off with my brother. I never seen him. That battle was awful, awful, awful! Well, I certainly was scared to death. They never got out of Missouri with my brother. In 1872 he went to St. Louis to my mother. She was cooking there. My father went with the Yankees and was at Jefferson Barracks in the army during the War. He was there when we got stole but she went later on before he died. He was there three months. He took pneumonia. They brought me in to Kansas and back by Ft. Smith.

"Talking about hard times, war times is all the hard times I ever seen. No foolin'! It was really hard times. We had no bread, shoot down a cow and cut out what we wanted, take it on. We et it raw. Sometimes we would cook it but we et more raw than cooked. When we got to Ft. Smith we struck good times. Folks was living on parched corn and sorghum molasses. They had no mills to grind up the corn. Times was hard they thought. Further south we come better times got. When we landed at Arkadelphia we stayed all night and I was sold next day. Mr. Spence was the hotel keeper. He bought me. He give one hundred fifty dollars and a fine saddle horse for me. I never heard the trade but that is what I heard 'em say afterwards. Mr. Spence was a cripple man. John Merrican left me. He been mean to me. He was rough. Hit me over the head, beat me. He was mean. He lived down 'bout Warren, down somewhere in the southern part of the state. I never seen him no more. Mr. Spence was good to me since I come to think about it but then I didn't think so. We had plenty plain victuals at the hotel. He meant to be good to me but I expected too much I reckon. Then it being a public place I heard lots what was said around. I come to think I ought to be treated good as the boarders.

Now I see it different. Mr. Spence walked on a stick and a crutch. He couldn't be very cruel to me if he had wanted to. He wasn't mean a bit. I was the bellboy and swept 'round some and gardened.

"In 1866, in May, I run off. I went to Dallas County across Ouachita River. I stayed there with Matlocks and Russells and Welches till I was good and grown. Mr. Spence never tried to find me. I hoped he would. They wasn't so bad but I had to work harder. They never give me nothing. I seen Mr. Spence twice after I left but he never seen me. If he did he never let on. I never seen his wife no more after I left her. I didn't see him for four years after I left, then in three more years I seen him but the hotel had burned.

Freedom

"Mr. Spence told me I was free. I didn't leave. I didn't have sense to know where to go. I didn't know what freedom was. So he went to the free mens' bureau and had me bound to him till I was twenty-one years old. He told me what he had done. He was to clothe me, feed me, send me to school so many months a year, give me a horse and bridle and saddle and one hundred fifty dollars when I was twenty-one years old. That would have been eight or nine years. Seemed too long a time to wait. I thought I could do better than that. I never done half that good. I never went to school a day in my life. I was sorry I run off after it was too late.

"I heard too much talking at the hotel. They argued a whole heap more than they do now. They set around and talk about slavery and freedom and everything else. It made me restless and I run off. I was ashamed to be seen much less go back. Folks used to have shame.

Ku Klux

"In 1868 I lived with John Welch one year. I seen the going out and coming in. I heard what they was doing. I wasn't afraid of them then. I lived with one of 'em and I wasn't afraid of 'em. I learned a good deal about it. They called it uprising and I found out their purpose was to hold down the nigger. They said they wanted to make them submissive. They catch 'em and beat 'em half to death. I heard they hung some of 'em. No, I didn't see it. I knew one or two they beat. They took some of the niggers right out of the cotton patch and dressed them up and drilled 'em. When they come back they was boastful. Then they had to beat it out of 'em. Some of 'em didn't want to go back to work. Since I growed up I thought it out that Mr. Spence was reasonably good to me but I didn't think so then. It was a restlessness then like it is now 'mong the young class of folks. The truth is they don't know what they want nor what to do and they don't do nothing much no time.

"I went to see my mother. I wrote and wrote, had my white folks write till I found my folks. I went back several times. Mother died in 1902. We used to could beat rides on freight trains—that was mighty dangerous. We could work our way on the boats. I got to rambling trying to do better. I come to Phillips County. They cut it up, named it Lee. I got down in here and married. I was jus' rambling 'round. I been in Lee County sixty-one years. I married toreckly after I come here. I been married twice, both wives dead. I was about twenty-three years old when I married. I had four children. My last child got killed. A limb fell on him twenty years ago in April. He was grown and at work in the timber.

"I farmed all my life—seventy years of it. I like it now and if I was able I would not set up here in town a minute. Jus' till I could get out there is all time it would take for me to get back to farming. I owned two little places. I sold the first fifty acres when my wife was sick so I could do for her. She died. My last wife got sick. I was no 'count and had to quit work. Mr. Dupree built that little house for me, he said for all I had done for 'im. He said it would be my home long as I live. He keeps another old man living out there the same way. Mr. Dupree is sick—in bad health—skin disease of some sort. We lives back behind this house. Mr. Dupree is in this house now. (Mr. Dupree has eczema.) I used to work for him on the farm and in the store.

"I never was a drunkard. That is ruining this country. It is every Saturday night trade and every day trade with some of them. No, but I set here and see plenty.

"The present times is better than it used to be 'cause people are cleverer and considerate in way of living. A sixteen-year-old boy knows a heap now. Five-year-old boy knows much as a ten-year-old boy used to know. I don't think the world is going to pieces. It is advancing way I see it. The Bible says we are to get weaker and wiser. Young folks not much 'count now to do hard work. Some can.

"I get eight dollars and I work about this place all I am able. It keeps us both going."

www.ingramcontent.com/pod-product-compliance
Lightning Source LLC
Chambersburg PA
CBHW071645160426
43195CB00012B/1364